MONEYTHINK

MONEYTHINK

Financial Planning Finally Made Easy

ADRIANE G. BERG

THE PILGRIM PRESS

NEW YORK

Library of Congress Cataloging in Publication Data

Berg, Adriane Gilda, 1948-
  Moneythink.

  Includes index.
  1. Finance, Personal.   I. Title.
HG179.B45 1982   332.024   82-12384
ISBN 0-8298-0497-8

The Pilgrim Press, 132 West 31 Street, New York, NY 10001

FOR MY MOTHER

I wish to thank the many people who have contributed so generously to the writing and preparation of this book.

Special thanks to: Hyman Clurfeld of the law firm of Clurfeld, Ross & Krevitz; Melvyn J. Feldman, C.L.U.; Mitchel Hochberg & Myron Bloom, of the accounting firm of Bloom Hochberg & Company; Stephen Stark, Partner, L. F. Rothschild, Unterberg, Towbin; Rosie L. James, Trust Officer, and Maureen Bateman, Esq., of Bankers Trust Company; Lee G. Gamage, Executive Vice President of the Springfield Marine Bank; Lawrence P. Murphy, Jr., Senior Law Assistant, and Armand J. Sarace, Chief Clerk, of the Brooklyn Surrogates Court; Gerald Hass, Manager of Mt. Ararat Cemetery; and James Goodfellow, Vice President of the Morgan Guaranty Trust Company.

I wish specially to thank Judy Block who was so generous in allowing me to print portions of an article entitled "How to Talk to Your Lawyer" which we co-authored. The value and lucidity of that section of this book is due largely to Judy's extraordinary writing and editing ability.

I wish to thank Esther Cohen, my editor at Pilgrim Press for her encouragement and interest and also for laughing at my jokes.

A special thanks to Shelley Larsen for her excellent secretarial skills and her enthusiasm regarding the project.

I wish also to thank Ruth Van Doren, Director of the Human Relations Department of the New School For Social Research for having the foresight to include courses for laypeople in this important area long before it was fashionable to do so.

I wish to thank my husband, Stuart Bochner, for tolerating endless chatter regarding "The Book" during almost every day of the past two years.

Finally, a special thanks to Dorte Schreiber who was my original inspiration in showing the need for this kind of book.

CONTENTS

ix

x   *Contents*

*professionals—consulting, organizing your thoughts,
asking questions, settling fees, speaking up,
demanding service, discharging where
necessary ● Special advice for women*

MONEYTHINK

INTRODUCTION

Moneythink and How to Do It

Did you hear the one about the beggar?

There was once a beggar who for some twenty-eight years stood upon the very same street corner in a small Bavarian town. One day the beggar went to City Hall and sought out the Burgermeister to complain. "Sir," he said, "for twenty-eight years I have diligently stood upon the same street corner and begged; and yet, in all these years, I have never been given even one coin. What shall I do?" "Beggar," said the Burgermeister, "did you ever consider crossing the street and begging on the other side?" "What?" said the beggar, "and leave such a good spot!"

Well, that's the story. I don't know about you, but I would like to grab this poor beggar by the shoulders and say, "Pal, you wanted advice, you got advice. Why don't you take it?" But I already know the answer. He can't overcome his emotional investment in standing on that same crummy corner; he's been there too long, and the longer he stays the harder it gets. The beggar's tragic flaw is not that he picked a bad corner in the first place, or that he stayed, but that even after getting good advice he couldn't budge.

That's why I wrote this book: to get you off whatever financial street corner is not working for you, and to help you get moving in the right direction. I know how hard this is. I've handled hundreds of clients who come to me, get good advice, and still

3

can't move. Through the years I've developed a method called Moneythink, a way to crash personal barriers and help people get off their old street corners. It works!

You see, that wasn't the only possible ending to the beggar story. There is a much more optimistic version. In this version, the beggar didn't say anything, he just fainted. He was overcome by the enormity of the advice, its simplicity, its excellence. He hit his forehead and thought, "Of course, why didn't I think of that?" That's what I want from you. I want you to have a financial revelation. I know you will.

I also wrote this book to help you relax about money. I've seen more money worries and related physical ailments than many doctors. Americans are trained to worry about money, but never really do anything about it except perpetuate their own anxieties. Moneythink is a way of realizing your own personal psychology of money. It makes you happy and confident. It gets rid of a lot of myths you've been carrying around too long. You will have the information and the nerve to cross the street to a better financial life.

Once you have opened yourself up to thinking clearly and without emotional conflict about money, how you earn it, how you invest it, how you spend it, you still need something else. That something else is information, good, truthful, hard-core information. This book provides it. It gives you both my techniques for practicing Moneythink and solid information regarding hundreds of aspects of financial planning, everything from divorces to retirement to taxes. The book, too, has been Reaganized. Where the new federal laws have made a drastic change, it tells you. You get the old way and the new way, so you can understand what's happening as well as how things were until recently.

Most people, even wealthy ones, believe they can't grasp technical, legal, and financial information. It's not true. As a teacher, I know that if people don't learn, it's the instructor's fault. Consider this conversation I overheard between a mother and an eight-year-old child:

Child: "Mommy, how big are my eyes?"
Mother: "Oh, about an eighth of an inch long."
Child: "Mommy, how big is that building over there?"
Mother: "That's the Empire State Building, a very tall building. It must be thousands of feet high."

Child: "Mommy, which is bigger? The Empire State Building or my eye?"

Mother: "Of course the Empire State Building is much bigger, thousands of times bigger!"

Child: "That can't be!"

Mother: "Why not?"

Child: "Because that building, that big building, it fits inside my eye."

You can perceive much more than you are. You can learn and analyze. A human being has a mighty power and shouldn't be intimidated by a little thing like estate or financial planning or by the experts in the field. This book helps you know yourself, perhaps a part of yourself that you have not explored recently, the self that thinks about, worries about, even agonizes over finances but never really does anything about them because it seems to be too complicated, too boring, too hard, or too troublesome. Step by step, by knowing more you will do more. The lucky part is that knowledge is itself power in this area. Just by knowing, you will have accomplished something that will help you every day.

The device I use is Moneythink.

GETTING TO THE BOTTOM OF IT

In the past half decade I have gone through "getting to the bottom of it" sessions with hundreds of clients. This was necessary because many of them could not even begin a financial plan or an estate plan, since they could not focus on their own financial personalities. The barriers that prevent us from focusing realistically on dollars and cents are most often leftovers from childhood. They are there for almost every one of us; it has nothing to do with special trauma, or neurosis; it is universal. Some people are more paralyzed than others, but few are altogether sane about money.

What to do about it? Keep on probing. One technique for getting started came to me out of an experience I had while training mental health professionals who were learning to use the new technique of divorce mediation. My role was to help the counselors deal with the need of any divorcing couple to arrive at a financial agreement covering such matters as child support, division of property, and what used to be called alimony but is now called maintenance in many states. Budgeting, tax planning, and estate planning are also involved. All this can be very complicated, and yet there is no time for endless speculation or self-searching or debate. Besides, the very idea of mediation is to move fast while there is still a spirit of cooperation and communication between the couple, so that they can reach an amiable agreement at a difficult and usually adversarial time.

The mediator-trainees soon reported that couples had great difficulty zeroing in on financial matters under such pressure. Instead, they brought up old quarrels, offered only partial information about income and assets, and even drew a complete blank about finances, each relying on the other spouse, even though they were about to divorce! Husbands claimed that wives knew all about the bill-paying, and wives that husbands had a monopoly on information regarding income.

I was asked to devise a homework assignment for couples, designed to unblock them and get them to Moneythink. The result was the quickest and most pleasant technique I can imagine for getting to the bottom of the problem. Find out who you were as a money baby, and in that way get an understanding of your true money self in adulthood. The technique is very simple; it consists of actively observing children dealing with money. I sent those people who were absolutely blocked to, of all places, amusement parks!

If you can't start your Moneythink assignment, take a trip to a local amusement park. Make sure it is one that offers choices among souvenirs, candy, games, and rides. Don't go to a "one price covers all" place. Go where children or the adults with them must choose their enjoyments, where everything must be paid for separately.

What to do when you get there? You could have fun, and I'll bet you will. You certainly don't have to go alone. Take your own kids, spouse, or a friend, and enjoy. But while you are browsing around the amusement center, eavesdrop on all the children you can hear in the souvenir shops and near the rides. See how they ask their parents to buy them balloons, hear how the parents reply. Observe how the children react. Some will be making real choices, some will be given everything they wish, and others will be deprived altogether. Some will have their parents push toys or rides on them; other parents will obviously want to avoid spending anything. You will find that brother and sister teams will be treated differently. Even twins will get different treatment.

I was struck recently by the behavior of two small children and their very serious-looking parents at a craft shop. The children wanted to buy something. Each had been given money and was expected to make a purchase. They had double pressure. They had to buy, and at the same time they had to buy within a dollar limit. Over and over again the children tested the parents to see if they would approve of a purchase before it was a final decision. The little girl saw a bell and asked the father, "I think that has value; does that have real value?" Depending on her father's reactions, she would like the bell and buy it or not. Neither child was making independent choices, for fear of parental disapproval. The basis of their choice would be value, not true value, their own value, but rather value in terms of how their parents saw it.

Some of your eavesdropping will be heartwarmingly positive. For example, one day on a bus I observed a little girl (perhaps four years old) with a package of M & M candy. She asked her father, who had obviously bought it for her, how much it cost. The subject was raised by the child, not the father, who was paying the fare. The father explained to the little girl that the candy cost different amounts in different stores and gave her some prices. The girl looked at the candy, paused for a moment, looked up at her father, and said "Gee, I really appreciate this." It was a startling statement from a four-year-old, and clearly heartfelt. The child was learning value through her own random experiences.

It doesn't really matter, though, whether your eavesdropping warms or curdles your heart. This isn't an exercise in passing judgment. Neither your own parents nor their parents nor you yourself are the object of criticism in this homework assignment. What you are supposed to do at the amusement park is react, and see which of the many things you will hear touch you personally. You will find someone whose Moneythink as a little child reminds you of yours. Instances of the past will come flooding back. You will become nostalgic, sometimes sentimental, and certainly in touch with your money past. If you have no reaction whatsoever, and it is not a result of your trying to hide your reactions, that too is highly significant. I have never met anyone in any walk of life who did not react to the assignment of eavesdropping in an amusement park. But if you have no recall whatsoever regarding your money personality, then you must conclude that some of your problems regarding positive, constructive, adult Moneythink may have to do with the loneliness it brings to you, since you have no childhood money past.

The amusement park homework is a one-time quick means of immersing yourself in Moneythink when you need fast results. There are hundreds of events around you, if you have more time, of which you can become aware. Did you collect for UNICEF? Have you had the experience of asking people for charity for others? For yourself? And, very important, did you work when you were a child and earn money? How old were you? How much did you earn? What did you do with it? How did you feel about earning money? Were you taught that hard work is best?

In Bardstown, Kentucky, the town where the original Old Kentucky Home is located, an old-fashioned pageant depicting the life of Stephen Foster is shown on summer evenings. It happens that Foster was a young man in Pittsburgh around the same time that Andrew Carnegie, the self-made millionaire, lived there as a small boy. There is speculation in the pageant that Carnegie took flute lessons from Foster. Carnegie is portrayed as a ten-year-old who knows exactly what to do with a buck. The pageant shows him earning whatever money he can from doing odd jobs, and investing in single shares of stock in growing corporations. When he wins two dollars in an essay contest, the man presenting the prize asks, "What will you do with it, young Andrew?" Andrew answers, "I'll buy one share in your corporation for a dollar, sir, and with the other dollar I will take flute lessons." What would you have done with two dollars when you were a child?

MONEY WORRIES CAN BE HAZARDOUS TO YOUR HEALTH

Every dollar bill should have a notation of health hazard printed on it, signed by the Surgeon General. Stress is now known to be a major cause of heart disease, high blood pressure, stroke, and more. Money worries lead to stress and can be as disabling as the death of a spouse or divorce. Notice that I did not say money *problems* but money *worries*. They are two different things. Most thoughts about money fall into the worry column. Only on rare occasions do people feel good about their financial situations. This is true across the board, regardless of income. Among the middle class, the largest American financial category, the worries are greatest. Caught between the realization that they will never reach the perfect financial freedom of their dreams, and the pressure to pay their own way for everything, members of the middle class feel both guilty and cheated. Those who are poor worry about money for survival, and those who are rich worry about money because they have so much to lose. We are a society, in fact, that looks down upon those who do not worry about money. We call them spendthrifts, wastrels, nogoodnicks, and bums.

But let's face it, we really don't want to worry about money. It spoils our fun; it is boring and destructive. Why do we worry so much and do so little? Why do we find that our worries are always the same, year after year, and that we continue to worry even if we become wealthier and actually do better? The answer is: *We worry about money because we don't know a thing about it; and we are particularly ignorant about our own money matters!*

We refuse to engage in Moneythink, a healthy concentration on our own private financial situation as it really exists. We will do almost anything to avoid this, including worry excessively. Here are some excuses for avoiding Moneythink:

- I am no good at math and I hate math.
- It's too boring.
- I can't find copies of all the bills and other records that I need, so it's useless anyway.
- Even if I understood my money picture, I am not shrewd enough to make the right investments.
- I need lawyers and accountants, and I can't afford them.
- My spouse is better at it. It is his/her job, not mine.
- I am starting a new business or job, and I will look at my finances later on when there is more to look at.

Excuses would be fine if they actually stopped us from worrying, but they don't. The antidote for the poison of worry—and it can be a poison that keeps you up at night, makes you sour with your friends and family, and even causes illness and fatigue (it takes a lot of energy to worry)—is information, coupled with an attitude that lets you put the information to work. For at least a decade I have concentrated on the financial problems of clients. Many of them are women who have gone through divorces and have been forced to concentrate on money matters for the first time. The example of these women applies to us all. First they panic. Having been used to years of not engaging in Moneythink, they consider themselves helpless and hopeless. Then they resign themselves to approaching the task, since they must live and decide alone. At this point, if they take my advice, they do some thinking about their own attitudes toward money; they get rid of their doubts, fears and myths. Once money is demystified, they're able to learn and they proceed to become informed regarding their own budgeting, debts, and investments. Finally they feel power, liberation, self-worth, and sometimes even pure joy at being in control of their own financial situation.

Moneythink means that you deal objectively and unemotionally with your own dollars.

The excuses for avoiding Moneythink could be multiplied indefinitely. But they're all phony. All our real reasons for avoiding Moneythink have nothing to do with the excuses. Some people will use excuses that are embarrassing or self-deprecating, like saying that they are too stupid to understand money matters, rather than really look at the true reasons. The best thing you can accomplish is to break through the barriers of Moneythink and unblock the emotional resistance to dealing with dollars. You don't need seven years of therapy; you don't need thousands of dollars in legal and accounting consultation fees. You don't even need a pencil and paper with a bunch of charts and forms to fill out. You might eventually want some of these things, but none of them is a first step. Seeing professionals, dealing with money in therapy, making charts and filling out budget forms are second steps. The first step is to work hard at answering the key question: What kind of money personality are you? It seems remarkable that almost no book, lecture, or discussion on the subject of money ever focuses on the basic question of what is your money personality. Instead of making you dizzy with forms, promises of instant riches, or stories of what other people are doing, money experts ought to focus first on you personally. When I began to write this book I reviewed dozens of others already on the market. I noticed that every one of them began something like this: "John and Martha are members of a two-paycheck family and they have found that because of changes in tax laws they are now able to accumulate a surplus of $10,000 a year and would like to invest it."

Well, I doubt that you could care less about John and Martha. It's you that you should be concerned about. A book full of anecdotes about what other people are doing will ultimately do you little good; it may even keep you from really working at your money worries. In this book we will soon look at some examples of what other people have said about their money personalities, but, to put first things first, we start with you.

As I've already suggested, to find your money self, focus on what kind of money baby you were. Our personal Moneythink is dictated by our childhood as much as are our attitudes toward sex, religion, personal relationships, and career. Yet the money baby in us is always ignored. In his book *The Psychoanalysis of Money,* Dr. Ernest Borneman begins by telling us that our toilet training often accounts for our view of money. He discusses the anal and oral personalities and how each type handles money differently. Differences range from going on spending binges to holding tightfistedly to the loot.

The way we think about money is consolidated in our adult life, but is a very fundamental part of our childhood. So, instead of immediately analyzing your present budget, ask and answer some of the following questions about yourself as a child:

- Did you get an allowance?
- Was it too much or too little?
- Did you think that you were rich when you were growing up, or did you think that you were poor? (Forget about what you really were.) What did you perceive yourself to be as you grew older?
- Were you deprived of things like toys or movies?

- What was happening in the world when you were a child?
- Were you a Depression baby? Were you part of the baby boom, or did you come along later?
- How did you compare to your friends? Were you all about equal in your allowance and toys, or were you in a poorer or richer crowd?
- Did you ever move into a new money environment because your family suffered a financial disaster, or because your family was upwardly mobile? How did you react to the move in your childhood?
- Were there discussions when you were a kid about whom you should marry? Did any of them revolve around money? Were you told to break a leg in front of a hospital so that you could marry a rich doctor? Did you think that was funny? Did you resent it? Did you believe it? Did you think marrying money was a goal you had to achieve to please your parents?
- Was there a death in the family, creating a big gap in funds, or any financial upheaval?
- Do you remember discussions between your parents about money? Did they fight about it all the time, or did it seem never to be an issue?

Well, you get the idea. Your particular style of worrying about money didn't come out of nowhere. If you reminisce about its sources (and I don't mean only for the time it takes to read this chapter) I guarantee that two things will happen. First, new revelations about your money attitudes will come to you. Second, you will get mighty uncomfortable. Few people in our society live through their childhood without some kind of money anxiety. It can rise out of a disaster like personal bankruptcy. As a child, you don't know what that means, but all the others in the family are hush-hush around you, whispering little secrets and passing on their worries to you. It can be caused by financial success as well: a parent gets a better job, but it means you have to move and leave your friends. Anxiety about money, I found, in one client came from the fact that a family member won the sweepstakes. The sudden windfall of money was greatly resented by the rest of the family. That memory had made my client fearful of taking risks because he might win!

This is not unusual. Money worries do not always stem from real money problems. I have said this before regarding ourselves as adults, and it is certainly true regarding ourselves as children. In her wonderful book, *Overcoming Your Fear of Success,* Dr. Martha Friedman points out that failure is sometimes a device to block something even more fearful—success.

MONEYTHINK FOR MONEY TASKS

Once the reminiscing process is complete barriers begin to fall. A movement takes place from recalling the baby money self to understanding the adult money self. Time and again, people who have really studied their money past, when asked what stops them from dealing realistically with finances, give new and more truthful answers. For example, I dealt for some time with a young lawyer who claimed that he was too busy to draw up a will or to focus on his estate. He changed a little when he learned he was about to become a father; for the first time he felt guilty about not focusing. He tried harder but still canceled one appointment after the other. After he had done some Moneythink exercises, I asked again what was really bothering him about focusing on his financial situation. His new answer was that he was afraid to focus on his money because if he knew too much about it, he would see its limitations, get scared that he would run out of money, and become dissatisfied with his job and career. He was one of those who as children continually had to scrimp. In fact, he recalled having to do his puzzle book mentally so that his younger sister could use the book after him without its being marked up. Although he was now far from being poor, he feared that budgeting would bring back his deprived past.

Over the years I have asked hundreds of other people, "What stops you from thinking clearly about money?" These were people who already had thought a great deal about money and who had even engaged in some Moneythink exercises. The funny part was that no one accused me of asking a loaded question. Every person acknowledged that he or she did not think clearly about money. Not one said the question did not apply.

Here are a few of the blocks that people experienced. A

young man with inherited wealth said, "I can't focus on my own money because I haven't got any. My father had money, and my children will have money, but I have none. It was inherited, and it's my job to keep it for the kids. It makes me mad, and I have trouble getting over the anger."

A teacher in the New York City public school system: "I had opportunities to go into business but I took a steady position instead, to shoot for a pension. I'm afraid to think about money because I don't believe I can do much about it; I need my security."

A wife about to divorce: "For most of my adulthood I let my husband think about money; I believed that was the right thing to do. Now it feels like having to learn to walk for the first time. Frankly, I'm terrified."

A young intern: "I expect to be making a lot of money in the future, and I think I'm going to be very worried about it all the time. It's funny, but having no money now is a big relief; it's like being finished with one job and having another one lined up with two weeks' vacation. You really don't have to do much, but you rely on the future."

A person about to retire: "I recently realized that money reminds me of death. I'm afraid to deal with money because I don't want to have to measure my life and time by it. Some friends of mine talk in terms of years; they have enough money to keep going for ten years or fifteen years, but what happens after that?"

A highly successful businesswoman: "I don't think about money because I know I am not doing as well with it as I could be. I spend my money on luxuries instead of putting it into the business. It's my way of showing that I made it, even in a man's field."

Once the adult fears are focused on, things begin to come very naturally. There is not much hard work after this.

THE MONEYTHINK PAYOFF

To make the final transition to recognizing yourself as a money person, try the following exercise. Write down those things that you find the most difficult to do, the most boring, or the most distasteful. The usual examples are

- getting all the documents together to see what your assets are
- doing the necessary mathematics
- reviewing your old income tax returns
- shopping for and paying an attorney or accountant to help you
- preparing a budget
- determining the money goal you really wish to reach

Once you have your list, take the next step. With your newfound sense of money self, answer the question, *Why?*

Why is it hard for me to keep records, set investment goals? What really stops me from making a budget? Instead of answering that it's boring, when you know that money is a fascinating topic, perhaps you will realize that a budget pushes your limitations in your face.

Is it math that's the problem? Ask: Why do I hate to do the math? Who told me that math is distasteful, or that girls can't do math, or that boys should be excellent at math, and I'm a boy and I'm not that great? Go from one distasteful act to another and simply face it.

Believe it or not, that is enough to get you off your street corner. It doesn't mean you will learn to love math or get any better at it. It doesn't mean that you will not mutter under your breath while digging through your pile of documents.

It only means that finally, after all these years, you'll do it! Remember, you don't have to like it, you just have to do it. The whole point of Moneythink is to get you to act. A colleague of mine once popped into my law office in the middle of the day and asked, "Are we what we think or are we what we do?" He thought that he was asking a tough philosophical question. Of course, real thinking is itself a form of doing, and it leads to more doing. If your thinking (at least about money) doesn't move you to action, it's not thinking but fretting.

Now, sit still and really read this book. From this point on, you'll find that much of it is highly technical and loaded with information. But you'll also find that each chapter starts with a Moneythink project to help you understand and do something positive about your daily finances. The chapters themselves will teach what you need to know; the Moneythink exercises will teach you how to learn. Let's begin by asking a few more questions.

1
WHAT KIND OF ESTATE PLANNER ARE YOU?

What kind of estate planner are you?

"What kind of question is that? If I knew what kind of estate planner I was, I wouldn't be reading your book! In fact, I think I'm probably no kind of estate planner at all. I don't know the first thing about estate planning. I'm not even sure I want to know anything about estate planning."

All right, so you don't think you're an estate planner. You're wrong. Everybody is an estate planner, even people who believe that the "quality of life" would be ruined by too much thinking about the future. All of us, in our own ways, engage in estate planning. Everybody who has ever earned a dime, everybody who has ever had to file an income tax return, everyone who has ever thought about retirement, wished for it early or been sorry for having chosen it. All parents who hoped that their kids would have a better life than they, or who thought that the kids should have to struggle for what they got. Everyone who has thought about getting married (or divorced), about buying a car or a house or taking a vacation, is an estate planner. We are all estate planners, but we hate to admit it. We hate to admit it because we hate to admit that we will ever have an estate to leave. Estate planning has long been associated with death and taxes, two inevitables that are universally hated and feared. The

16

notion that simply by not focusing on our estate we can avoid D and T has long been an unspoken motivator. But the truth is that failure to focus on estate planning really diminishes the control you have over your finances day to day and undermines your peace of mind in both the long and the short run.

"Living well," it's said, "is the best revenge." Won't worrying about your estate get in the way?

Well, no. Not if by living well you mean having more control over your resources, paying less in taxes so that you can make your own choices about the use of your money, feeling free to marry and divorce without adding financial worries to the already intense emotional strains, being prepared to move to bigger quarters or smaller quarters, to make the lifetime purchase that you have been dreaming about, to protect your children or make sure they can protect themselves. Estate planning helps in all these ways. In all these ways you can be "living better."

Like all Moneythink, estate planning is really a matter of making basic human choices about spending, saving, and leaving what we earn or have. We all think about these choices quite a lot. Unfortunately, most estate-planning books are frankly dull. They look upon estate planning as a matter of structure, mathematics, records, and at best offer some interesting schemes to save on taxes or make sure your kids get their due. But the answer to the question "What kind of estate planner am I?" has nothing to do with math. It may not even really have to do with money. It certainly does not have to do with the *amount* of money you have. It has to do with your goals and the whole fabric of your personality. For every one of you there is a slightly different answer regarding estate planning, and I cannot categorize our whole population. But I can give you some ideas on how to be able to think about your own goals and needs right now.

Remember the following three basic rules: (1) No estate-planning goal is wrong. No one has the magic formula for the best estate plan, which will fit everyone's life style and needs. *So never play another person's game.* (2) You can learn everything you need to know about estate planning. You may not want to, or think you need to, but everything, even the most technical subject matter, is within your grasp as long as you are literate, and regardless of your education or training. *So don't let anybody fool you into thinking you're not smart enough to understand estate planning.* (3) You are not alone in estate planning. You have a partner named Uncle Sam. Taxes play such an important part in estate planning that ignoring them, avoiding them, or not using them to your best advantage is the quickest way to fail in meeting your goals. *So make Uncle Sam your friend.*

To find out what kind of estate planner you are, Moneythink about the following:

I can't find where I wrote it down.   One kind of estate planner is filled with good intentions, often expressed by beginning a new book of items that are tax deductible, and keeping new records. This estate planner has stacks on stacks of notebooks, assignment books, calendars, budget records, special budget envelopes, special stationery with pockets in which to put loose papers and receipts. The trouble is that estate planners in this category can hardly remember where they put anything once they have abandoned their scheme or been overcome by its tedium. They are like two-day dieters, the kind who are always going to start on Monday, and wind up stopping on Wednesday. Once the book is bought and neatly lined, the index cards are headed, and a good $25 or $30 has been spent on sharpened pencils, rulers, and new books about estate planning, the estate plan ends. Actually I have a sneaking affection for the type: this is the estate planner who will surely buy my book. Whether he or she will read it is another story.

What shall I choose?   When I was a kid my aunt used to take me to the toy counter at Woolworth's every week. There was an amazing array of items for children, including tiny dolls for fifteen cents, paddles with a string and a rubber ball attached, sets of jacks, Classic Comic books. But there were also huge stuffed animals, pink plastic suitcases filled with lipstick, nail polish, and toilet water (all fake), and dolls with doll clothes, usually called something like Little Princess. Every week we went to the toy counter, and every week my aunt asked me the same question: "What would you like today, one big thing or lots of little things?" Every week I pondered, sometimes for a whole five minutes. This was a very serious question, and I considered it solemnly. I knew that we didn't have all the money in the world but that we did have some. I knew that I had to make a significant choice here—one big thing or a lot of little things. Every week I thought about it, and every week I came to the same conclusion, "I'll take a lot of little things." It never seemed sufficient to come home with one large item. I might get bored with it, or break it, or lose it. With a lot of little things, even though each was individually inferior, I had a chance to hedge my bets. If I got tired of playing jacks, I could always paddle that ball against the board. If I lost a jack I could always read the Classic Comics. In short, even then I had a Money Self, and it preferred to diversify. Not everybody likes to diversify. J.P. Morgan advised putting all your eggs in one basket and then watching that basket. He didn't do so badly. Think about yourself. If you have to make financial purchases and plans and work at financial security, ask yourself what makes you more comfortable, one big thing or a lot of little things.

How can I retire early? Not everybody wants to retire early. That surprises the people who long for the day that they can bask in the sun. Some people even get mad about early retirement. I have consulted for many years with groups that are advocates for the aging, and I've talked against early retirement and forced retirement every time I got the opportunity. But there are many people who long for retirement. Their goal is to plan well enough so that they can retire comfortably at the earliest possible opportunity. For them, the needs of estate planning are very much bound up with day-to-day financial planning and tax savings. For them, estate planning is for the here and now.

I hate lawyers. Me too. I do my best to stay away from parties and boat trips that are chock-a-block with my own colleagues, but I can't always do it. If you're a lawyer-hater, I freely confirm that you've got reasons. Most people are suspicious of lawyers: they can't understand them, they think they are being cheated or at best condescended to. They want to have a tax plan, they want to have an estate plan, they want to be up on financial matters, but they don't want to pay someone to help them, especially someone they don't trust, who makes them feel uncomfortable. This book will not help you avoid lawyers, but it will teach you how to talk to one, how to use one and how to get the most out of your relationship. You will find that there are many honest lawyers, after all. None of them will help you very much unless you know something first. The same goes for accountants, bankers and trustees.

The children must have a better life than I.   If the children's future is your concern, then you're a good old-fashioned type of estate planner. You'll soon read that most estate-planning techniques teach you how to leave your money to others after your death so that they get the most out of it. For those of you who care about this, you're in luck. Almost the whole world of estate planning is based on this.

I'm too young to do estate planning.   I'm not going to lecture you about this. I'm just going to tell you a story. Once there was a young lawyer who specialized in taxes and was also a CPA. He had a wife and one child and a rosy future. He had gone through a period of upward mobility, and things were just about to break. Of course, being young, he didn't think it was necessary to make an estate plan. He really didn't have much extra cash anyway, and everything was being used for the new car, the new furniture, and vacations. He probably would have said that he didn't have any estate to plan yet. Of course, he did have a small life insurance policy on which he still had his mother named as beneficiary, since he had never bothered to change the designation after marriage. He had no will and no other life insurance. But why worry? He was so young.

One day he died, nearly instantaneously, of a cerebral hemorrhage. He left his family without an income, without insurance (although of course his mother gave the family the small policy). The surviving spouse and child lived first on savings, then on state aid. Then the wife went to work. Her first job was stapling rolls of toilet paper in a Brooklyn factory. Finally she became a bookkeeper, and the family did better.

That's my personal life story. I was the child. As in many such tragedies, good things could and did emerge. For one thing, independence; for another, Moneythink: it is likely that a good deal of my self-earned holdings result from hard effort to compensate for the loss. Barbra Streisand, in her autobiography, asserts this same need to make up for an early loss. But frankly, who needs it? Instead of having your family become aware of estate planning through an upheaval in your home, why not learn from my experience? If you still think you're too young to plan, you'll get no sympathy from me.

I'm too old to estate plan. If not now, when? I assure you that some retirement plans can be made after retirement begins. Investments can be made all your life. Tax savings can even take place after death. If you are at the point of retirement, the way you budget and spend is already about to change. You're going to have to Moneythink anyway. Not everyone becomes a millionaire at thirty. Some do at seventy-five. If you're beyond retirement age, you have the advantage of knowing yourself better than before, and Moneythink will come more easily.

Whatever kind of estate planner you are, you're ready to learn the tools of estate planning.

2
Wills

Wills are like teeth: few people enjoy attending to them. They are, after all, a testament to our mortality, and it is much more fun to shop for new sporting equipment. In fact, people would rather spend a lot of money trying to avoid writing a will than a little money taking care of it. All kinds of interesting devices—some that work, some that don't—have been set up to avoid wills. Some people who put money into bank accounts for grandchildren and children leave it there just to avoid writing a will which says that they leave their money to their children.

In general, that's silly. A will can be a very good thing to have. Even if you decide not to have a will, you should at least know why you so decided. There are three basic reasons to have a will, and from each of them stem the other rules regarding estate planning. You can think of a will as the hub of a wheel from which there are many spokes making up your all-round plan.

The three basic purposes of a will are (1) to get your assets to the people whom you want to have them; (2) to do your best tax planning; and (3) to pick the executors, trustees and other fiduciaries that are going to administer your estate. A healthy by-product of will making is that it forces you to learn a little about estate planning and requires that you put together a list of your assets so that you can begin to Moneythink about how you're holding money right now.

Your will is a document that should be tailored to your needs like a good suit. It can provide for anything you please, so long as it is not illegal. Short of this, your will should reflect your wishes, covering your needs and your family's needs.

Will provisions are fairly standard in form, but that doesn't make them easy to read: typically, they're expressed in legalese. There are reasons for that. A will is one of the few documents for which I do not suggest the use of plain language understandable by laypeople. The problem with plain talk is that while you may understand it, a judge may not. There are many time-honored phrases (we will look at them in a moment) that you must have in a will. Years of experience with these words have given them precise meaning to the courts, so that these major words become symbols that leave the courts no room for doubt. I have found that if you vary from these time-honored phrases, judges get confused, and lawsuits spring up. Remember, it will be the judge who will decide; you won't be around to help interpret. Spend the effort now to make clear to your lawyer what you want, then make him or her explain the language that will be used.

A will is only one document, but it takes the place of many more complex devices. If after you have read about will clauses you still don't want a will, you can do some things to substitute for one. Study this diagram of will substitutes.

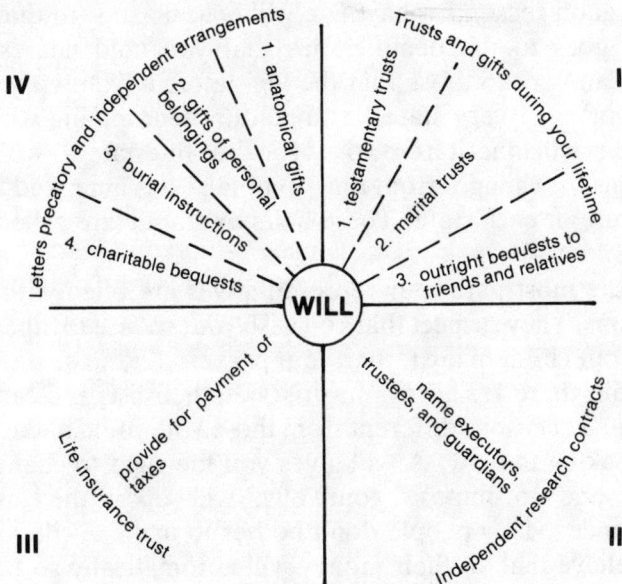

Section I of my "spoke diagram" shows that to leave your assets to particular beneficiaries you must give them gifts or make trusts during your lifetime. This takes the place of charitable bequests, marital bequests, and the residuary bequests, all of which we will consider later.

Section II shows that to pick those who are your best fiduciaries you can research and interview during your lifetime and enter into various contracts and agreements with them instead of having a will that names executors and trustees.

Section III helps if you want to provide for the payment of estate taxes, which you will have with or without a will. You can do this through insurance trusts which pay the taxes for your estate as long as the premiums are kept up.

Finally, Section IV is useful if you wish to have special burial instructions or give your personal belongings to friends and relatives. You can do so by giving gifts or preparing a letter for your administrator. These are all will substitutes. But there is no one document, no one way that can accomplish so much with respect to getting the right things to the right people as a will. It is true that probate can be expensive but the substitutes for it are equally costly and difficult, if not more so. Furthermore, if you don't make a will, the government can end up choosing your beneficiaries for you.

One good reason for having a will is to make sure that your money goes to the beneficiaries that you hold nearest and dearest and not to those that the legislators in your state think most worthy. Every state has a statute determining which of your heirs will inherit from you if you die "intestate"—without a will. This list changes from time to time as it is amended by the legislature of each state. These heirs by statute are called your "distributees."

For the most part your representatives are filled with good intentions. They suspect that you wish your spouse to inherit the most, your children next, then your parents, and so on down the line. Still, there are always surprises on their list, and certainly they make decisions different from those you would make if you were making the law. A will gives you the right to change the statute and to impose your own will upon the laws of inheritance. Many people don't bother to make a will because they believe that all their money will automatically go to their spouses, or because they don't feel they have any heirs that they wish to protect. Even the many couples in our country who are living together but are not married may vaguely believe that somehow their money will go to the person they are living with, never realizing that if they don't make a will it may go to a sister or relative many times removed whom they've never seen.

New York State has a fairly representative statute which will give you a good idea of what happens to money when there is no will.

In New York, if only your spouse survives you, he or she will inherit everything, provided you had a valid marriage at the time of death. If you are survived by a spouse and one child, the legislature has concocted the following distribution of property: First, $4,000 in money or personal property is given to the spouse, and then the rest of the estate is divided equally between the spouse and the surviving child. If you are survived by your spouse and grandchildren, you will find that the same $4,000 in money or personal property goes to the spouse, together with half of the estate; the other half will go to your grandchild. Most people, if they are survived by their spouse and a grandchild, would like all the money to go to the spouse, with perhaps a small sum to the grandchild.

If you are survived by your spouse and more than one child then your spouse gets the $4,000 and only one third of the rest; the children divide the other two thirds equally. If one of the children has died but had a child, that grandchild will take a share. How about Mom and Dad? If you are survived by your spouse, no children, and both parents or only one parent, then the first $25,000 will go to your spouse. The remainder of your estate will be divided in half, one half to your folks and the other half to your spouse.

What if you have no surviving spouse but just children? In that case everything will go to the kids to divide equally. If you are survived only by parents, your entire estate will go to them. If you are survived only by your brothers and sisters, then your brothers and sisters will inherit everything equally. If one of them has died, his or her children will take their parent's share. If you are survived only by your grandparents, they will inherit everything. Next, your estate goes to first cousins, first cousins once removed, and so forth. Your so-called "distributees" must be traced to a common grandparent. This is truly a statute to protect the friendless orphan. While the statute provides for distributions to great-grandparents, great-great-grandparents and their descendents nothing is ever provided for someone you are living with, no matter for how long. You might be interested to know that your own parents can be disqualified if they treated you so brutally that their parental rights could have been terminated. The law gives nothing to the abusing parent. And this is only New York. Every other state has its own plan for "intestate" distribution.

The point of all this is, of course, that you don't have to stand for it. You can make your own will and leave your property to whomever you please. Here is your big chance to do what you have wished you could do all along, to do what you know is right for you.

WILLS AND MONEYTHINK

To set your mind at rest, I surveyed a dozen of my older colleagues who have been in the estate planning business for forty years or more and asked them whether they could remember any time when a client of theirs died immediately after making a will. None of them had had any such experience. Wills are not hazardous to your health. In over 490 years of combined legal experience, not one person was brought low by making a will.

You can also have many wills during your lifetime. Get over the notion that wills are written in stone. You will soon see that the beauty of a will is that it can be changed many times.

At the end of this book I have included forms for you to fill out that will help you talk to a lawyer about a will and to think clearly about it. The type A Estate Planner—the one who loves forms and sharp pencils—will get a real kick out of these forms. The rest of you will have to dutifully fill them out. If you find that you're letting it slide, do your Moneythink exercises again. Why can't you sit down and fill out some simple forms? Where does the block come from?

Getting started is often the hardest part, so begin with the simplest task. Write down who your beneficiaries are. Whom do you want to leave your money to? Most of you know the answer and don't need help. Your spouse, children, grandchildren, usually in that order.

You can even disinherit an heir—with one exception, your spouse. Almost every state forces you to provide something for your spouse in a still-surviving marriage. In New Jersey, for example, you must give your surviving spouse at least one third of your estate if there are any children. Most states let you leave it in trust; the inheritance need not be an outright gift. For example, in New York, if you want to leave money to a spouse in the most restricted way, you can leave a cash amount of $10,000 and place the rest of the one third in trust for him or her. States differ. Pennsylvania used to be a state where you could cut out your spouse. But even there you are now required to give something to your spouse. This is so definite that even if you put in your will that you disinherit your spouse, that portion of your will would be invalid. The spouse could elect to take his or her share even if disinherited. That's why this statutory share is called the spouse's "Elective Share."

After your spouse, consider your children. Are there any you want to favor? Are any minors? Do any have special needs? Don't forget your children can easily be disinherited by a will, even if your spouse can't.

Are your children adopted? Remember, adopted children are no different from natural children. If you want to disinherit them you can and you don't have to give a reason. But if a will leaves property or money to "my children" the word children will include adopted children. On the other hand, if you have "illegitimate" children—the law's word for a child born of parents who are not legally married and don't get married afterward—they will get nothing if you just use the word child or children in your will. To leave them something, you must specifically name them.

The rights of illegitimate children are still very skimpy. In many states, illegitimates inherit from their mother's family, if there is no will, but not from their father's unless there was a paternity suit first. Two clients of mine are in the forefront of asserting the rights of illegitimates. Their parents led a kind of Back Street life. The father, a prominent businessman, had a so-called legitimate family living completely separate from his second family. When the "illegitimates" learned of the other family and of their own illegitimacy, the pain was staggering. Shortly after their father died, they learned that the law gave them no rights at all. In fact, they weren't even entitled to a formal notice of a probate proceeding. After months of research in this specialized field, I was appalled to conclude that the law in the area is practically medieval. For example, if you want to start doing legal research in the field, you begin with the Law of Bastards.

My first client in estate planning was the parent of an illegitimate baby. He was married and had two children of his own with his wife. She knew nothing about the illegitimate child. I worked out an elaborate estate plan for him and his family when he told me about his dilemma. If he left his illegitimate child a legacy, it would shock and distress his legitimate family, but he did want to provide for the baby. What should he do? The answer, of course, was a life insurance policy significant enough to be meaningful as a death benefit. This policy, as you will see in future chapters, is paid to the beneficiary without going through the estate and without being mentioned in the will and is even tax free as long as the father gave total ownership of it to the mother of his illegitimate child. He did this. It turned out to be a happy and workable solution for everyone.

If your beneficiaries are children, you must think of their children too. There are two phrases used in will legalese all the time that you should know. They are *per capita* and *per stirpes*. Knowing these words will help you talk to your counselor and also help you Moneythink. In fact, the way people regard these words tells a lot about them.

Per Capita means that you leave your money in such a way that it is distributed equally among those individuals of an equal degree of relation to you. The share of anyone who dies is divided up equally by the other beneficiaries of equal kinship. *Per stirpes* means that if one beneficiary dies before you the heirs of that beneficiary divide up the share. Literally, their heirs sit in their "stirrups" and inherit by right of their deceased ancestor. Here are examples:

Per Capita   Your children, A, B, and C, are beneficiaries. If C dies, A and B divide C's share. If C had two children, C's kids get nothing.

Per Stirpes Your children, A, B, and C, are beneficiaries. If C dies, his share is divided between his kids, D and E, equally. A and B keep their original share.

Do you want your money to go to your grandchildren equally, even though one of your children has had many offspring and the others have had only a few? Or do you want the grandchild with many brothers and sisters to have less from you than the grandchild who is alone or has only one sibling? There is no right answer. Most people choose *per stirpes,* so that the grandchildren get more if their parents have had fewer children. Again, the only child wins out. Most grandparents believe that grandchildren should not get more than their parent would have gotten in the first place.

Next, think about the other people who are your heirs. Whom would you like to leave a lump sum to? A charity, a friend, a sister, a brother, a parent?

Once you've gotten your beneficiaries straight, consider the amounts you want to go to each of them. Don't think that you must put specific amounts in a will. Usually you can't, since you don't know how to predict the future. Instead put in percentages. Whether you have five million or only five dollars you can still give 1% of your estate away.

Next, decide how much you want your spouse to have—in terms of power, not money. If you want your spouse to have complete control over what's left to him or her, give it outright. If not, leave it in trust for his or her lifetime. You'll see how later.

Decide who your trustees and your executors will be. This book contains a good deal of advice on selecting them. For this Moneythink exercise, just list everyone, including lawyers, institutions and family, that you would even consider.

Do some Moneythink about your dreams for the future. Can you envision yourself retired? Where would you be living? Will your dependents be working? If you're young and you can't possibly answer these questions, don't. Have a simple will as your first shot and then make it more specific as you get older and your estate is clearer.

Typically, a first will leaves everything to your spouse. A second will leaves the bulk of your estate to your spouse outright or in trust and provides for the kids too. Variations of later wills create more sophisticated trusts for the wife and children, naming tested professionals as executors and trustees, together with the major beneficiaries. This is typical, but it may not be right for you. Still, it may give you a framework in which to begin your Moneythink.

Information of course is needed too, and you'll get plenty of that in the next section. Meanwhile, before reading further, learn this short glossary of terms:

Bequest or Legacy—A gift of personal property made in a will to a legatee; a gift of real property made in a will to a devisee.

Legatee—One who gets a gift of personal property in a will.

Devisee—One who gets a gift of real property in a will.

Specific Bequest or Legacy—A gift of an identified item.

General Bequest or Legacy—A gift that isn't specific, demonstrative or residuary—usually a sum of money.

Demonstrative Bequest or Legacy—A gift of property to be taken out of a larger holding of specific identified property.

Residuary Bequest or Legacy—A gift of the balance of property after payment of taxes, debts, expenses and specific, demonstrative, or general bequests or legacies.

ANATOMY OF A WILL

Since all wills have a similar format, let's dissect a standard will and see its anatomy. We will examine a will clause by clause so you can learn the jargon and the meaning behind the words.

The Revocation Clause

Typically wills begin simply enough with the statement that they revoke (replace) all other wills or codicils previously made. A codicil is an amendment to a will if there is some change you would like to see but don't want your attorney to remake the whole will. It saves time and paper, but that's all it saves. Most attorneys will agree that you are better off having one will rather than a will and a codicil. Frequently clients come into the office with a will and many codicils. If any of them were lost or misplaced, their wishes would not be followed. Limit yourself to one document, and use a codicil only in the event that you are going on a trip or are rushed and must get an amendment out quickly.

Remember, you can make and revoke a will at will. I have one client who has made sixteen wills in his lifetime; each subsequent will replaces the former. Only the last one counts. The usual language is: "I, (your name) of (your address), do make, publish and declare this my Last Will and Testament, hereby revoking all former wills and codicils made by me."

In fact, this is so typical many lawyers use preprinted fancy embossed stationery for it, and other lawyers have their word-processing machines set up to type these words automatically.

Let's look at this revocation business.

Simply stated, subsequent wills revoke prior wills. This will be true for you even if you don't write it in your will. But what if the second will is not valid? In some states a person who makes a subsequent but invalid will ends up having no will at all. In other states the prior will is *revived*. When we talk about revival in estate practice, we are talking about the rule that a subsequent invalid will in some states is void and the provisions of a prior existing will are revived when the subsequent will is struck down. This is why you read about heirs contesting the validity of existing wills, and coming up with old wills under which they have been named beneficiary.

If you do have a will but feel that it is inadequate and plan to make a new one after reading this book, make sure that your old will is properly destroyed. Tell your attorney to make a note for the file stating that you destroyed your old will. Then take the old will and throw it in the fire. Don't let that old will survive! In states where an invalid subsequent will does not revive an old will, the law of intestacy will apply; in other words, those old State laws will take over again. Be sure to make a new valid will.

Tax and Debt Clause or All Right Already Uncle Sam

After you have told the world that you intend to revoke all your prior wills and codicils, you go on to assure the government that taxes will be paid, and your creditors that your debts will be paid. There are many ways to do this, depending on where you want the tax and debt payments to come from. Consider this example:

> I direct that my Executors pay all my debts, including my funeral and administrative expenses and all estate, inheritance and similar taxes imposed by the government of the United States or by any other state or territory with respect to all the property that is required to be included in my gross estate whether the property passes under this Will or otherwise. Such expenses, debts and taxes shall be paid from (choice number 1) Residuary estate; (choice number 2) A portion from each beneficiary; (choice number 3) Paid from the bequest to (a stated heir).

Many attorneys will prepare this clause for you without discussion, but there are some significant things to think about. For example, your estate taxes can be paid right off the top of your gross estate or from the residuary portion of the estate. We will talk a lot about residuary clauses; for now it suffices to say that the residue of your estate will be the property and money left after everything specifically mentioned is distributed. It usually goes to your major heir, the person most important and close to you. If the taxes and debts are paid only from the residue, then your nearest and dearest will bear the full burden. If you have a few residuary beneficiaries, taxes will be apportioned among them unless you say otherwise. For example, if one third of the residue goes to charity and two thirds to your spouse, there will be proportionate tax payments, *unless* you say to take it from the top first. If the taxes and debts are paid from the entire estate, then all the beneficiaries will be contributing. But you might have reasons for wanting one of the beneficiaries to pay everybody's taxes.

If you leave real estate to someone in your will and the real estate taxes were paid by the estate, the beneficiary of the property will have to reimburse the estate for those taxes. The beneficiary also picks up the mortgage unless you say otherwise. If you want the beneficiary who obtained the real estate to be free from existing taxes on it, say so; your fiduciaries (executors) will then pay the taxes from the rest of the estate.

This clause also directs the payment of debts like your funeral expenses, including masses and perpetual care, and any lingering medical bills. Give some basic thought to the question of whom you wish to pay for these expenses and put your decision into this tax and debt clause. If you are content to take the amounts off the top of the estate at the beginning, you will be in good company, since this is the most usual way of doing things. Avoid using the phrase "just debts," which appears in many wills. A debt may be just, but legally unenforceable; e.g., a charitable contribution or a debt barred by the statute of limitations (the creditor waited too long to collect). Don't leave your executors guessing about this.

Personal Property

The clause called the "specific legacy" clause is what most people think about when they think of making a will. This is the place where you get to give away specific items of tangible personal property to the people you would most like to see have them. Specific stocks, bonds and other cash substitutes are also given here. This is the place to get a little sentimental and to be specific in regard to what you give away. Remember, the rest of the clauses will be very general, leaving pretty much whatever is left to the other heirs. Remember too that moving expenses, if any, are the responsibility of the legatee unless you say otherwise, and so are any liens against the property you leave. So if you really want to get even with someone leave him or her the baby grand piano which you have bought on credit.

An example of a specific legacy clause is:

"I give the ruby ring known as the Kimmelman stone to my niece Sophie if she survives me."

Don't imagine that if you leave a specific piece of property, you are obligated to keep that property for the rest of your life. Many people who leave their gold earrings, say, think that they must change their will if they lose one of them, or if they decide to cash them in because the price of gold has gone soaring. Not so. If you die without owning that specific piece of property, the legatee will simply not get anything. This is called ademption or a "failed bequest."

What if you don't want the bequest to fail? You can state that in the event the personal property no longer exists the legatee will get the dollar equivalent or another gift that you also describe.

Description of the items is the most important thing in this part of the will. Many attorneys do not want to work out the descriptions for you. They call this the pots and pans part of estate planning. Make your description clear. Take a tip from Martha Washington, the childless mother of our country. Since she had so many wonderful things to give away she drew little pictures on her will to make sure everyone knew exactly what she was talking about! You too should be specific.

Letters Precatory

Despite all the foregoing advice, there can be good reasons for leaving out specific bequests. Perhaps you do not want everyone to know who is to get your retirement watch or your engagement ring. The alternative to announcing the facts in a will is the "letter precatory." A letter precatory is a letter written in your own handwriting, signed by you and given to your executor. It can list all the odds and ends of personal property, both valuable and sentimental, without publishing who gets them in the will. The executor, of course, must be someone trusted who will carry out your wishes. I suggest that you do list very valuable items in the will. For sentimental items, don't clutter up your will but prepare a letter precatory.

Alternatively, the will can permit your executor, particularly if he or she is a spouse, to divide things up at his or her discretion. You could say for example: "I leave my doll collection to my beloved daughters, and direct my husband John as executor to divide them among our daughters at his absolute discretion having due regard for our daughters' preferences. John's decision shall be binding and conclusive."

To make life easy, you can leave your personal property in a general way. Try this:

> I give, devise and bequeath all of my jewelry, clothing, books, personal effects, household furnishings and equipment, automobiles and other tangible personal property, wherever situate, which I own at the time of my death, together with my insurance policies to my children share and share alike.

Money Clauses

Next come the money clauses. Your will can give money and property to people in many ways. You can give a general legacy that is a specific amount of money, which is not taken from a specific fund, to be paid off from the cash available in your estate. If there is not enough cash at the time of your death, then only a part of that legacy, or perhaps none, will be paid. Another way of giving is through a percentage of your estate rather than a specific amount of money. Here you give one third or one half or some other fraction or percentage of your estate to your heirs. You can make the gift flexible. For example, you can leave a stated sum, say $50,000, provided that this does not exceed 5% of your estate and in the event that it does the gift will be reduced to 5%, leaving the remainder to your more important heirs, such as your spouse and children.

There is even a type of legacy called the demonstrative bequest. This means that you give a certain amount of cash and state where the cash is to be taken from. For example, you can give $10,000 out of a specific bank account. The beneficiary will not get the $10,000 unless the bank account itself is still in existence, even if there is $10,000 in the estate. In that case, specific and general bequests are paid, then the demonstrative bequest is considered.

If you want to give stocks and bonds, pay attention to whether you are giving them as a specific bequest or as a demonstrative bequest. If you want your beneficiary to get a particular stock that you own at the time you make your will, then name the stock and put down the certificate number right in the will. (You can still sell the stock, and if you do, that beneficiary will not get anything.) Otherwise, if you just leave a general disposition of AT&T, then it's possible that your executors will actually have to go out and buy some of that stock in the open market at a time when you would not have recommended such a purchase. Remember if you do give a specific stock, it carries with it any stock splits that may occur after you have executed your will.

No one can tell you whether to be specific or general in your bequests, but I can tell you which type of legacy will be paid and which will fail if you don't have enough money to cover everything. Such failure is called "abatement" and it proceeds in this order:

- Gifts to a spouse that qualify for an estate tax deduction are paid first.
- Specific legacies, if the item still exists, are paid next.
- Demonstrative legacies are paid next if the fund they are taken from still exists.
- General legacies are paid next.
- Demonstrative legacies are paid next if the fund specified does not exist, but other money is left.
- Residuary gifts are paid last.

The order varies from state to state and sometimes the legislature makes changes, but these guidelines are widely used.

Trusts

Trusts are a separate and useful part of estate planning, and no anatomy of a will would be complete without reminding you that trusts, if you want them, can be set out right in your will. A trust is a method by which someone you name (the trustee) will manage a bequest for the beneficiary instead of the beneficiary getting the money outright. These kinds of trusts don't come into existence until you die and the will is probated. If you do create one, you can change it anytime you want, merely by changing your will.

The Residuary Clause

Everything that you have not given away in your specific bequests, and everything that the government hasn't taken from you in taxes and everything that you have not paid out to your attorneys, fiduciaries, doctors, and creditors is called the residue of your estate. Since the bulk of your estate is likely to be involved here, the person or persons who generally inherit the residue of the estate are those who are closest and most important to you. They are called the residuary legatees, and the clause that gives them everything is called the residuary clause.

The words are fairly standard and very significant. They state that the testator will leave the "rest, residue and remainder of my estate wherever situated, whether real (that means real estate) or personal (that means all personal property including

stocks, bonds, bank accounts, etc.), to my residuary legatees."
In other words, everything, including any specific bequest that
has "failed" (remember that).

You can leave this significant portion outright or place it in
trust for your family.

Don't forget that you can give someone a specific bequest,
like an automobile or a painting, and also make that person a
residuary beneficiary.

Burial Instructions

You may include instructions for burial in a will,
according to your needs and wishes. The older person should
pay some attention to this subject. No one ever died
prematurely from writing up a burial clause. While it may take
ten minutes of painful thinking and conversation with your
loved ones, let them know what arrangements you've made and
where the documents can be found. Sometimes giving them this
peace of mind is the best legacy you can leave.

Because of the fears stirred up by focusing on burial, most
people know nothing about it. A discussion with Mr. Gerald
Hass, manager of the Mt. Ararat Cemetery in New York, put it
in a nutshell; in New York, as in many states, the control of
cemetery plots goes directly to the surviving children, with the
surviving spouse having the right of burial. If you don't want
your children to inherit the plot you must either have them sign a
release to the cemetery waiving their right (the cemetery will
provide the forms for you) or specifically leave the plot to
someone else in your will. In many states burial plots do not go
to the person named residuary beneficiary in a will; instead they
are governed by state law unless specific mention is made in the
will directing otherwise. Unless you've given it some thought,
whoever it was that you intended to use a family plot could
literally be without space when the time comes.

Most states also have new statutes which cover anatomical
gifts. If you want to give a portion of your body to science, say so
in your will but also separately fill out donor cards. Call local
hospitals for information. Speed is of the essence, and there will
be no time to do a real service for humanity if a donee has to wait
for your will to be probated in order to get the gift.

Simultaneous Death Clauses

What happens if you and your beneficiary die at the same time, or examination can't determine who died first? Wills cover this, too, in simultaneous death clauses. Frequently, when beneficiaries plan their wills together these clauses crisscross, so that each one is considered to have predeceased the other. This means that whatever legacy you leave will go directly to your beneficiary's choice of beneficiary. The same will happen to the person who died with you.

For example, take a brother and sister who die together in a crash, each having made a will leaving everything to the other. If the brother was considered to have died first, the sister (even though already dead) would inherit, and an estate tax would be paid. The inheritance would then be paid out directly to her heirs, named in her will. It would be taxed again in her estate. By the time her heirs received it, two tax bites would have been taken.

If the sister is considered to have predeceased the brother, then the legacies would go directly to the brother's other heirs. One tax bite would be saved.

Brother's will	Sister's will
Heir is sister, or if she dies	Heir is brother, or if he dies
Nephew	Same nephew

If the brother and sister die together with a simultaneous death clause in each of their wills providing that when in doubt as to who died first the testator (the one who made the will) is presumed to have predeceased, this is what will happen:

Criss-cross problem

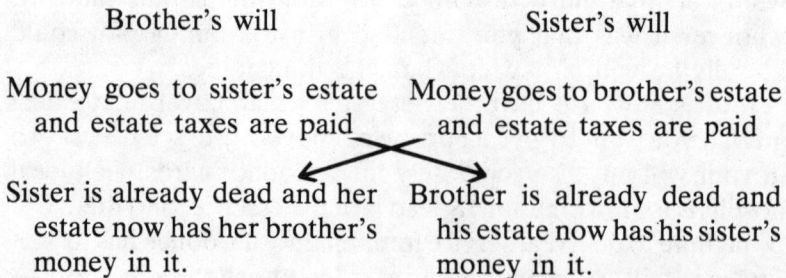

Brother's will	Sister's will
Money goes to sister's estate and estate taxes are paid	Money goes to brother's estate and estate taxes are paid
Sister is already dead and her estate now has her brother's money in it.	Brother is already dead and his estate now has his sister's money in it.

| The nephew inherits after a second estate tax based on the sister's estate is paid | The nephew inherits after a second estate tax based on the brother's estate is paid |

Nephew

Here are the same wills, except that the simultaneous death clause doesn't criss-cross. The sister's will says she survives and the brother's will says he survives:

Sister	Brother
Brother gets nothing because sister is presumed to be survivor—no tax	Sister gets nothing because brother is presumed to be survivor—no tax
One estate tax	One estate tax

Nephew gets everything

Before including a simultaneous death clause, consider whom you want to inherit in such a situation. Let your attorney consider and explain the tax aspects.

The In Terrorem Clause

I have told you a lot about getting your property to the right people, but what if there are people whom you don't wish to inherit anything at all? There is a will clause with the frightening name of In Terrorem. This is a clause that says in no uncertain terms that you do not intend to leave anything to the person named. In most states you can disinherit your children. You might wish to disinherit one and not the other. Usually it is only the spouse that you cannot disinherit altogether. Suppose that you have only brothers and sisters, some of whom you want to help, others who in your judgment don't need help or don't deserve it. If there is any danger that people you want to exclude might contest the will, this is the time to use the In Terrorem clause. It states that you have no intention of giving them anything and that if they should contest the will, the very fact that they caused trouble will result in their bequest failing.

Special Terms

Also in the category of clauses that withhold rather than give are those provisions that deal with people who may be in a nursing home or receiving other care at the time of your death. You may know that in order to get medical aid, the government requires the recipient to spend down and keep only $2,150 in his or her bank account. If you leave money bequests to such persons, the government will force them to spend it first, perhaps by paying bills to the institution in which they may be living. They will not be able to keep more than $2,150 for extra things to make them comfortable. To prevent that, there is a saving clause that you can use which states that a bequest will lapse if the beneficiary is in an institution and government aid is available. With this, your beneficiary will not inherit money that will be paid out to the government. On the other hand, if the beneficiary doesn't need government aid, he or she will be able to inherit the money.

The Home

Unless you specifically want to leave your real estate to a particular person, it is not necessary to have a special clause regarding it. It goes into the residuary and is left to the residuary legatee. However, some states require that at least the marital home (the home that the couple last lived in before one of the spouses died) be given automatically to the other spouse. That right to real estate is called the Right of Dower when given to the wife and the Right of Courtesy when given to the husband.

What you should include in your will is the giving of a cooperative apartment. Remember that a co-op is not real estate. Because it looks like shelter, many people are not clear on this. When you own a co-op you own shares in a corporation. The corporation—not you—owns the real estate. That means that you have to abide by the shareholder's agreement, usually embodied in the proprietary lease or in the by-laws of the corporation. Most co-ops permit you to leave your corporate shares to your spouse without interference by the board of directors. Some extend this to the rest of your family; others do not. Therefore, if you do own a co-op check the by-laws and check the lease. A simple clause stating that you plan to give your shares to your spouse or next of kin will suffice.

Executors and Trustees

The next part of your will generally names your trustees and executors. Here is the individual that will administer your estate and be responsible for the welfare of your kin. The clause itself is innocent enough; it generally reads "I appoint my wife (or a bank or son or family lawyer) to be the Executor (Executrix) of my will. If he (or she) fails to qualify or ceases to act, then I appoint my sister-in-law as the successor Executrix."

This is the portion of your will that contains those all-important decisions as to whether to have your major beneficiary act as the executor alone or together with a professional executor. In general, persons or banks or attorneys named as executors must post a bond securing their responsibility. But a will can (and most wills do) exonerate them from having to post that bond. What the testator (will-maker) cannot do is exonerate the executor from liability for failure to exercise due care. You wouldn't want to anyway; the whole idea is to have your fiduciaries be the most upright, forthright, and efficient persons you could find.

Guardians of a child can also be named; however, a surviving parent (even if the parents are divorced) can defeat the guardianship appointment.

Signing the Will

After a will is drawn, you generally come into a lawyer's office for what is called the will ceremony. This gives the lawyer the opportunity to tell bad jokes about estate planning and to have everyone sit uncomfortably in a forcibly light atmosphere: lawyers call this "putting the client at ease." I suggest you make the visit to your lawyer more palatable by ending it with champagne. Bring a glass for the lawyer, too, especially if it's me. The will ceremony includes the attestation clause. In that clause, you sign the will and state that you have read it, understood it, and attest that it is your will. This little ceremony is witnessed by two or three persons, depending on the State in which you sign the will.

I always play a little game with my clients when they finally come in to sign their wills. In the presence of witnesses I ask them what day it is, in order to show that they are of sound mind. Every single one of them looks at his or her digital watch and then gives me the answer. If they're sane enough to look at a watch, they're sane enough to sign the will.

The best witnesses are generally the secretaries or paralegals present in your lawyer's office when you sign the will. After your death, it will be time-consuming and expensive, if not impossible, to bring together all of these strangers to swear that the will is yours, in the event that there is some sort of contest. Even in the absence of a contest, this is the kind of nonsense that makes probate so expensive. Check with a lawyer to see if your particular state permits the special attestation clause, which avoids the need to bring in witnesses at the time of actual probate. This simple piece of paper, which reads as follows, is enough to do the job:

Each of the undersigned, individually and severally being duly sworn, deposes and says:

The foregoing instrument was subscribed in our presence and sight at the end thereof by   (your name) hereinafter referred to as the Testator, on the   day of   19   at

The Testator at the time of making such subscription declared the foregoing instrument so subscribed to be his last Will.

Each of the undersigned thereupon signed his name as a witness at the end of the foregoing Will at the request of the Testator and in his presence and sight and in the presence and sight of each other.

The Testator was, at the time of so executing the foregoing Will, over the age of 18 years and, in the respective opinions of the undersigned, of sound mind, memory and understanding and not under any restraint or in any respect incompetent to make a Will.

The Testator, in the respective opinions of the undersigned, could read, write and converse in the English language and was suffering from no defect of sight, hearing or speech, or from any other physical or mental impairment which would affect his capacity to make a valid Will. The foregoing Will was executed as a single, original instrument and was not executed in counterparts.

Each of the undersigned was acquainted with the Testator at such time and makes this affidavit at his request.

Answers from the Surrogate Court

Thanks to Chief Clerk Armand J. Starace of the Brooklyn Surrogate's Court and that Court's Senior Law Assistant Laurence P. Murphy Jr., I learned the answers to some of the questions most asked by laypeople on the subject of wills.

Q. Should I use a letter precatory or list personal property in a will?

A. To be entirely sure that property will go to the beneficiary of your choice make your designation in the will, do not use a letter precatory.

Q. What is one of the biggest mistakes laypeople make in talking to an attorney?

A. They fail to prepare an accurate family tree and the failure to notify all distributees and legatees causes delay.

Q. Why does administration of estates take so long?

A. Some reasons are: many parties have rights and contest the proceedings; assets may be complex and difficult to get together; administration can be delayed when out-of-state executors have been named; estate tax audits, if they occur, can be time consuming.

Q. Where should I keep my will?

A. Your best assurance that the will is not misplaced is to file it with the Surrogate Court. If not, keep the will in a safety deposit box or bring it to your lawyer or executor for safe keeping, and keep a conformed copy for yourself with a notation stating the location of the original.

A final word of caution: *Make all the wills you want and all the changes you require. Keep changing when there is change in your life.* If you have a child, if you divorce, remarry, marry for the first time, become wealthier or significantly poorer, change your will. Change your will now because taxes have become Reaganized. Take guidance from your lawyers, who, if they are on their toes, will send you letters every once in a while when there are major tax or other legal changes. Come in and keep your will up-to-date.

An out-of-date will can be worse than no will at all. Probate can be hell when wills have been made thoughtlessly. One situation I handled was like a law school example of what not to do. First, the executors and trustees were older than the will-maker, and by the time he died they were ancient. Second, they lived out of state (in two different states). Every piece of paper had to be sent to them separately, with endless time in between for signing and returns. Third, the will was made when the maker was married to one woman and never changed after he divorced her and married another. Worse, he finally separated from his second wife and made no new provisions there either, leaving her with the right to get the maximum marital share (remember you can't disinherit your spouse unless there was a divorce). The burial plot was left to the first wife when the law gives it to the surviving spouse, not a surviving ex-spouse.

I could go on. The moral is: Once you have broken through your resistance to making a will, keep your Moneythink active. If nothing special happens, review it every five years anyway. You can use the five year interval to set new goals and do financial and investment Moneythink and tax planning too.

If you keep aware of your estate needs, you won't have to knock yourself out to avoid probate because the eventual procedure won't be so bad.

3

EXECUTORS

People often appoint executors without much thought, naming their child or spouse or whoever seems to be handy at the time. It is hard to realize that the work of the executor is very substantial and can take years. What do executors do anyway? Of course they shepherd the will through probate. But they also take care of the estate assets while probate and distribution are going on.

Statutes of each state give powers "as long as your arm" to the executor, even though those powers go unmentioned in the will. In most states the executor may:

- retain property
- make investments
- hire professionals
- manage real estate
- dispose of personal property
- participate in corporate matters
- collect debts
- vote shares
- borrow
- exercise options
- pay debts
- marshal and distribute assets
- appoint custodians

45

- pay taxes
- defend will contests

Even greater powers are often included in wills. Some significant additions include marketing works of art or copyrights, and running small, family-owned corporations while an estate is being probated.

Almost anyone can be named as your executor, except infants, incompetents, aliens, felons, and persons who are habitually drunk, dishonest or improvident. This is no easy job.

Unless you say otherwise in your will, the executor you appoint is required to file a bond insuring good conduct. Most wills waive a bond.

Family members may be required to serve without being compensated or may serve in return for a gift given to them in the will. Gifts given in the will are not taxable to the persons named as executors on their personal income returns. On the other hand, commissions given to them are deductible from the estate before estate taxes are figured, while gifts are not.

Even if you do name a family member, it is useful to have a professional as back-up. Because probate should be quick, people minimize the importance of the executor. Actually an estate can be administered over a very long period of time. Sometimes this is actually advantageous. It can save both estate and income taxes. For this kind of fancy estate administration there is nothing like a professional.

Attorneys with small firms or individual practices are often the best bets. Unquestionably I am biased. Since my own background is with the hard-working specialist in the area of trusts and estates I see that type of professional as the backbone of the trust and estate planning process. Most such attorneys will set their fee based on the statute and a discussion with you.

Rates regarding executors vary regionally. You will find that individual attorneys, institutions and larger law firms throughout the country cater to the special needs of their locality. For example, in those states where a major portion of family wealth is represented by land and farms you can find institutions that specialize in administering those types of estates. I spoke with Lee G. Gamage, Executive Vice President of the Springfield Marine Bank in Springfield, Illinois. Springfield Marine not only performs the usual trustee and executor functions but it also provides farm management services. Mr. Gamage gave me a run-down of the services performed by Marine for those families that have farms to manage.

> Our farm management services include selection of tenants, fertilizer and chemical programs, selection of crops, supervision of conservation practices and disposition of grain. In other words, we take the place of the owner in all activities in connection with the farming operation. We furnish tax information and accounting statements to the owner. Our fee for this service is 6% of the owner's gross income with a minimum of $5.00 per acre and a maximum of $10.00 per acre annually.

SPECIAL TASKS AND POWERS

It can be a very good idea to continue to have the executor operate a business, whether it be a retail jewelry store or a cattle ranch, and accumulate income. So, in deciding whether you need a professional, ask: Does a major portion of my wealth consist of stock in a closely held business? If so, the federal taxes can be paid in annual installments. In other cases estate taxes can be deferred for up to five years, after which, again, one can pay out in installments. In order to avoid acceleration of this kind of plan, income that is accumulated should be distributed during the administration of the estate. Giving the executor the power to do this can be very important.

Sometimes an estate accumulates capital gains (income from the sale of investments). If the executor is authorized to distribute capital gains and does this, the taxes shift to the beneficiary and are not paid by the estate. Often this results in a large tax saving, and a happy beneficiary when the capital gains tax is lower than the estate tax bite. So you may want to give special power to distribute capital gains.

The executor also must be concerned with taking the appropriate deductions for depreciation of property held by the estate. Many of these areas are best handled by an accountant. I cannot emphasize too strongly that in protecting your beneficiaries a good accountant brought in early in the game can save a lot of headaches.

Among the other tasks of an executor is to balance the income tax and estate taxes against each other. But the executor also has the power to determine which of the beneficiaries will pay the taxes, unless you put limits in the will. Sometimes this causes great antagonism between different kinds of beneficiaries: beneficiaries of income of an estate and beneficiaries of principal. You might specifically wish to give your tangibles (a car, a necklace) tax free because you do not wish the beneficiaries to pay the tax. Or gifts to employees may be small, and you may want them to receive the sum outright without paying a tax. Also important can be exempting charities and your spouse from paying taxes.

Remember a good part of what you leave spouses and charities is deducted from your gross estate before taxes are considered. By making them pay taxes on what they have inherited you are diminishing their benefit and often playing havoc with the best formula for determining the marital and charitable deductions and exemptions. If you have been paying attention you know all this already.

However, here it is again in a nutshell: The executor evaluates the estate for estate tax purposes, determines what property is distributed to satisfy a bequest, pays the taxes and winds up the estate.

ACTING AS AN EXECUTOR

Let's say you have convinced the members of your family that you're an expert in estate planning. You've taken the right courses, read the right books, and you're determined not to let accountants and attorneys take over the family fortune. You plan to do it all yourself. Or maybe you are named co-executor with a professional. If either title is going to mean anything at all, you must take on great responsibility and understand the role of executor or executrix. If you want to do more than merely have the attorney pat you on the hand now and then while he or she takes care of the real business of the estate, you are going to have to learn how to swim. The waters of probate, tax returns and planning can be pretty muddy. For any substantial estate they should not be maneuvered alone. It is essential to be surrounded by good attorneys, bankers and accountants—but without some knowledge of your own you won't know what "good" means. Also, you will not feel free to discharge a professional who is not doing a proper job. Besides, any professional will treat you differently if you know what you're doing, and you will be more comfortable under all the circumstances.

An executor must have a feeling for the needs of the family. You, as a member of the family or a close relative, should have that feeling, and if you don't there is no book that can help. What I will give you here is some of the technical knowledge that you need. Later I'll provide information about how to talk to your lawyer and accountant.

The procedures that you will be going through are probate, distribution of assets and tax paying. The technical aspects—the filing of forms, the preparation of an accounting showing all the assets of the estate, the preparation of the tax return—will be done by the professional co-executor or by the lawyer and accountant that you hire. Most family executors simply hire professionals and let it go at that. They don't participate much in the process and they hope that they have selected the best professional. But even people who seek medical attention know they are better off if they have a background that can help them deal with the doctor and sometimes even challenge him.

If I have any message for you it is that there is no magic. There is no secret to being a good executor. There is no one rule to follow that can guarantee you will do well. Remember that the role of executor is finite. Once the estate has been completed and everything has been distributed, you are no longer an executor. Unlike a trustee, who may labor for decades, you will serve for only a short, definite period of time. Probate requires the filing of forms and working with an attorney to make sure that everything is done on time. Paying taxes requires balancing of interests among heirs and a good deal of mathematics; your role is to do as little as possible while urging the accountants to do things on time.

Your ability to handle these professionals is largely a matter of your own personality. I know from experience that anyone willing to get educated will be able to do the best possible job. Once informed, you will have the composure and confidence to speak up when you think something is going wrong, even if you don't have the information to understand quite what is amiss. You will also have the guts to insist on being given explanations.

From time to time you will find that family members are making conflicting demands upon you. This happens, for example, when there is substantial jewelry or art and you have been given discretionary power to distribute these items among family members.

You may very well find that while you are working without compensation to keep the family fortune intact, you are being faulted rather than thanked by the rest of the family members. Expect it. Take on the job as executor because you think you would enjoy it, or because you are the major beneficiary in the estate and have the most to lose if things go wrong, or because it's a job that has to be done and you know you can cope. Don't take it on to earn gratitude. Your rewards will be small.

If you have any doubts, remember that you don't have to be an executor if you don't want to. If you are approached by family members and you would rather say no, say it. Professional executors are paid very well for performing their duties. You will get no compensation and, as I told you, very little thanks. It is a lot of work and it can happen that you become the object of a good deal of family anger. There is also a lot of responsibility involved: moral, emotional, but also legal. Under the law the executor of an estate is a fiduciary of the beneficiaries. As discussed in other chapters, this puts a legal burden on you not to act negligently or carelessly.

Often, a family member is asked to act as executor because the person making a will does not want to spend money on professional help and believes that going to a family member will cut costs. From your viewpoint, that may not seem such a convincing reason. But sometimes it is difficult to say no because you have been chosen by the person making the will on the basis of what he or she thinks to be your superior intelligence and grasp of financial matters. This is all very flattering and you certainly may feel that you're letting the family down if you refuse. And yet there is nothing worse for a family than bringing an executor into the picture like a reluctant bride, unwilling and unenthusiastic.

Often people name distant relatives as executors—"distant"

both literally and figuratively. The relatives may have no real stake in the immediate family or may live so far away that administration of the estate is cumbersome, time-consuming and costly.

Having to say no is not easy and varies in every situation. To help you cope here are a few tips. To be an executor you must know all the details of the will maker's business and finances. If you are unwilling to take on the job without information, say so. The will maker may very well think that you are prying and take back the request to make you executor. If that happens you are certainly better off not having been involved in the first place. You may also say that you expect to move and would not want to burden the estate with an executor who is far away. That may get you off the hook. Or assert that you don't mind being a co-executor or a successor executor if there is no one else around, but that you prefer not to take on the whole responsibility yourself. Finally you may just very well have to say no, that you don't feel capable of taking on the responsibility. In the long run this will cause a lot less trouble than if you sheepishly take on a position you don't wish to hold. But if you do want to be executor or can't refuse to be, you must prepare yourself. Start with the following simple preparations.

Preparations and Procedures

Know where all the papers are. Try to find out where the will, social security numbers, insurance policies, and other important documents are kept. Suggest that they be placed in a safe deposit box to which you have the key and access. Your name can be jointly placed on the box, or the bank can be given instructions to permit you to open it in the event of death. In most states you will not be able to remove cash but you will be able to remove needed documents. Another idea is simply to keep the documents in a desk drawer with an easy access and without any need for bank supervision. If you wish to act in a professional way, explain to the will maker that you are preparing a file and intend to keep copies or originals of all important documents. It would be best for you if you had the originals, but I predict you will find reluctance in the will maker to give up the originals of life insurance policies and the like. Of course, if you are the spouse, you may know where all these things are, but frankly I doubt it. Rule one is to find out.

Be informed.   Once you know where the documents are, read them. There is no excuse for an executor never having seen the contents of a will maker's will until after death. Of course it may not be the last will, but there is nothing wrong with keeping up to date as the wills are changed. Even more important is to read the insurance policy, at least to find out the size of the death benefit. Be informed of the will maker's pension plan or other death benefits.

Talk to the professionals.   Find out who the will maker is using as a lawyer and introduce yourself. The same with the accountant, banker and the insurance agent. Find out from the insurance agent what papers you need in order to get the death benefit quickly and have them handy. Don't let these people tell you that they will take care of things. They will, but they are busy, busy, busy, and you're there to do the legwork so that there is no delay for your family. Talk to the personnel office if the will maker is employed by a corporation. Read over the pension benefits package with respect to death benefits. Know how these are to be applied for.

Get a power of attorney or know who has one.   If the will maker becomes ill before death it may be necessary to withdraw funds or sell stocks and bonds. You need not bother someone who is suffering in a hospital if you have a power of attorney made out to you. The power of attorney can be limited so you have the right to do only certain things at the will maker's choice. If there are stocks involved, every stock brokerage house has its own type of power of attorney for the transfer or sale of shares. Contact the broker where the will maker has the most holdings so you can go into action quickly.

Get ten copies of the death certificate.   It is usually the funeral home that provides death certificates. You will find that even to begin to put everything together you will need quite a few death certificates. To save you or another loved one from going down to the hall of records and spending a day going through that bureaucratic operation, have the presence of mind to ask the funeral home to get at least ten copies for you.

Know where the appraisals are.   In this chapter and many others we talk about the value of property which may have been appraised or for which there may have been receipts. These are very important in tax planning. Know where they are.

Know where the witnesses to the will are. If you don't have the special certificate we discussed earlier, you will have to get affidavits from the witnesses to the will before you can even go to court and file probate papers. Witnesses themselves may have moved, left town or died. If you're using an attorney who did not draft the will, know where to find the witnesses when the time comes. Keep this knowledge up to date as wills are changed. It will help the attorney too—always a worthwhile thing to do.

Rely on the professionals. As long as you are knowledgeable and assertive there is nothing to be ashamed of in relying on the professionals. The likelihood is that you will have made a good selection or the will maker will have done so. It is only those who are too dependent that must watch out. Don't be afraid to give the professionals their due. They will be paid for it; you are not expected to become a financier, C.P.A. and tax attorney overnight.

Coordinate with your co-executor. If you are not the sole executor and you are sharing the ship, recognize that there are no captains. The law makes each executor equal. You have equal rights and responsibilities. Never be afraid to speak up if the executor is a professional; on the other hand, don't expect that you can be "the boss." The law holds all executors responsible for the deeds of the others and for opposing decisions they believe to be mistaken.

Read the complex rules made simple. Next are rules that you should know. Read them. Do what you must do to suffer through, but read them!

Complex Rules Made Simple

An executor who is on his toes knows that he can:

Postpone the payment of estate taxes if necessary. If there is reasonable cause to do so, estate taxes can be deferred for a twelve-month period. Usually taxes have to be paid within nine months of death. But if you can show any reason why they cannot be paid on time, an additional year will be given.

If things are even worse than that and you can show undue hardship, an extension of ten years can be given. Undue hardship includes the probability that an important asset would have to be sacrificed in a distress sale in order to raise the money for taxes, or that the stocks of a family-owned corporation would have to be sold to strangers. The government wants to help you avoid such undue hardship and will give up to a ten-year delay in making payments.

If a substantial portion of the estate is made up of the stock in a family-owned corporation, then a mandatory extension can be gotten without showing any undue hardship. Hardship is presumed. As long as you elect to do so prior to the end of the first nine months after death you can pay estate taxes in twelve equal installments over twelve years.

Substantial is defined as more than 35% of the value of the gross estate made up of this type of stock. If the decedent owned an interest in more than one closely held corporation, the interests can be lumped together to get the 35%. If through the years there is a change in the holdings of the company so that 50% of the value is withdrawn by the family or if you fail to make an installment payment on time, the whole schedule of tax payments can be accelerated. These mandatory extensions are also available for sole proprietorships and partnerships under certain circumstances. I urge the use of a professional executor if a family business comprises the bulk of an estate.

Warning to executor: You are personally liable for the unpaid taxes. If during the ten-year period there is too little money in the estate to pay the taxes, the executor remains *personally* liable for the tax.

To give you peace of mind—but possibly at a price—you can ask the I.R.S. for a discharge from personal liability. The I.R.S. has one year from the time you make the request to notify you if there is a deficiency or if they are satisfied with the tax payment. If they are satisfied, you are off the hook. Do this only if you are really concerned, because by filing this form you are forcing the I.R.S. to look closely at the estate forms and taxes paid to see whether they are ready to guarantee that the right thing has been done. Whenever the I.R.S. has to look so closely at something they might as well make an audit. So beware.

It is also possible, however, that Uncle Sam will require that a bond be posted in an amount double that of the taxes due. Check the cost of posting such a bond; it may be prohibitive or perhaps even unavailable. Do this by looking at the Yellow Pages under bonding companies and you will find knowledgeable people ready to give you an answer. For the most part, the accountants and attorneys will be working on this, but it puts you on top of things to understand what's going on.

Choose among beneficiaries. This is the most delicate job of all. If you have a will that includes any kind of trust, there are usually two groups of people who will benefit: the persons who receive the income from the trust as it goes along and the persons who get the principal when the trust is over. Most of the time the trustee has great power to determine who will benefit more, the income beneficiary or the principal beneficiary (the remainderman, that is, the person who gets the remainder of the trust when it's all over).

Be that as it may, the executor too holds a lot of decision-making power that has an effect on principal and income beneficiaries. You may have to make decisions that favor one beneficiary over the other. Even by deciding to extend the payment of estate taxes you may be favoring the income beneficiary. When less is paid for taxes, more stays in the estate to produce income, which the income beneficiary gets. On the other hand, the tax is generally paid from the principal; yet the tax deduction is taken from the income earned in the year that the tax was paid. Again the income beneficiary benefits.

Choose the evaluation date. The amount that's in an estate in the first place depends on how the assets are evaluated. The executor is given a choice of evaluating assets (1) at death, (2) six months after death, or (3) on the date at which the asset is sold or distributed to a beneficiary if that took place during the six month period. To pick just mark the box on the Federal Estate Tax Return. You can't, however, change your selection once the time for filing, including extensions and paying of the tax, has elapsed. If the taxes are not filed on time you may lose this choice.

Most of the time you want the lowest value, to get the smallest tax. But sometimes for small estates it's worth using the higher value. If an estate is small enough not to have any estate taxes in the first place, a higher evaluation can save the capital gains tax. For example, take a share of stock worth $10 at the time of death and $20 six months later. If the executor chooses the $20 evaluation, and the stock is actually sold, say, three months later at $35, the capital gain that the estate made is only $15 not $25. This way the executor is selecting the basis or the value on which capital gains are figured. If the whole estate is so small in the first place that no estate tax return need be filed you will not be spending an extra dime in estate taxes and you will be saving some money on capital gains. Besides, in an estate that small only the date-of-death value can be used. Again you'll want to consult an accountant but at least you're going to know enough to ask whether you can save capital gains taxes by choosing a higher evaluation. With a little extra work the accountant can decide what will yield the best results. Similar vigilance should be shown by executors who are handling the estate of someone who has died insolvent. While there would be no federal estate tax, it is possible an income tax would be paid. It's important in such cases to watch the capital gains and less important to watch the estate taxes.

A question frequently asked of me by executors is whether we should try to sell or distribute assets during the first six months so that we have a choice of evaluation dates. My general answer is no. There is no reason to make sales or distributions just for tax purposes. Sales should be made when the market is best so that the most money can be realized for the asset. Executors engage in a "distress sale" or "estate sale" partially because they feel that the profits will be eaten up by estate taxes anyway, and partially because the money they are counting is not their own. Well, if you sell during your lifetime, part of the profits is eaten up by income taxes or capital gains, but you still don't decide to take a lower profit just because you'll suffer a lesser tax. There should be no difference in estate sales.

As for distributions directly to heirs without a sale, these should be made after the six month period unless the property has declined a great deal before six months elapse. If so, distribute the property at the time of its lowest value, even though the full time period has not expired. Some property, especially fluctuating stock, may increase in value if you wait.

Warning: Whenever you are making a decision think about

the other decisions you have to make and how they are affected. For example, if you evaluate shares in a closed corporation as very low, you may find that you are not meeting the 35% requirement, discussed earlier, that would permit you to pay taxes in installments. If not having to pay all the taxes right away is very important to the family, don't fool around by trying to make the value of the shares so low that other assets in the estate bulk larger and the business no longer accounts for the 35% of the gross estate needed to meet the installment requirements test.

Flower bonds are a poetically named government bond specially suited to use in the payment of estate taxes. Actually they are Uncle Sam's way of giving you a bargain. These bonds can be redeemed at the time of death at their par, or face value at maturity, even though at death they have not yet reached the maturity date. Their value at maturity is accelerated so that you can get their full value at date of death. Also, because they pay so little interest and are not a good investment for building income or capital, they are usually very cheap to buy and are actually sold at a discount in the first place. Therefore you get a double savings. The bond is sold at a price lower than its value at the time of purchase and its highest value at maturity becomes due at the time of death, even though that is before the maturity date. This happens only in the event they are used to pay federal taxes. It is Uncle Sam's way of admitting that he too has a collection problem and would like to give a discount for cash. Remember that the flower bonds must be bought prior to death and are therefore evaluated in the estate at par value. But no income tax is paid when they are sold.

Deal with the surviving spouse. If you are the executor of an estate and are not the surviving spouse, you may have to contend with one; particularly if the spouse has been excluded from the will. You will remember that as long as a spouse has not abandoned the deceased, or gotten a divorce or separation, he or she is entitled to a portion of the estate. This "elective" portion varies by state law. States also vary in listing the bad acts of a survivor which would deprive him or her of any claim on the estate. You may have no choice about dealing with an irate spouse if one turns up.

Not every decision to take an elective share is made by an

angry and excluded spouse. In some cases a loving spouse who has not been deliberately left out might be interested in the election. Here's how this works. Let's say a woman dies leaving everything to her son by a first marriage. She has a surviving spouse but she has left him nothing. He has independent wealth and has no interest in taking a penny away from his late wife's son. Still, unless he has signed an agreement waiving his rights, he is entitled to a portion of the estate. If he took it there would be a big estate tax saving. If he then gave the money to the son he would pay a gift tax but it would still be far less than the estate tax deduction is worth in some estates. This is purely a matter of mathematics and should be considered as part of the executor's post-mortem planning job in any case where there is a surviving spouse who has been given nothing under a will.

Suggest disclaimers. Would anybody want to disclaim an inheritance? Well, you might if you were going to save taxes and be able to do what you wish with the money anyway. There is a disclaimer form that has to be filed through which one beneficiary can disclaim a legacy in favor of another. Here too the attorney will be able to provide you with details.

This was done very successfully by one of my clients who was given all of her husband's estate. She was already very well provided for and didn't need the money. She was also getting on in years and planned to leave everything to an only son. She knew that the estate would first be taxed when she inherited (because in pre-E.R.T.A. days the marital deduction would be equivalent to only half of the estate) and then a second time when she died and left everything to her son. She decided then and there to disclaim her inheritance in favor of her son. This way the money did not pass to her at all and was not taxed upon her eventual death. Of course she gave up the right to use the money when she was alive. But this was a decision she made knowingly. Consider disclaimers when a party is very well provided for already and would probably give the money to another heir anyway. Disclaimers can also be made in favor of charities.

Disclaimers are governed by both state and federal laws. There are many rules, but at minimum disclaimers should be written, timely, show a complete refusal to accept the property and contain *no* designation of who gets the disclaimed property. Who does get a disclaimed gift? That's a matter of local law. Remember the disclaimer device if a legatee is incompetent to handle his or her own affairs.

Consider Subchapter S. If a family-owned corporation is an important part of an estate the executor may find himself in the position of having to decide whether or not the company should be a Subchapter S corporation. Subchapter S is a part of the Internal Revenue Code which permits certain small companies with ten or fewer individual shareholders to take the losses of a business from their own personal income tax returns and gives other benefits as well.

Subchapter S can be a good thing or bad thing. The decision to be Subchapter S is made on a yearly basis and must be signed by every shareholder in the company. When one shareholder dies, his or her executor has to make the decision on behalf of the estate. If nine of the shareholders wish to be Subchapter S and you as executor don't, you will be able to stop them from getting the benefits they want. Few non-professional executors can figure out the full financial ramifications of making this choice. Check with the attorney for the business as well as the attorney for the estate. Speak with both accountants as well. Hear their suggestions and their reasons. But do it fast; you may not have much time to make the choice.

Pay the income tax. Even estates pay income tax. As they go along they may be earning interest on undistributed income from investments. Income tax is paid on the fifteenth day of the fourth month following the close of the estate's taxable year. Here too you can choose to pay the income tax in monthly installments without interest. Because an estate tax is paid as well as an income tax, you sometimes have the opportunity to juggle the deductions (see the following rule) and determine whether they will be used as estate income tax deductions, estate tax deductions or deductions from income of the decedent's last personal income tax filing. Take a look.

Take deductions. Administrative expenses that can be taken as deductions from either estate taxes or the estate's income tax are such things as filing costs, fees to notaries, appraisers, attorneys and accountants, medical expenses, brokerage fees, traveling expenses, storage expenses, executors' commissions and casualty losses that may have occurred after death. The executor decides whether to take these as estate tax deductions or income tax deductions. If the estate is small, deduct from income tax. If the executor waits until the estate is terminated, the deduction can be passed along to the individual beneficiaries to be deducted from their personal income taxes. This is useful when the estate's income tax and estate tax are small and the beneficiaries can use the deduction to better purpose on their personal taxes. Of course this requires a knowledge of the needs of all the beneficiaries and the estate. Again, the lawyer and accountant usually can help, but it is important for you to know enough to be able to ask questions regarding deductions and deductibility. Deductions are taken only in the year when payment is made, so sometimes it is useful to make payment in the year that you wish to take the deduction. Warning: Funeral expenses can be deducted only from estate taxes; deductions for foreign, state and city income taxes paid on income of the estate are deductible only from the income tax of the estate. A decision must be made for each item, and certain deductions can even be split between income and estate tax deductions.

There can be a conflict between the income beneficiary and remainderman of a trust. If the estate is to be held in trust rather than passing to the beneficiaries outright, shifting deductions to the income tax return will ordinarily reduce the tax burden on the income beneficiaries and increase the tax burden on the remainderman. Some courts require the remainderman to be compensated for this.

File the final income tax and gift tax return. Though this is the accountant's job, it is your responsibility as executor to make sure that all the gift taxes that should have been filed in the last year of the decedent's life and his personal income tax returns are filed. Check with your local professional.

4

PRObATE

For some time now the general public has had a vague notion that probate is something to avoid. Sad to say, while most people wish to avoid probate, few of them know what it is. Maybe they think of "probate" the way some people think of "obscenity"—to paraphrase one of our Justices of the Supreme Court of the United States, "I can't explain it but I'll know it when I see it!" The trouble with probate is that once in it, you do indeed see it and you can't avoid it.

I give you two choices. You can do everything necessary to avoid probate (this takes work, planning and money) or you can do everything to take advantage of what probate has to offer and minimize its bad effects (this too takes work, planning, and money). What you can do, practically free, is understand it enough to make the right choice for you. First, you need to forget some myths.

Myth Number 1: If you avoid probate you save taxes. On a true or false test the answer to this is false. Probate has nothing whatever to do with taxation. Taxes are based entirely upon the assets that people have in their control when they die. If money is in your control the government is going to find a way to tax it. A good deal of this book helps you take money out of your control for tax purposes and still be able to use it efficiently for the purposes that you choose. If you avoid probate entirely you

61

will still be taxed under the same rules and in the same amount as if your estate was probated.

Myth Number 2: Probate is handled by the Internal Revenue Service. This is also false on a true or false test. Probate takes place in the state court, in the state where a person resides at the time of death. These courts are often called widows' and orphans' courts, or chancery courts. A fancy name is the surrogate's court. "Surrogate" is another word for substitute; the idea is that the judge in these courts is a substitute for the deceased. If there is any question as to what the deceased meant in his or her will or intended at the time of death, the surrogate or substitute (the judge) will decide. Surrogate's court judges are given the job of acting in the place of the deceased to carry out his or her wishes. If there is a will, the will must be submitted to probate.

The legal set-up is similar in all states. The executor named in the will files it and a probate petition with the surrogate. The surrogate, after determining that the will is genuine and valid in its form, accepts it for probate and orders that legatees (those you left money to) and distributees (those the legislator wanted you to leave money to) are notified, so they can present claims against the estate, if there are any. Sometimes you see such notices in local newspapers.

This is the time when heirs who are disinherited get into the act to try to set aside the will; e.g., the wife deprived of her elective share. Once all the assets are before the court, and either no claims by disappointed heirs have been made or claims made have been settled and the fees of administration have been paid, the probate is complete. At this time I.R.S. forms are presented separately and taxes paid.

Myth Number 3: If you have no will you will not need probate. False again on the true-false test. If you have no will, then the court must appoint an administrator since there is no executor named in a will. That alone requires a member of your family to go to the probate court to be designated as administrator. Unfortunately, the problem with estate planning is that few people do it until it is too late. Only five minutes ago, while writing this very portion of the book, I received a call from a client whose mother had died suddenly over the weekend. She had only $1,000 in a joint account upstate and a few hundred dollars in an individual checking account. There was a life insurance policy of $2,000. She had left no will because the estate was so small. My client could not obtain the money in the individual checking account, as I explained to her, without first going to the local county surrogate's court, applying to be named administrator and being so named. Only then could she apply for the tax waivers necessary to withdraw the funds. Her mother certainly had not avoided probate by not having a will.

Myth Number 4: Probate takes place in only one state. False again. Residence is the key to probate. The problem is that in our mobile society often people reside in more than one place. The older couple who keep their condominium in Florida and perhaps a vacation home in Connecticut can have double trouble when it comes to probate. Where do they reside? Today there are many middle-class couples who cannot afford a large home but can afford a small rental apartment and a small country house. There was a time when multiple residences were for the rich. Today, just because housing is so expensive, many people put their estate dollars in a small country place in another state and pay rent in their main state of residence. The court will look to where the deceased voted, kept property, kept bank accounts, worked and had friends to determine residence. The residence you list in your will is not binding on the court.

Generally a residence will be established. Sometimes a side (ancillary) proceeding is needed just to probate a single piece of real estate that exists elsewhere.

Myth Number 5: It is cheaper to have a family member as executor rather than a lawyer or other professional. This is the kind of true-false question that you used to hate because the best answer is maybe. An attorney will of course charge a fee. Your relative will not charge a fee and your will can even state that the executor shall serve without a fee. What does happen, however, is that the family member executor must know what he or she is doing or it will be necessary to hire an attorney to help every step of the way. Attorneys may charge on an hourly basis or a percentage of the estate; either way they may earn at least what they would have earned had they been named in the will. So the simple answer is either obtain professional help or have a knowledgeable family executor. A knowledgeable executor can work with an attorney to minimize costs and not be at the mercy of the professional's superior knowledge. In fact that's what this book is all about.

Myth Number 6:   While probate is proceeding no money is being distributed from the estate. False again, luckily for you and your beneficiaries. A good executor (one with a heart and a head) knows the needs of the beneficiaries and makes every effort to distribute the funds as probate goes along, particularly if the probate proceeding will take a long period of time. Probate can be lengthy—often annoyingly so, sometimes hair-raisingly so. Meanwhile the money is tied up. Rather than letting your beneficiaries go begging to an executor, make sure that the beneficiary has sufficient funds to live on for awhile as soon as death occurs.

Do this by having an insurance policy payable directly to your beneficiary. Such policies do not go through probate, even if you do have a will and even if the estate itself is going through probate. One of my good friends and one of the best insurance agents in the world suggests that the first person a beneficiary should call upon death is an agent. While I might not go so far as to advise that you keep your insurance agent's telephone number next to your phone, it's not a bad idea. It's also a great idea to give a simple power of attorney to your beneficiary to permit her or him to withdraw funds from your account while you are ill; it will avoid disturbing you in a sickbed in order to take money from the bank. Insurance policies, power of attorney, and a wise choice of executors all permit money to be collected even while probate is going on and even while an estate is being "tied up."

Myth Number 7:   If I put everything in joint names, I can avoid probate. False. Joint ownership has pitfalls that are to be avoided even more than probate itself. There are many kinds of joint ownership. Ownership with right of survivorship means that the survivor will automatically inherit. This automatic inheritance *does* avoid probate. But not all joint ownerships have the right of survivorship; most, in fact, do not. In general, regardless of what state we are talking of, if property, real estate, stocks, bonds and most other assets are held jointly and there are no special provisions for right of survivorship, they are *not* owned that way. Another type of joint ownership is called tenancy in common and has no right of survivorship. The deceased's half must be probated and will be left to his or her next of kin according to the rules of intestacy. No probate has been avoided.

Even if you do carefully use the magic words "right of survivorship," a problem arises if there is a common disaster and both you and your joint owner die simultaneously. Once again, who takes what must be probated. The same occurs if your joint owner becomes institutionalized. The wife that outlives her husband for years but who becomes mentally incompetent soon after his death may end up being the owner without probate but is really incapable of using and preserving the money. What happens? A friend or relative usually applies for a conservatorship to conserve the assets. Where is this application made? Back in the probate or surrogate's court.

So if you do want to avoid probate by joint ownership, make sure that you use the words "right of survivorship" wherever they are required and hope that your co-owner survives you in good shape and good health.

Myth Number 8: There is a magic, foolproof, painless formula to avoid probate. Yes, and there is also an Easter Bunny, Santa Claus, and the Tooth Fairy. What has been suggested as a method of avoiding probate altogether is something called an *inter vivos* trust, which we've already encountered in an earlier chapter, *inter* meaning during and *vivos* meaning lifetime.

If property is given in trust to someone during the lifetime of the person who sets up the trust, upon the settlor's death the beneficiary of the trust will automatically remain the beneficiary of the funds in the trust. Because it is clear, once you make a trust, who your beneficiary is, it is not necessary to go through probate to have a judge decide who gets the property. Also, it is not necessary to make a will telling everyone who your beneficiaries are, since each individual trust does that for you. This way you avoid probate by taking every type of property that you have and setting up a separate trust naming one of your loved ones as beneficiary.

Here is an example that will explain it to you. Say you happen to own a home and wish to have your sister inherit the house after your death. You have no wife and you have no will. You would like to avoid making a will so that no probate takes place just for the purpose of making sure that your sister gets the house. What can you do? You set up a trust naming your sister beneficiary, naming the house the subject of the trust and naming yourself the trustee. In the trust document you give yourself the right to live in the house for your own lifetime. You also name a successor beneficiary should your sister die before you. You also state that upon your death the trust will terminate and your sister who is the beneficiary of the trust will receive all of the property. You leave this trust document with your important papers just as you would a will. Since there is no question that the property will go to your sister, no will is needed to leave the property to her and therefore you avoid probate of a will.

Wills must go to probate, and trusts do not go to probate. By replacing all of your will provisions with separate trusts you avoid probate. Also, since an attorney will charge you a percentage of your estate based upon the value of the estate property that is considered for probate, you save legal fees by having as little property as possible go to probate. It sounds so easy you might wonder why everybody doesn't do this. There are plenty of reasons.

1. To begin with, to truly avoid probate you must have trusts which cover all your property—including stocks, bonds, bank accounts, real estate and anything else you may own—and all your beneficiaries. The preparation of the trusts—unless you really expect to do everything yourself—is ten times more expensive than the preparation of one single will.

2. When you make a trust during your lifetime you are giving a gift to that trust and so must file a gift tax return. You will surely be using up all of your gift tax exemptions pretty fast. Also, since gift tax may have to be paid right away (anytime you give a gift worth $25,000 or more you must file a return), you may be paying the tax during your own lifetime and taking the tax money out of your own pocket while you are alive rather than out of your estate after your death. It comes from you either way, but I presume that you would rather pay taxes after your death than during your lifetime when you can use the money yourself.

3. Unless you dispose of each piece of property, you will need a

will anyway. Hence, the expenses of preparing a will and of a smaller probate proceeding can't be avoided unless you diligently prepare a trust every single time you get new property.

4. Since life, I hope, is dynamic and you are constantly buying and selling, owning and giving up types of property, you must be on top of these endless trusts over and over again. A will too should be changed every once in a while: for example, if you have a new child, or remarry, or someone dies, or you become substantially richer or poorer. Still, you hardly have to worry about it everyday, whereas with a trust you must be constantly vigilant with respect to what you are earning, owning, and giving up.

5. Then there are emotions to consider. If you have created a will, no one need know about it. It can stay in your drawer, and you can privately and silently change it anytime you wish. With a lifetime trust, the beneficiary knows that the trust has been created, and if you wish to change it, it is going to be very difficult for you to do so without causing hard feelings. You can make the trust irrevocable. That might get you some tax savings, but it also deprives you of the use of your own money. No one, including those lawyers who swear by the use of trusts to avoid probate, suggests that you make these trusts irrevocable. That would stop you from selling, buying, and giving away your own money and property.

6. No taxes are saved by making trusts during your lifetime that are revocable. Again I warn you not to confuse the avoidance of probate with the avoidance of taxes. One thing has nothing to do with the other. If that is all you learn from these pages, that would be good enough. Taxes refer to the money the government wants after your death; probate refers to the procedure for determining who your heirs are after you die. That procedure can be expensive and lengthy, and all schemes to avoid probate are to avoid that, not to avoid taxes.

What, then, should you do? The answer is easy, but very individual. Have a will, but create an *inter vivos* trust to save estate or income taxes and diminish the size of your assets at death.

5

Taxes

Americans panic when it's time to pay taxes; in fact, tax
worries are a great American obsession. After all, we started a
revolution over them! Yet all estate and financial planning deals
with taxes. If it doesn't it's no good. This doesn't mean that taxes
are the only element of a plan or that they should fill you with
worry: *Don't be paralyzed by taxes*.

Remember, it is for the purpose of *saving* taxes that we plan.
The result of no planning or improper planning is that we do not
save taxes or we do not save enough taxes. However, tax
planning can become a disease when the goal of every financial
transaction is saving taxes. What I try to bring home to every
client is that while tax planning is very important, it is only one
goal of financial planning. Other goals, which must always be
before you, are: getting the money to the right people; not
divesting yourself of your own money too early in life so that you
cannot enjoy it; and keeping your money growing through
investments.

Tax planning is nothing to worry about, it is something to
understand and to do. Weigh each tax planning move against
whether or not it fulfills your other needs, or whether it suits
your own personal life style and your desire to leave legacies.
Tax planning is one goal out of many, never the only goal. It is
no shame to conclude that you would rather pay an extra tax and
not tie up your resources.

There are several kinds of taxes you have to consider in order to engage in proper financial planning. These taxes are not hard to understand. Since so much of our strategy goes into saving taxes it's important to distinguish between them. Investments, trusts, and even the post mortem decisions of your executor can depend on tax considerations.

We will not concern ourselves with real estate tax, sales tax, excise tax and custom duties. It's more than enough to look at the big three:

• Estate tax
• Income tax (with an emphasis on Capital Gains tax)
• Gift tax

ESTATE TAX

Estate tax is imposed only against the property owned and controlled by a person at the time of his or her death. From this simple principle come all of our tax saving techniques. If you don't control the property at the time of your death, you can't be taxed on it. If you do control it, a tax will be imposed.

When we create trusts that are irrevocable (that is, trusts we can't take back), we are losing control of resources in such a way that Uncle Sam can't include them in imposing an estate tax. If our trusts were revocable (meaning that we can undo them at our option) Uncle Sam gets a chance to take some of our resources since we did have control over them at our death. A life insurance policy giving ownership to a beneficiary instead of ourself is not taxed, and our beneficiary gets the proceeds of the policy as intended. If we give away money as an outright gift, that also avoids estate tax.

In addition to the rule of No Control there are three other rules:

1. A certain amount of money is exempt from estate tax; if your estate comes under that amount there is no tax.
2. Gifts you have given in the past are included in calculating the total amount of your estate at death.
3. Uncle Sam favors certain beneficiaries, like charities and

spouses, and allows deductions for the part of your estate you leave to them.

We'll look at each of these rules now, but see also the chapter on charitable gifts for more information about taking charitable deductions from your estate.

Amounts exempt from estate taxes.   For decades we have had no estate taxes imposed upon certain small estates. Recently the estate tax deductions and credits were increased a good deal, and our tax strategy will probably change in the next five years because of this. Certainly you have to act differently now than you did just six months ago. At present deductions from the gross estate are scaled to increase as follows: $225,000 in 1982, $275,000 in 1983, $325,000 in 1984, $400,000 in 1985, $500,000 in 1986, levelling off at $600,000 in 1987. See Appendix II to learn the equivalent credits. If the value of the property which you own and control at your death is over the amount you are subject to estate taxes; if it is under that amount, you aren't. This doesn't mean you don't have to estate plan, it just means you worry less about estate taxes.

This increase is not the only change made recently. A new tax law, called the Economic Recovery Tax Act or E.R.T.A., was passed, and most provisions became effective January 1, 1982. It was strongly championed by President Reagan, who made a speech to the nation regarding it. Before you go on you may want to read Appendix II—"Reaganization in a Nutshell"—for a quick review of the new law compared to the old law.

Including past gifts when calculating your estate.   There are many ways in which you may have given gifts during your lifetime, such as outright presents of money or things, trust funds, life insurance policies, conversion of your property to joint ownership, even under certain circumstances transfers made because of a divorce. In such cases you take something belonging to you and give up its ownership and control. If there were no restrictions upon this practice, it would be easy to diminish an estate, let's say by giving everything away in old age, so that no one ever paid estate taxes.

To avoid this, Uncle Sam combines the gifts given during your lifetime with the amount in your control at the time of death to calculate your estate. On January 1, 1977, the Unified Estate and Gift Tax was imposed, using the same tax tables for lifetime gift tax and estate tax. If the combined total comes under the exemption you are estate tax free. If you have already paid a gift tax on gifts given, you will get an estate tax credit for it—you are never taxed twice. Some gifts are not included if they are less than $10,000 per year for any one donee (gift getter). This is the gift tax exemption which we will discuss later in this chapter. After the total of estate and gifts is calculated, the standard deductions—$225,000 in 1982, $600,000 by 1987—are applied, plus any gift tax you have already paid. Estate taxes are paid only on the remainder after these and other deductions, discussed later, are taken.

Favored beneficiaries.   One of the cardinal rules of estate tax planning is that you will get a bonus if you give your resources to those beneficiaries that the federal government considers particularly worthy. We've had a long history of special benefits to spouses and a policy of encouraging both marriage and the support of the nuclear family. Someday with all the hullabaloo now going on regarding cohabitation, benefits for bequests between non-married couples who are economically interdependent may be sanctioned. But for now Uncle Sam is still a good old-fashioned boy. He wants to see you support your husband or wife and leave your money to them. If you do that, you get a big reward.

Beginning in 1982 (Post Reaganization) an unlimited amount can be given to your spouse and be deducted from your estate before estate taxes are imposed. This means that you can give all of your estate to your spouse, no matter how great (even more than $600,000), and pay no estate tax. This is a major change from the old rule that you could give no more than one half of your estate or $250,000, whichever was *greater,* to your spouse.

So far this sounds pretty easy. No doubt, you planned to give just about everything to your beloved wife or husband, anyway, and here comes Uncle Sam to give you a tax benefit for doing what you planned to do all along. Actually, it gets even better. Uncle Sam knows that you may not want to give large sums of money to your spouse outright so he makes an allowance for that. You don't need to give your spouse the money outright. (Some states, however, do require a small amount of outright gift to a spouse; in New York it's $10,000.) Instead, you may put the money in trust, with the income going to your spouse for his or her life, while the principal is left to your children. It seems easy and convenient, but don't be fooled. Uncle Sam has been in the tax business a long time. While you were taking your children to visit the Liberty Bell in Philadelphia to celebrate our bicentennial year or down to Battery Park to watch the ships come into New York Harbor, Uncle Sam was creating new rules, in the Tax Reform Act of 1976. In 1981 it happened again.

Let's look at some of the constraints surrounding the marital deduction that I am eager to help you understand.

Rules of the Marital Deduction Game

The game is played by three players, a husband, a wife and Uncle Sam. The decedent must be a citizen or resident of the United States. The surviving spouse must be validly married to the decedent but need not be a citizen or resident.

The "playing pieces" consist of all the property in the decedent's gross estate that passes directly from the decedent to the surviving spouse, including community property. Most important, in order to win the game, the decedent must make sure that the surviving spouse is given control over the income from the playing pieces during his or her lifetime. This means that if money is left in trust, rather than given outright, the spouse must get a portion or all of the income from it, but the will-maker can still retain control over the principal and can designate who inherits it at the surviving spouse's death. The surviving spouse must survive the decedent by at least six months. Income generated by the playing pieces must be paid to the spouse at least annually, if not more frequently. Most people have it paid quarterly.

You can't leave the surviving spouse money for only a term of years and then leave the money to the children. This does not give the surviving spouse sufficient control. The income must go to your spouse for his or her entire lifetime. Nor can the decedent leave money in trust for the spouse only until she marries again and then to the children. In the fancy language that you may hear your attorney speak, to qualify for the marital deduction the bequest must not be "tainted by a terminable interest." In English this means that you have either to give your money to your surviving spouse outright, so that he or she can do whatever he wishes with it, or, if you want to put it in trust, he or she must get the income freely throughout his entire lifetime. The right to the income can't "terminate" on remarriage or any other event. What you can do (and this is a major change brought by E.R.T.A.) is name the remainderman in your will. This means that you retain ultimate control of the principal while granting your spouse a lifetime right to the income. This compromise is called a Qualified Terminable Interest in Property, or QTIP. The executor must check the appropriate box on the estate tax return to have a trust treated as a QTIP trust entitled to the marital deduction.

You may, of course, allow the surviving spouse to pick the one who gets the principal on his or her death. You do this by granting a "power of appointment" (the right to designate the principal beneficiary), which we'll discuss later.

Since, in the case of a trust, a lifetime income must be payable to the spouse, the corpus (trust fund) can't be non-income producing—like swampland. If you have that to leave, leave it outright.

By now you can see that the regulations make sure that you do not unduly limit the use of an inheritance by your spouse for his or her lifetime support. Conversely, if you do give control to your spouse, you will have a good and qualifying marital deduction. Once more, then, the ways to achieve this deduction are: To leave everything to your spouse outright, including joint property, insurance proceeds, bank accounts. To leave everything in trust for your spouse, with the principal left to his or her estate, so that he or she controls what ultimately happens to the money. To leave your spouse a life estate and designate in your will who inherits after your spouse's death.

Variations in How To Play

What happens when the surviving spouse dies? If she or he dies with control over the money because it was left outright or in a QTIP trust, estate taxes will now be imposed. There can be a hefty tax at this point, because for the survivor there is no marital deduction.

To avoid disaster in the estate of the surviving spouse there are many roads, all of them new because E.R.T.A. is so new. Discuss these possibilities with your lawyer:

1. Not giving everything to your spouse if your estate is large, or he or she has money of his own. Give at least the full amount of the estate tax deduction to other heirs.
2. Consider a disclaimer, discussed in the section on Executors. This permits your spouse to give up some of the money you leave to him or her at the time the estate is administered and give it to a different person, for example, your children.

In fact E.R.T.A. has unified the disclaimer procedure that used to vary from state to state. To disclaim you must say so in writing within nine months of the time you are entitled to receive a gift or a bequest. Send copies to the executor, the holder of the property, and the one who gets your disclaimed gifts. Work with the executor in planning disclaimers. Who gets the gift you disclaim? The law of each state is still different; usually the rules of inheritance for those people dying without a will applies.

3. Try a "by-pass" trust. Give your spouse all of the estate save the amount of the deduction. Put that in trust for your spouse's lifetime and name the heir who gets the principal. This way the credit is not wasted.

Calculating Your Estate Tax

Your lawyer or accountant can calculate estate taxes for you when you plan your estate. But if you wish to get a very rough idea, first add up your gross estate. This includes everything that you may have control over at the time of your death. It *does not include* irrevocable trusts, life insurance to beneficiaries who own the policy, gifts that you have already made in the past which are $3,000 or less per year, per person, or gifts which you will make starting in 1982 which are $10,000 or less per year, per person.

It does include one-half the value of property owned jointly with your spouse, and all the other property actually in your ownership or control at death, and any non-exempt gifts that you gave throughout your lifetime.

Next deduct your likely administrative expenses and debts, such as lawyers' fees, executors' fees, debts of the estate. Then deduct all you leave to your spouse, and any amount you leave to charity. What remains is roughly your taxable estate. Then use the chart in Appendix III to calculate the tax. Give yourself your tax credit, found in Appendix II.

Once you know your Federal taxes you have to look at State taxes. State taxes vary since they are a matter of state law. In some states they are called estate taxes and in others inheritance taxes. Different tax tables are used, the amounts of exemptions differ and the amounts of tax credits differ. For example, Arizona, Alaska, Alabama and many others base their tax on the estate tax credit given to you by the Federal government. California, on the other hand, has both an estate and an inheritance tax, with different amounts of exemptions depending on who your heirs are. The surviving spouse gets a $60,000 exemption, a minor child a $12,000 exemption, and a brother or sister a $2,000 exemption. The sun belt states and retirement havens have little or no tax. That's why older people are often Miami-bound; but if you stay in the East you'll be hit with a state tax. Each state has still to make its own decision as to whether to follow the Reaganized estate tax formula.

INCOME TAX

Income taxes are, as you know, imposed on the amount of money that you earned or received in a given calendar year. In some countries the taxes are calculated by the government itself. We have self calculation. We make our own judgments and if Uncle Sam thinks we're wrong, he sends a messenger from the IRS to tell us so. Income tax is based upon our total net earnings. It, too, has been Reaganized. But for our purposes here, the important tax is the capital gains or investment tax.

A capital gains tax is an incentive, not a special annoyance. Capital gains is a tax imposed on profits made from the investment of money (capital). The government encourages investment of capital in things. The government would rather you spend your money investing in oil wells than buying personal luxuries. To encourage you Uncle Sam gives you a break on profits from investments. Let's see how this works.

There are two kinds of capital gains—a long term and a short term. If you own an asset for one year or less and then sell it, this is short term. If ownership is for over a year, it is long term. It is the long-term gains that get the special income tax treatment; a short-term gain does not. This is why people hold assets for at least a year. Under the terms of the special treatment the tax rate is the same as for your ordinary income, but the capital gains tax is imposed on only 40% of the profit you receive. Sixty percent of the profit is subtracted from your gross income before the gain is taxed.

Capital gains tax is figured not on the gross profit or gain, but on the net profit or gain, called "basis." To figure out the basis take the sale price and deduct the "adjusted basis." The adjusted basis is your original purchase price plus additional money you spent as capital improvements. This gives us the formula:

Basis = sale price minus adjusted basis (original purchase price plus capital expenditures).

For example, if land is sold at a profit, you have capital gains tax to pay, not ordinary income tax. If you bought the land for $25,000 and you sell it for $35,000 after putting in a $1,000 septic tank, you have an adjusted basis of $26,000. Your net profit or basis is then $9,000. It is on this amount that the tax is imposed. If you had bad luck and the selling price is less than the adjusted basis you have a capital loss.

You may have heard that since E.R.T.A. capital gains tax has been reduced to a maximum of 20%; the old maximum was 28%. How is this calculated? Under E.R.T.A. the maximum tax rate is 50% on any type of income. However, a profit from the investment of capital is not taxed entirely, only 40% of the profit is taxed at the maximum rate of 50%. So 50% of 40% is 20%! Therefore if you do have a gain from the investment of capital, the tax you pay is a maximum of 20% of the net profit. If you are not in the top 50% bracket, your "maximum tax" will be even less, i.e., 40% of profit times the amount in your tax bracket = capital gains tax. By the way, this 20% maximum tax applies to profits made June 9, 1981, or thereafter.

A good thing to do with certain property is to take depreciations. Since you haven't actually sold the property, there is no real loss. Yet Uncle Sam lets you deduct about a fifth of the value of the property from your tax each year. If you then do sell the property at a gain all this depreciation has to be subtracted from the original purchase price to reach the adjusted basis.

Those of you 55 or older, or with a spouse 55 or older, can save a whopping capital gain tax when you sell your home. You may exclude up to $125,000 of the profit provided it is your primary residence (house, co-op or condominium) and you owned and occupied it for at least three of the five preceding years. This exemption applies to residences sold July 20, 1981, or thereafter. For anybody else, the gain is not taxed if you reinvest the proceeds in another primary residence within 24 months after you make the sale. More than one sale and purchase is permitted if the relocation takes place because of employment.

What if you have capital losses? With short term losses (property held for one year or less) you get a dollar for dollar deduction from gross income. For long-term losses (property held for one year or more), only up to 50% can be used to offset ordinary income and then up to a $3,000 maximum. Any loss over this amount can be carried forward to the next years. Uncle Sam isn't giving anything away. You can't create losses with sales between husbands and wives. Nor can you take a loss if you have a wash sale—that is, a sale of securities at a loss made thirty days before or after the purchase of identical securities. For example, if you owned $10,000 worth of a stock and needed the money quickly, you could sell it at $34 instead of your purchase price of $35. However, if two weeks later you rebought the stock in exactly the same amounts you could not take a loss.

THE GIFT TAX GAME

Now let's consider the gift tax game. Actually, this is merely a spectator sport for the gift getter because the gift tax is paid by the person who gives the gift, not the one who receives it. You will see this in more detail in the gift chapter. Someone generous enough to give a gift must also pay a tax on it if its value is $10,000 or more (this amount has also been Reaganized—the old amount was $3,000). This $10,000 amount can be increased by gift splitting.

What is gift splitting? A husband and wife can each give $10,000 per person, per year, without taxation. Often one of the spouses has less money than the other. For example, the husband might have the money to give a child $20,000. The wife may not have $10,000 to give the child. Uncle Sam permits the husband and wife to give the $20,000 gift together, as if $10,000 came from her and $10,000 came from him. This way there is no gift tax since each is within the $10,000 exclusion.

Under the new Economic Recovery Tax Act each of us can give a gift of $10,000 tax free in any year to as many people as we like. We can also pay unlimited tuition or medical care expenses for anyone without paying a gift tax. Caveat: Such payments must be made directly to the institution, not be covered by insurance, and not made on behalf of someone you have a legal obligation to support.

If we do give more than $10,000 to one person in any year the gift tax rate is the same as the estate tax rate. This is only true for federal gift taxes, not state. Also, as you already know from reading about estate taxes, the gifts you give are counted in determining whether you have used up your estate tax exemption.

Most important, since Reaganization, there is no limit to the amount of gifts you may give to a spouse. No gift tax will be imposed on spousal transfers during your lifetime; nor will you use up any of your estate tax exemptions.

In order to figure out how much gift tax to pay you have to know the value of the gift itself. The tax is imposed on the fair market value (what a willing buyer will take for it and what a willing seller will pay for it) of the gift when given. It is *not* based on the value of the gift when first purchased. To discover the fair market value you may need appraisals or research into book values.

The gift tax return is filed annually on April 15th of the year following that in which you gave the gift. Remember, no tax need be paid; only the return must be filed. The gift tax can be deferred and paid later on. No filing is necessary for gifts between spouses since under Reaganization there is an unlimited exemption for such gifts. And no filing is necessary if you are under the amount of unified gift and estate tax credit. As already said, the gift tax rate is identical to the estate tax rate;

after evaluating the gift see Appendix III to calculate the tax. Many states like California, Colorado, Delaware, Louisiana, Minnesota, New York, North Carolina, Oklahoma, Oregon, Rhode Island, South Carolina, Tennessee, Vermont, Virginia, Washington, Wisconsin, and Puerto Rico have gift taxes too.

When should you give a gift? Everyone with some extra cash and children to support ought to be making gifts if there is danger of paying estate taxes in the long run. A standard gift-giving program can be a useful thing for college, marriage and other special needs. Another good time to give a gift is when property has appreciated in value so much that to sell would create a large capital gain. Take a look at the gift giving chapter. Charitable gifts are important too. Now that you grasp the tax aspects it's time to look at the rest of the picture.

6
TRUSTS

Many people think they can create a workable trust by
stowing away some extra money in a regular savings bank
account at low interest rates, and filling out the account card in
their name and the name of a loved one "in trust for." They
think that the beneficiary for whom the money is held in trust
can secretly close the account at the moment of their death,
getting the money without paying any estate tax. Meanwhile,
during their lifetime, they will have complete control over the
account and can remove the money at will if they need it. Many
grandmas who think of themselves as quite clever don't even tell
their grandchildren that the money has been left in trust because
they don't want them to count on the money coming to them in
the future.

Two things are wrong with this rosy picture. First, such
accounts are subject to estate taxes. This kind of trust, a simple
bank-account trust, actually has a formal name. It is called a
Totten Trust. It is useful for the purposes of avoiding probate
and avoiding making a will, but it does not save taxes. You can
put money into a bank account in trust for someone else. During
your lifetime you can handle the money, use it and even spend it
without accounting to the intended beneficiary. At death, the
money will automatically go to the person for whom it is held in
trust.

This is useful because it avoids leaving the money specifically to them in a will, and if there is very little money in an estate it can help avoid probate. At least there can be no question as to who will inherit the money.

But since wills themselves are inexpensive, particularly simple ones, this is no great saving. What it doesn't do is avoid paying estate taxes. Upon the death of the person who opened the account, that money must be accounted for to the government. Remember, if the decedent has less than a taxable estate to begin with, there will be no taxation. What a Totten Trust does is to designate the beneficiary, but it does not in any way save estate taxes.

The second thing wrong with such a plan is that there are better ones. Most people who open Totten Trusts have not actually explored the use of trusts and have no idea how they could better open one with the same amount of money. They don't realize that other kinds of trusts can save estate taxes and income taxes, can help you see how your money will be managed after you are gone, and can insure that those dependent on you will be taken care of. Trusts can even create a barrier between your loved ones and creditors who are ready to pounce upon their money. Trusts can do all this and they are quite simple to create, but they are not going to be created if you insist on thinking only about the simple bank-account trusts.

To understand trusts it is best to learn the lingo, and to classify trusts in your mind. I am not going to pamper you with simple words. In order to deal with your attorney effectively it will be helpful to remember these few definitions:

- Trust: a trust is a written document whose purpose is to put your money in the hands of a third party, so that the third party can use it only for the benefit of your loved one.
- Trustee: a trustee is the person to whom you give the money, so that he or she can handle it for your loved one.
- Beneficiary: the beneficiary is the loved one, the person you wish to get the benefit of the money.
- Corpus: this is Latin for "body," but here it means the money itself or the bonds, stocks, diamonds or whatever else you wish to give to the trustee for the benefit of the beneficiary.
- Settlor or grantor: the settlor aka grantor is you, the person who created the trust.

- Revocable trust: a revocable trust is a trust that the settlor can revoke and stop.
- Irrevocable trust: an irrevocable trust is a trust that the settlor cannot terminate; it goes on without control by the settlor once it has been made.
- Inter vivos trusts: the Latin literally means "between" (inter) and "living persons" (vivos). These are trusts that you create during your lifetime. You can even be the trustee. The trust can terminate on your death or during your own lifetime. One that you create during your lifetime can pour over into another trust in your will so that it continues even after your death.
- Testamentary trusts: These trusts are created only in your will and come into action only upon your death. They are part of your *last will and testament*. If you change your will you can eliminate them. Of course, if you already have an inter vivos trust, you can instruct in your will what to do with it. This is called a "pour-over" provision if your instructions are to take inter vivos trust funds and "pour" them into a testamentary (set up by will) trust fund.

Here is a comparison of how the inter vivos and testamentary trusts work.

Inter vivos	*Testamentary or Trusts in Wills*
Saves estate and income taxes. Allows you to see how your fiduciaries control and use funds.	Controls the use of money even after death. Allows long range tax planning.
Takes effect during your lifetime.	Takes effect at your death.
Gives property away irrevocably if estate taxes are to be saved.	Property remains yours during your lifetime.
Can be revocable; but no estate taxes will be saved.	Property is taxed along with the rest of your estate.
Can save on income taxes because they will be paid either at the trust's rate or at the beneficiaries' rate.	No income tax advantage.

Allows you to designate a beneficiary of the income and a beneficiary of the principal when the income beneficiary dies.	Same.

An inter vivos trust (lifetime) can save you estate taxes. As with everything else in estate planning, remember that the government is interested only in taxing the estate for money in your control and possession at death. If you manage to take money out of your control and place it instead in the control of a trustee irrevocably, then upon your death the government will not tax the money. If on the other hand the trust is revocable (such as Totten or bank-account trusts where the money can be withdrawn at any time), then the government will tax whatever amount of money is in the trust. So if it is estate taxes you wish to save, create an irrevocable inter vivos trust.

Another great use for a trust is to reduce income tax. This happens because a trust, like a corporation, is a new entity, separate from you—like a legal clone. That entity, not the settlor (you), pays the income tax. The trust may be in a lower tax bracket than you are. This means that you may be taking money that ordinarily would be in a taxable saving account or other taxable investment and putting it in a trust which is in a lower bracket.

Tax bites are measured by two things. First, the tax rate, and second, the tax bracket. The tax rate applicable to the taxable income of a trust is the same as that applied to married persons filing separate returns and therefore is higher than those applicable to single individuals, heads of household or married persons filing joint returns. However, if there is a mandatory pay out of trust income to a beneficiary, the amount paid is deducted from the trust income and the distributed amount is taxed at the rate of the beneficiary. So if either of these rates is less than yours, the trust's income tax is less. More important, since the trust has only the amount of money you put in it, the trust's tax bracket will be lower than yours. Or, if the beneficiary is a child with only trust money as income, the child's bracket too will be far lower than yours.

You can save capital gains tax too when the corpus (what you put in the trust) is a highly appreciating asset. If you have stock, real estate, etc., that you do not want to sell, but that is appreciating rapidly, you can get some benefit by gifting it to a trust. You will pay the gift tax, based on the value of the gift to the beneficiary as of the date you made the transfer. It is then out of your estate and the higher value which will accumulate years later will not be entirely added to your estate for estate tax purposes. I say entirely because there is a catch back that must be discussed with your accountant.

Caution: To save income taxes the trust income cannot be used to support you or someone (i.e., a child) for whom you are legally responsible; to fulfill your legal obligations (i.e., to creditors); to pay your or your spouse's life insurance, or to be accumulated for you or your spouse.

Gift taxes can be saved too. When a transfer of money is made to a trust, this too is a gift with the usual gift tax payments. Still, the gift tax itself is deductible from the eventual estate tax, and the overall tax savings are enormous. Let's say you want to set up a trust for your daughter who has children of her own. If you put in $50,000 and make your daughter the income beneficiary, the first thing that happens is that $10,000 of the original $50,000 has no gift tax. Second, $10,000 worth of income every year is also excluded from the gift tax. Gift taxes on trusts are often figured at the termination of the trust, as part of the estate tax computation, rather than when the transfer is made, so you probably won't pay a gift tax immediately.

If a trust created by you during your lifetime does not terminate at your death, but continues until the death of your income beneficiary, there are lots of non-tax advantages too. For example, there will be a continuity of investment handling. Even if you become unable to handle your money in old age, the person you name in the trust as your successor will take over; not someone appointed by the court. There will be a continuous flow of income to the beneficiary, and of course probate is avoided for the funds in the trust. A will leaving money to an heir who is already a beneficiary of a living trust can provide that the money left in the will be added to the corpus of the existing trust. There is no tax advantage, but continuity of management is preserved. This is particularly important if you expect a challenge by a person for whom you have not provided any legacy or gift. Probate is stymied when a challenge to a will takes place, and your heirs will get no distribution from your estate during this time. On the other hand, during a challenge to a trust, the trustee continues the administration and payment to beneficiaries. It's also procedurally more complicated to contest.

The Crummey Provision: Trusts and Gifts

Crummey is the name of one of the more famous cases in trusts and estate history. The result of the *Crummey* case is that if you do create a trust your beneficiary can demand up to $10,000 a year from it, which is then considered the same as your giving a gift of that amount. As you know, such a gift is completely tax free. It is not included as income to the gift getter nor is it included in determining a gift tax or estate tax for the gift giver. In making a trust with a *Crummey* provision you are actually creating another donor who is entitled to give $10,000 a year tax free. This newly created donor is the trust itself.

To take advantage of *Crummey* the beneficiary need only demand the $10,000. However, there are some simple limits to these *Crummey* provisions: (1) The beneficiary can demand the $10,000 only once in any calendar year. If he or she permits the year to go by without demanding the money, that year is up and the money can no longer be paid. (2) The beneficiary will get the money only if a transfer is made to the trust itself. (3) The beneficiary must have notice of the right to withdraw and a reasonable opportunity to exercise the right.

Here's something interesting. In case your beneficiary does not call for the $10,000 gift and lets it lapse, the Internal Revenue Service considers this a gift by your beneficiary to the trust. By not accepting a gift your beneficiary has augmented the amount in the trust merely by leaving the money there.

However, the Internal Revenue Service does permit a beneficiary to leave up to $5,000, or five percent of the amount of the corpus in the trust (whichever is larger), without being subject to a gift tax. This is a great lesson in the workings of the I.R.S. It shows you how much the Service, as it is formally known, loves to create problems and then find ways to solve them.

TRUSTS AND MONEYTHINK

The greatest barrier between you and a trust is fear. People believe that only the wealthy should or can make a trust. They fear the costs of legal fees and accounting work and the eventual fees paid to trustees. For some reason trusts breed paranoia in the middle class. People look at a trust as a way of taking money out of their pockets and putting it into the control of another. Emotionally it's difficult. But remember, in the tax-paying game you *want* to take money out of your control.

Moneythink can help you through. Also, you'll soon see that you can be the trustee of a lifetime trust. True, this defeats the estate tax savings, but it gives you all the other pluses and keeps you in control.

To Moneythink properly you have to ask yourself the following questions: Who are my real dependents? Will I be spending money on them whether I create a trust or not? Do I have college funds tucked away that I dare not touch? Do I have other money in a low-interest bank account that I consider untouchable because it's needed to pay for my children's education or marriage?

In another vein you must ask even tougher questions: Do I want my spouse to have all the family money outright, or do I want restraints on my spouse after my death? Do I want to protect my children from a spendthrift spouse? Do I want to protect my spouse from spendthrift children? What is the likelihood of my spouse's remarrying?

Now some easier questions: Do I have too much income tax to pay on my investments? Am I a good investor or should I really be using a professional? Is there anyone I would be willing to pay to handle money for me? Do I feel comfortable with institutions or only with individuals in handling my finances?

And finally: Would I like a chance to experiment with a small trust during my lifetime to see how it works? Would I like some extra control over what happens to my money after my death? Do I have dependents who may need special care throughout their lifetime?

SOME TYPES OF TRUSTS

Trusts for the Children

It is both wise and popular to create trusts for your children because such trusts pack a four-punch wallop. First, they provide for the health and welfare of the children. Second, the trust income, if paid out and not needed for the direct support of the child, is taxed at the child's rate (which is presumably much lower than the parent's rate). Third, any future increase in the value of the property belongs to the child and not to the settlor and therefore is out of the estate for estate tax purposes if the trust is irrevocable. Finally, when the trust is set up a gift tax is paid, and the gift tax itself is deductible from estate taxes.

In the chapter on gifts you will learn that you can give gifts to children (1) outright, putting the money or property in their names; (2) under the Uniform Gift to Minors Act; or (3) under a custodianship arrangement. These all have their drawbacks.

For example, an outright gift belongs to the child and becomes his when he reaches the age of eighteen or twenty-one, depending on the state in which you live. If the child should die, the money will go directly to the child's other parent, which may not be what you have in mind. Until a guardian is appointed for a young child the gift will be frozen and cannot be used. To set up a guardianship entails a great deal of expensive legal red tape. The same is true for a custodianship arrangement because you, the donor, cannot act as the custodian. If you do, the property is included in your estate should you predecease your child.

Some special trusts for children, both minor and adult, hold fascination for parents. For example, an incentive trust may be used for children with questionable futures. The trust income can vary as the child's own earnings vary. Or if for some reason you dislike or distrust your child's spouse, you may use an incentive trust to provide for a beneficiary of the principal upon your child's death. There is thus no chance that the spouse will inherit, as he or she would if you gave your child the money outright.

Trusts for Yourself

A trust can also be made by you, naming yourself as income beneficiary and another as remainderman upon your death. This creates no tax savings but it does produce probate savings. If you have a business and wish to have it continue after your death, you might put it in trust for yourself as beneficiary, naming someone else as your successor-manager and trustee. This will ensure continuity of your business after your death. Take a look at the section on the business person's will for more ideas on this.

If you just want to relieve the burden of managing your own money, this too can be done by placing your investment funds in trust to be managed by trustees, with you as the settlor and beneficiary. There are no tax savings, but you get good management and peace of mind if you pick the right trustees.

Short-term Trusts

If you don't want to tie your money up forever but do want to get income tax reductions, there is an instrument called the short-term or Clifford trust. This trust must last for more than ten years, or until the death of the beneficiary, whichever comes sooner. It is irrevocable during that period of time, but after ten years it is terminated. Most important, upon termination the settlor gets the trust fund back. The income is *not* taxed to the grantor but to the beneficiary. The income can be accumulated and not paid out. The major purpose of these short-term or Clifford trusts is to devote the income from the corpus to others so that they, not the grantor, pay tax upon it, presumably at a lower rate.

Who is usually the beneficiary of such trusts? Persons whom the grantor does not have to support legally, but whom he would choose to support voluntarily. A Clifford trust is often used for dependent parents.

Uncle Sam's rules for short-term trusts are really very simple. The trust must continue for ten or more years, or be reasonably expected to do so, or it must continue for the lives of the beneficiaries, or for the lives of the beneficiaries or ten years, whichever is shorter. So a grantor can create a trust to continue for a minimum period of ten years, or for the life of the beneficiary or his own life, provided that he is healthy enough to have a life expectancy of ten years or more. The ten year term begins at the time the assets are transferred to the trust, not at the time the instrument is signed. The corpus can be cash or securities.

Don't forget that you must pay a gift tax when the money is transferred to such a trust. However, it is only a portion of the value of the corpus, since it is not an indefinite trust. Remember also that a short-term trust is no way to avoid estate taxes. If the grantor dies within the term of the trust, the trust corpus is counted in his estate. If the short term does not terminate upon his death, then the amount the remainderman would get is measured at the date of death and is included in the estate.

Accumulation Trusts

Accumulation trusts can be set up with no income paid to the beneficiary. Instead, the money is accumulated in the trust. The money earned by the trust is taxed every year at the tax rate set for the trust's own tax bracket. When it is finally paid out to the beneficiary there is a special tax imposed at the beneficiary's bracket, as if the income had been paid to him in the years it was being earned. The taxes the trust itself has paid now come back to the beneficiary as a credit against the new taxes (this is called throwback). Meanwhile, the extra tax the beneficiary would have had to pay through the years has been invested elsewhere. Better yet, if the income was accumulated before the beneficiary reached the age of twenty-one, only the tax the trust paid is imposed. If the money is paid out after the child is twenty-one the tax may be slightly higher; the added tax is the difference between the amount the trust has actually paid and the amount the beneficiary would have had to pay after age twenty-one had the trust income been paid to him or her.

Trusts for the Spendthrift

Spendthrift trusts are a creation of the rich who found that their spoiled children often spent trust income before it was distributed to them. Creditors such as jewelry stores and automobile salespeople were often willing to accept a marker giving them the right to collect future trust-guaranteed income. The would-be heir often had all future income pledged to creditors. A spendthrift trust protects these people from themselves. It doesn't give them any interest on the income until it is distributed, so that they can't give it away beforehand. Such trusts can also empower the trustee to make only direct payments for the needs of the beneficiary instead of giving them income.

Discretionary Trusts

The discretionary trust is so called because the trustee is given the power to distribute income among many beneficiaries as needed. This discretionary power can be very helpful when there are several beneficiaries with different kinds of needs and a trustee who really understands the family. A discretionary trust (also called a sprinkling, pot or spray trust if there is more than one potential beneficiary) can be used also to protect mentally handicapped dependents. Parents of mentally retarded, developmentally disabled, and mentally ill children are often in a quandary over what to do to protect these children after they are gone.

Hyman Clurfeld, an attorney and lecturer on the law relating to the mentally retarded and developmentally disabled, deals with these problems in estate planning every day. He suggests a program that has been highly successful through the years.

First, nothing should be left outright to the mentally handicapped dependent, either by will or by lifetime gift, including joint accounts or trusts. Clurfeld warns that if you have such dependents, you should be sure to review your employee benefit plans, life insurance policies and other documents that merely require a check mark or other simple designation next to the name of the beneficiary. It is possible that years ago you did check the word "child" or "children," and the mentally handicapped dependent may be entitled to the direct payment of a sum of money.

Second, once you have made certain that there are no funds or other assets flowing directly to the dependent, you should, through a discretionary trust, give the trustee the absolute discretion to pay or apply the income from the trust for the benefit of the mentally handicapped child or to any other beneficiary named. The beneficiaries could be the mentally handicapped person, other children, other relatives or even a charity. You may also wish to give the trustees discretion to invade the principal of the trust, but only for the benefit of the mentally handicapped child since the invasion of the principal for other beneficiaries could deplete the trust assets and perhaps terminate it.

Third, the key to the use of the discretionary trust for mentally handicapped dependents is to include a provision that forbids the trustee to apply any income or principal to the payment of charges by any governmental authority or public institution, and another provision that allows the trustee to terminate the trust in the event of the enactment of a law which would require such invasion. The government may reduce or deny benefits, or require their repayment, if the dependent has a right to income or principal from a trust. The trust should give the trustee no powers whatsoever to relieve any obligations on the part of the dependent to a governmental agency. The object of this is to avoid substitution of the parents' assets for the expenses of the government. This is crucial since, as Clurfeld points out, attempts have been made in some states to require the use of estate assets to relieve government of its expenses for the mentally handicapped. You should check with a knowledgeable attorney in the field. If a mentally handicapped person is receiving governmental aid, the trustees may need especially sound judgment in the exercise of their discretion in order to avoid loss of benefits, sometimes amounting to a dollar for dollar loss to the trust.

Here, perhaps more than in other situations, the trustee is crucial. After all, this is a discretionary trust. Nevertheless, the same criteria set out in the chapter on choosing trustees should apply. A bank or trust company may be too expensive, or they may reject the appointment because of its highly discretionary nature or because the trust is not large enough. The family's private attorney, the attorney who did the estate planning in the first place, or the non-handicapped potential beneficiary (brother or sister) are likely candidates as trustees. (This provides a balance of expertise and sensitivity to the needs of the mentally handicapped person). Clurfeld suggests three trustees in order to insure continuity, honesty and the exercise of sound judgment in the investment and disbursement of trust funds.

Trusts for the Children of the Children

For years the very rich have known what you are learning right now, that if you take money out of your control prior to your death it is not taxable in your estate and can go to your beneficiaries' estate tax fee. But they wanted more. They wanted their money to descend through many generations without any estate tax. To accomplish this they created a trust, made a child the beneficiary during his lifetime, and provided that upon the child's death the remainder of the trust would go to the grandchildren outright.

The trust rules permitted both income and principal to be distributed from time to time throughout the lifetime of the child. This meant that the trustees could make sure that the child had plenty of money to live on. When the child died the trust money went to the grandchildren directly. Or the process could be prolonged, skipping from one generation to another. That is, the trust income could be distributed for the lifetime of the child, then the grandchild, then the great-grandchild, then the great-great-grandchild, and finally fall outright into the hands of the great-great-great-great-grandchild.

The result was that the money would not be taxed in the settlor's estate because it was not in the settlor's control at the time of death, and it would continue to pass through several generations and not be taxed, since none of the younger generations were in control at the time they died. Uncle Sam was being cheated out of taxes. So, in 1976 a generation-skipping tax was imposed. Most trusts you are interested in will *not* be subject to a generation-skipping tax; only a few are. It is extremely unlikely that any of my readers will be involved in creating such a trust. I include it for the sake of completeness.

In order to be subject to taxation the trust must have all of the following features: there must be two or more beneficiaries. At least two must be of different generations from each other, and each generation must be younger than the generation of the settlor. The most common form is a trust leaving money to your children and then to your grandchildren. They are in two different generations and both of those generations are younger than you. These trusts can be made inter vivos or testamentary. The tax is the same.

In other words, trusts to your children only don't pay extra tax, trusts to your grandchildren only don't pay extra tax, trusts to your spouse and then upon your spouse's death to your child don't pay extra tax (your spouse is considered in the same generation as you despite any actual age difference). Furthermore, even if you do have a real generation skip (your child and grandchild for example) the first quarter of a million dollars is tax exempt altogether. This means that you must have a large trust corpus to worry at all about the tax.

If the beneficiaries are a child and grandchild, there is a $250,000 exclusion per child. So when the time comes to pay the tax $250,000 is subtracted to get the taxable amount, but only if the younger generations are your children's heirs. Even then the tax is imposed only if a transfer of the money or a termination of the right to get the money takes place. In the unlikely but possible event that the younger generation dies before the older generation, there will not be a taxable event at all.

Warning! In 1976, when the generation skipping tax was first imposed, wills made prior to that date were exempt. Under E.R.T.A. this exemption has been continued for wills made before 1976 where the testator dies before January 1, 1983, but only for wills in which the generation skipping trust provision has not been altered. If you want to make a new will but had such a trust made pre-1976 watch out not to disturb the trust provision. Consider a codicil for any changes just to play safe.

The generation-skipping tax, when it is imposed, is an additional tax, separate from estate and gift tax. The tax will be paid not by the settlor but by the trust, based on the tax rate of the son or daughter. The tax is based upon the estate of the "deemed transferor." That means that the child is deemed to have made the transfer to his or her own child, not the settlor to the grandchildren. This makes it almost impossible for your children to prepare their own tax picture accurately. By leaving money to their children you perhaps interfere with their estate plan. If you are in this situation, consider creating separate trusts for each generation rather than giving money for life to your own children and then to your grandchildren upon your children's death.

TRUSTEES

Whom to appoint as trustee? The answer is different for everyone. Remember that the job of the executor ends when the will has been probated. On the other hand, the job of the trustee continues until the trust is terminated. This may be several years and perhaps a lifetime. Because of this, big institutions, banks and fiduciary organizations are all waiting in line to be appointed as trustees. Don't forget your family lawyer, who also makes part of his or her living from serving as trustee.

Many people consider their brother-in-law or a friend who is smart in business as possible trustees of both inter vivos and testamentary trusts. Often the problem of choosing trustees brings about family tensions. It is also a common place for male chauvinism to crop up. Frequently, a husband who has accumulated the family wealth and who has made a will leaving substantial amounts to his wife thinks that she is incapable of handling the estate. The result is that sometimes an incompetent male relative is appointed instead of the wife, who is given no right in the will to get rid of him and suffers as a consequence.

On the other hand, not every spouse, male or female, would make a good trustee. The Moneythink earlier in this chapter asked you to face seriously your view of your spouse. You can ask your spouse as well; but only you know what gives you peace of mind. It generally does not work to appoint other relatives as trustees. No one likes to be at the mercy of a family member. It is often better to work with paid professionals, no matter how conservative they are. People are reluctant to give information to their in-laws, or worse, their in-laws' spouses. For the most part you are going to want a paid professional. At least one—maybe even two. My suggestion is co-fiduciaries—one of them the major beneficiary, such as your spouse, the other a paid professional.

Always there is the second question: Whom should I use as a paid professional, an institution or an individual? Believe it or not, it may be wise to use both. The institution has the double advantage of continuity and personnel. It may have a large team of experts, so that should one expert leave or die, someone will be there to take over immediately.

The individual has the advantage of offering service,

understanding, and intimacy. An individual lawyer who knows the family and is sensitive as well as knowledgeable can singlehandedly make the investment suggestions best suited to individual cases. Remember that large institutions do not plan for you alone. They often have hundreds of other clients and make mass investment strategies.

The individual knows you personally and treats you separately. Frankly, individual experts may also be more in need of your business. They need you because you may make up one percent, instead of one millionth of one percent, of their business.

Of course there's a drawback. Individual trustees may discover problems they can't handle, and therefore have to hire other experts to help, using your money. Also, they may have no one to give the helm to if they should become disabled.

Today, the practicalities of estate practice are such that no one can really handle it alone. Even those who appear to be individual estate planners work with accountants, pension planners, Erisa specialists, and sometimes even other lawyers to make your complete plan. When you talk to your lawyer, ask about his or her back-up staff. You'll be surprised.

One solution is the double and even triple fiduciary relationship. The major beneficiary is appointed a trustee together with an institution and an individual counselor. The individual counselor keeps up the dialogue with the institution and has equal say. The institution uses its expertise for investment.

Your individual lawyer can work immediately; there is no bureaucracy. He or she will listen to your wishes and react quickly. That doesn't mean you'll get your way; it just means you'll be able to voice your opinion and as a fiduciary have a vote.

Conflicts can always occur, even between institutions and individuals—perhaps I should say especially between institutions and individuals. The solution to this is simple. The institutions are made up of highly professional people and the individual you choose must be a highly professional person. Get them together early. Even if your trust is made in your will, do the job of having them meet with and without you. Often enough, my clients have sent me to lunch with a bank manager or trust officer of the institution they have chosen. That's very wise. We have a relationship and we work together. When something has happened to the institutional fiduciary, I have been there all along to educate whoever takes over. If something happened to me, the institution's professional would be there to educate my successor.

Using the co-trustee may be just the way to keep a widow in touch with the money that is rightfully hers and still have her working side by side with a professional. You should also give her the right to fire the professional if the work is not being done properly, just so long as she appoints another one immediately. The problem with co-trustees is that they are both equal fiduciaries. The widow may feel small and unimportant next to the big, powerful corporation that is her co-trustee. This can sometimes lead to her not participating. In turn the corporate trustee begins to take over, and make investment decisions without consultation. The answer to this is to prepare your beneficiary. One good way is to have him or her read this book. To help co-fiduciaries further along, have an emergency clause for illness or disability; a delegation clause for temporary absence; a hold harmless clause if one trustee (like the shy spouse) doesn't participate. There can even be a difference of opinion clause in case there is an impasse. Majority rule is possible. Or something like this:

> In the event of a difference of opinion the (corporate) (individual) trustee's decision shall apply, provided it is given in writing to the other. The (corporate) (individual) trustee shall abide by the decision of the other and shall not be liable for the actions of the trustees made pursuant to the decision.

Use the individual as a special trustee with review powers for sprinkling, accumulation or invasion. For example, an attorney can be named as trustee for the sole purpose of determining whether income should be accumulated or distributed between beneficiaries, or even whether the principal should be invaded. An institution can have investment control. Be flexible and creative. Most things can be done. Just remember in judging fiduciaries the criteria are (1) continuity—will they be around long enough so that no one else has to stop and choose the fiduciary after you're gone?; (2) consistency—is it an institution that changes personnel all the time, is it an individual who passes you off to subordinates?; (3) conversation—is there a dialogue among you, your beneficiary and your fiduciary, a willingness to talk?; (4) calculation—how have they done in the past with other people's money? They will be able to give you some idea without breaching the confidentiality of their other clients.

Once you decide on using a bank or other institution as your fiduciary you have to take the next step and decide which bank to choose. Most of us are ill equipped to judge institutions. But, I wasn't surprised when I interviewed Rosie James, Trust Officer at Bankers Trust, and Maureen Bateman, one of Bankers Trust's attorneys, to find that here again good judgment and common sense are all you need.

How to judge a bank? Start with the people. How will the bank assign personnel to you to handle your account? The best institutions try to match customers to account executives and trust officers. Ideally, customers with similar needs will be served by the same person, who has expertise in the needed area. Ask the procedure for switching within the bank if you're not satisfied. Don't be shy about this; it can and does happen.

Talk to the people at the bank, or other institution, and have your spouse speak with them too. Watch the kind of advertising and outreach they are doing with the public. As with lawyers, there is no reason for an institution to create an image that it doesn't really want. Banks are not shy in disclosing the kind of business they want. It's up to you to express the kind of service you want.

Also compare the investment policies at various banks and institutions. For example, do they use their own common funds as the vehicle for investing money in a trust for which they have been named as trustee? They will give you performance records. Ask for three to five years' worth. Compare these with the performance records of other common funds. Use the following indicators, which can be found in your newspaper for comparison: Dow Jones industrial average, Standard & Poors Composite Index, New York Stock Exchange Index. Also ask what type of fund is being used. Is it one that emphasizes income, growth or tax free returns?

Compare also requirements for accepting you. Most institutions will not take a trust and act as trustee unless there is a certain amount of money in the trust. Some banks actively seek individual trust accounts, and are flexible. They may take a smaller trust if it is not a complex one and if it fits in easily with the kind of management they are used to.

See how institutions act with your individual co-trustees. For the most part they will insist on being paid as much as they would be if they were sole trustees. There are few variations, but you might look around. Even more important is the relationship between the family member, or individual lawyer, named as trustee and the bank. See the dialogue that they set up with each other. This is particularly important if you have special assets to manage like copyrights and royalties.

If you are considering a bank, and simply want to test the water, there are two ways of doing this before you name a permanent trustee. You can open an advisory account. The account is totally in your control, and no trust is set up. But the bank does give investment advice and handles your investments. The charge is slightly higher than for acting as trustee because it is not limited by statute. In states without statutory limitations the charges may be the same. It is the investment advice in which you are interested. Familiarizing yourself with a bank's investment performance can be very important. A second method of testing the water is to set up a revocable trust. This is one way to judge the performance of any trustee.

Finally, no trustee worth its salt will prevent you from including a discharge clause in your trust document. As you might want to change the trustee, it is also possible the trustee will wish to renounce its role during the course of the trust. Usually, however, if a trustee does not want to serve, it will simply not qualify at the time the inter vivos trust is created or the will is probated. Either eventuality gives another good reason to think carefully about your substitute trustees.

A few words now about costs. The expense of multiple trustees is not necessarily forbidding. Some states don't permit lawyers to double charge: they can't charge legal fees and fiduciary fees. Usually the legal fees are greater and prevail.

Some states provide statutory limits for charges by fiduciaries based upon the amount of principal in a trust each year. New York provides that three trustees must share the fee of two trustees if the trust is valued at between $100,000 and $200,000. If the trust is valued at more than $200,000 each trustee is entitled to one full statutory commission unless there are more than three, in which case a total of three commissions is apportioned.

So you might pay the same amount as you would if you had only one institutional fiduciary and still needed legal work. Banks and other institutions will provide rate schedules on demand, and require yearly minimum fees or they won't take the account.

Here is the current minimum rate schedule of Morgan Guarantee Trust:

Testamentary Trusts
    Entirely in Common Trust Funds (Sole Trustee) $2,000
    Not entirely in Common Trust Funds
      (Sole Trustee)   3,000
    With co-Trustee   4,000
Inter-Vivos Trusts
    During life of primary income beneficiary $5,000
    After death of primary income beneficiary   Minimums
                        same as for
                testamentary trusts

James Goodfellow, Vice President of Morgan Guaranty Trust Co., suggests the following when deciding among large institutions:

- Look for lawyers on the staff.
- Question the fiduciaries about the complexity of assets they are used to handling.
- Pick an institution that operates in all of the localities where you have assets and beneficiaries.
- Ask your lawyer to advise you and encourage coordination.
- Introduce your beneficiaries to the fiduciary and consider their response.

In deciding between family members and professionals, ask yourself whether you hold stock in a close corporation. Families whose major income comes from closely held corporations and farms should consider the paid professional executor more than any other.

In general, the thing least to be feared is that your money will be mishandled. People in this field are generally honest; if anything, they are overly conservative. The reason is that an executor or trustee is a fiduciary, and therefore has a special legal relationship to you and to your beneficiaries. Fiduciaries must exercise prudence, good judgment and reasonable care. If they do not they can be accused of negligence or gross negligence. This can mean fines, loss of reputation, replacement of money lost or even imprisonment.

If the Only Decent Conversation You Can Have is with Yourself

In deciding who should act as trustee of a living trust, your first thought will naturally turn to yourself. Who better to handle your money than you? This thought has crossed the mind of many a person who's thinking of starting a trust. Of course, you can be your own trustee but you may find that you don't love the tax consequences. As long as you remain the trustee, capable and powerful with respect to what happens to the money, you have not gotten rid of control, as Uncle Sam expects you to if you want estate tax shelter. The rule is that a person who is the grantor himself or any non-adverse party (that is, anyone who is not a beneficiary under the trust and who is controlled by the grantor) cannot be named as a trustee if that trustee has substantial powers. This means that neither you, your mother, your father, your kids, your brothers, sisters, or employees can be named as trustee without running into possible tax problems. There are in fact very specific things that a trustee who is the grantor himself, or someone controlled by him, cannot do without losing estate tax benefits. If you're in either situation, here are some precautions:

• You can't deal with trust property for less than adequate value. That is, you can't sell your trust assets to your own business for less than true value.
• You can't borrow without interest or security.
• You can't vote shares even in your own business held in the trust.
• You can't control investments.
• You can't substitute trust property.
• You can't freely make tax decisions between income and

principal beneficiaries, but must follow specific instructions in the trust.

Therefore, if you do plan to name yourself as trustee, see to it that you have very limited powers. You are practically forced, if you wish to have any flexibility in your trust, to name an independent trustee.

Nevertheless, if you find that the only decent conversation you can have these days is with yourself and you insist on being the trustee and grantor, you can do so. Be aware, though, that you can have only a simple and inflexible trust arrangement; for example, a trust that specifically states that all income is to be given in equal shares to the children with no opportunity to sprinkle the money around at will. While you can invade the principal in case of an emergency, the standards set forth in the trust for doing so must be specific—what the law calls "ascertainable standards." This puts restrictions on you. On the other hand, you will be free to make the investment decisions and if that is all you care about, then you can indeed make yourself the trustee of an inter vivos trust.

7
Gifts

With respect to taxes, it is better to receive than to give. The reason is that the donor (the person who gives the gift) pays a gift tax which is calculated according to the same tax tables as estate taxes. The donee (the person who gets the gift) pays no tax—not an estate nor an income nor a gift tax. (An exception occurs, however, if you get a gift and your donor defaults on the gift tax; Uncle Sam can then come after you.)

Remember that to determine estate taxes gifts, given throughout a person's lifetime are included in the gross estate, and the estate tax is calculated on the combined amount of those gifts and property owned or controlled at death. To avoid the inclusion of gifts in their gross estate later, many people elect to pay the gift tax as they give the gift.

How then can we talk about saving through giving? I recommend to my clients who are over fifty and who have children or grandchildren, and also to my clients younger than fifty who are well-off, to prepare a formal gift-giving program in order to save taxes. It works this way: You save estate taxes because the government wants to tax your estate only for that money in your control and ownership at the time of death. If you give something away the gift is no longer in your control and ownership, and as long as you have paid the gift tax on it it will not be counted for estate tax purposes. But since the tax rate for estate taxes and gifts are the same, why bother? Because for tax purposes the value of the gift is calculated at the time that the gift is given, which in these inflationary times is probably a lot less than its future value.

If you hold the asset and give it to your heirs in your will it probably will have appreciated in value. So if you have heavily appreciating property that you do not need to live on it is better to give it away now and pay the smaller gift tax than hold it for your estate and pay the greater estate tax.

You can save income tax too; if you have assets that are producing income you may want to give them away to someone who is in a lower income tax bracket than you. What you are doing is taking stocks, bonds, or other income-producing assets and giving them, let's say, to your minor children who are in a lower income tax bracket. They pay the income tax at their low rate and they own the asset and the income. *Since you as guardian are in control of these assets anyway* you really aren't losing much and you are saving taxes.

Further, the government permits you to give $10,000 per year per person as a gift without paying any gift tax at all and without including this in your eventual gross estate for estate tax purposes. Before E.R.T.A. it was $3,000. This means that if you had five grandchildren you could give away $50,000 of your wealth every year as gifts and be free of paying any gift or estate taxes on that money. If you are a husband-and-wife team, you can give $10,000 apiece. (If one of you doesn't have a full $10,000 you can as a couple give away $20,000 per year.)

Before giving anything away, however, ask yourself some hard questions, like these. How much do I really have to give away? Is there any chance I will need it? Would I be better off with a trust so that I can keep control? Deep down, do I expect anything in return other than tax savings, like loyalty or affection? Will a gift help my marriage? Will it equalize my spouse's financial position and mine? Do I want that? Yes, no, why? Am I going to leave my spouse or children or whomever a lot of money? Would I like to test their performance now?

Don't feel guilty about facing up to these questions. If you're not honest with yourself, who can you trust?

SOME WAYS OF GIVING GIFTS

Having reviewed your resources, it is wise to make a gift-giving plan. If you have excess wealth that you know will eventually fall into your estate and be taxed, begin a program, say around age fifty or so, of divesting yourself of some of this money by giving it to your heirs on a yearly basis at a rate of $10,000 per year per donee. You can give it to as many donees as you wish—they don't have to be relatives.

In addition to the $10,000 exclusion from gift tax, you pay no gift tax if you give medical or educational aid to someone for whom you are not legally obligated to provide, like a parent or your wife's child by a first marriage. Remember, the money for health or education must go directly to the institution, not to the friend or relative to pay the institution. This gift tax exclusion is unlimited and is separate from the usual $10,000 per year exclusion.

There are special ways you might wish to consider in giving gifts to youngsters. For example, there is the ever popular Uniform Gifts to Minors Act. It has been enacted by every state and is uniform nationwide. Any adult can make a gift of securities in bearer or registered form, or of cash, to a person who is under the age of twenty-one when the gift is made. To make the gift, merely deliver the funds to a custodian for the under-aged donee. The custodian can be any adult member of the minor's family, a guardian, a trust company, or a lawyer. If the gift is an unregistered security, the donor himself cannot be the custodian. If the gift is of securities in registered form, money, life insurance policies, or annuity contracts, the donor can be the custodian. The custodian has very broad powers to hold, manage, or invest this property. His or her duties include the usual fiduciary responsibilities, such as registering the securities, placing the money in a specific account and keeping good records for inspection. The custodian can sell or exchange the property and use the proceeds for the minor.

All the money automatically goes to the minor when he or she is twenty-one years old. If the minor dies before the age of twenty-one, the money becomes part of the child's gross estate. The gift once given belongs entirely to the minor and is irrevocable. While the custodian or donor controls and manages the money, the income earned on it is taxed only at the level of the trust, not at the level of the donor's income tax rate. Be aware, however, that if the donor names himself or herself as custodian and then dies before the minor reaches the age of twenty-one, the value of the property will be included in the donor's estate for estate tax purposes.

Here is how the Uniform Gifts to Minors Act works out as a tax saving device:

PRO	*CON*
1. The income from the investment is taxed at the lower income tax rate of the donee.	1. The gift is irrevocable; once given it cannot be taken back.
2. The use of the money (and the income from it) can be controlled by the donor throughout the minority of the donee; this includes using it for the health and welfare of the donee.	2. If the donee should die an early death the money will be taxed in his or her estate.
3. The gift will automatically go to the donee at age twenty-one—so that the right person is going to receive the funds.	3. If the donor should die before the minor reaches twenty-one, the money will be taxed in the donor's estate.

Banks love this Uniform Gifts to Minors Act and yours will give you a simple form to fill out if you want to set one up. If you get a professional to act as custodian, you will pay a fee, but family custodians need not be compensated.

Part of your gift-giving program should also include giving gifts to a spouse. Actuarial statistics tell us that the surviving spouse will usually be female. Therefore, most spousal gift-giving programs entail giving by the husband to the wife to divest property from his estate and place it in hers. The likelihood is that he will die first and the wealth will be taxed only once, upon her death. Gift giving to a spouse is encouraged by the federal government. We have already seen in the material on taxes that since E.R.T.A. interspousal gifts may be unlimited, and no gift tax is paid, no matter how much is transferred back and forth. This is similar to the unlimited marital deduction available to you for gifts given in wills. Gifts given to a spouse prior to January 1, 1982, go by the old rules, which were much more limited. Formerly, you could give $100,000 during your lifetime to your spouse without paying a gift tax and without its being included later in your gross estate for estate tax purposes. For gifts over $100,000 a gift tax was imposed and couples had to be aware of the tax implications. Today you need not make such gift tax calculations.

Gifts *causa mortis* (in contemplation of death) are treated as any other gift. The $10,000 exclusion or unlimited spousal exclusion applies. This is new, too. Prior to January 1, 1982, a gift given within the three years prior to death was counted in calculating estate or gift taxes—only the $3,000 exclusion applied. The government presumed that you were giving money away in old age to avoid estate taxes.

If you do plan to give gifts very late in life, or to wait until you are very ill, you should consider capital gains. Here is the dilemma. If you give a gift of appreciated property during your lifetime the recipient takes it with the same basis that you had. This means that when the recipient sells it the gain will be reckoned as the difference between the sale price and your original purchase price. On the other hand, if you leave the property in a will it is transferred on a stepped up basis; that is, its value is judged by its worth at the time it is transferred. When resold by the recipient, the gain is less, and the capital gains tax less as well. You must decide whether the extra estate tax paid by giving in a will instead of during your lifetime is more or less than the capital gains tax saving of a testamentary gift.

There are many types of gifts we might make everyday without really thinking about it. Here are some and their consequences.

- Opening a joint bank account in your name together with a child or another: No gift is made and no tax incurred until the other person makes a withdrawal. If you both contributed equally, there is no tax.
- Putting two names on United States bonds: The same formula applies, a tax is imposed when the other person cashes in the bonds. If you cash them and keep the money there is no gift tax.

- Buying joint stock: A gift is made as soon as you designate another as joint owner.
- Placing someone else's name on real estate: A gift is made when the new deed is executed.

Remember that no tax is imposed for transfers between spouses. This applies to the above everyday type of gift as well.

What happens when one joint owner dies? If the joint owners are husband and wife, one-half of the property is counted in the decedent's estate for estate tax purposes. The surviving spouse will automatically inherit the property unless a different designation is made. If the joint owners are not husband and wife, the amount of the property included in the decedent's estate is based upon who purchased and contributed to the property. It is possible for 100% of its value to be included.

CHARITABLE BEQUESTS

Uncle Sam wants to protect and encourage giving to certain especially worthy beneficiaries. Both income tax and estate tax deductions are available if you give money to charity. The idea is very similar to the marital deduction in that, here too, Uncle Sam has given you a bonus if you give your money to the right party. The government knows there are other institutions that do things people want, things the government can't do or can't do as well or doesn't want to monopolize. A charity can be selected from a large list, provided by the Federal Government, of types of institutions that qualify. They include religious, educational, and social organizations. You can even create your own charity if you have sufficient funds.

Here are some simple rules for how to give. Make sure that you actually inform the director of the organization that the charity is being named in your will. You may find that the organization has rules and regulations regarding the acceptance of bequests. Not every organization is out there welcoming your dollar. You may also want to give the money to a charity for special purposes, such as an educational scholarship. If so, it is wise for you to know the name of the fund or to have other information that you will insert into a will to make sure your money goes for the intended purpose.

If you want to put restraints on the use of a charitable gift, make sure that the charity is willing to abide by such rules. A year ago I visited a wonderful reconstructed plantation house in Louisiana, which had been left in a will to a church. The home had been the long-time residence of a family that wanted the church to preserve it as a monument to the family. If they would not do this then the church was to sell the home. The church never agreed to run it as a monument since it was not in the historic preservation business. The community was in real danger of having the property sold to a private owner, perhaps a developer, or of having it knocked down to make a parking lot. The will was hotly contested by the community, which finally paid the church $200,000 to sell its rights under the will.

Once you decide on your charity and inform it of your intentions, you must decide on the amount you want to leave. You get a dollar-for-dollar tax deduction from your gross estate for the amount you leave to charity. So you will be saving a good deal in estate tax dollars. A good idea is to give property like jewelry, small issues of stock and other items hard to evaluate. This way, if the gift is held up while evaluation is being made it will not be your individual heirs who are stymied for awhile. To save capital gains tax, give highly appreciated property. You'll learn more about this later.

It is especially worth giving to charity when you wish to save taxes; you have a limited number of heirs; you want a special kind of management; and you have a charitable inclination. For example, several of my clients have children who for one reason or another they are sure will never have heirs of their own. Often these people are very concerned about preserving their estate, getting a good tax deduction, and providing their children with a lifetime income. They do not want to give all their wealth to their children outright, and they know that if they did the tax bite would greatly reduce the value of their estate. For these people a charitable trust with income to the children for life is a good bet. It gives substantial tax deductions, takes care of the kids, and preserves the principal for the benefit of a worthy charity.

E.R.T.A. provides that certain trusts with remainders to charity (to be discussed later) will qualify for the marital deduction if the surviving spouse is the sole non-charitable income beneficiary. You can always set up a trust for your spouse's lifetime with income to him or her, naming whomever you wish as trustee, and giving the principal on your spouse's death directly to a charity. This has no lifetime tax benefits, but it qualifies for the full marital deduction, gets your money to charity, and permits the usual flexibility a trust has during your spouse's lifetime for the investment and invasion of principal for his or her needs. The charity does not act as trustee; it is just the ultimate beneficiary.

If you have no surviving spouse and set up a trust with a child or other non-spousal beneficiary as income beneficiary, the principal which will eventually go to a charity is deducted from your estate. You can also make a "reverse charitable trust"; the charity is income beneficiary and the remainderman is a child or other heir. Perhaps the income will go to the charity until the child reaches age thirty-five. The value of the expected income will be deducted from your estate for estate tax purposes.

Charitable gifts are important too for people with high income, particularly when they are not married. If you belong to that group, consider a lifetime gift to charity. Instead of leaving the money in a will give a large gift, if you can spare the cash, during your lifetime. Such a gift is without gift tax, is deductible from your income tax, and also reduces your gross estate at the end for tax purposes.

In giving to charity not only do you help a worthy cause, you save taxes in many ways. First, there is no gift tax on donations to eligible causes. Second, if you give a gift to charity that has appreciated in value from the time you bought it you will not pay any capital gains tax, even though the value of the gift will be set at the time that you give it, not the time you acquired it. This is important in selecting what you give to charity, something we will look at shortly. Finally, you get an income tax deduction if you give during your lifetime, or an estate tax deduction if you give in your will. Don't expect the income tax deduction to be dollar for dollar.

To begin with, charities are divided into what are called 50% and 20% charities. You are free to give any amount of money to them that you wish, but at best you will only get a deduction of up to 50% of your Adjusted Gross Income (A.G.I.). This works a bit like medical deductions: The amount that can be taken depends upon your income. If your A.G.I. is $30,000 you can give $15,000 to charity and get a deduction for the entire amount. If you give $16,000 you get only the $15,000 deduction. On the other hand, there are certain charities for which you can only deduct up to a maximum of 20% of your A.G.I. If you are making $30,000 only $6,000 could be deducted, even though you gave much more to the charity.

However, if you do give more than half your A.G.I. to a 50% charity, you can carry over the additional deductions for the next five years. You will not lose the full value of the deductions as long as you have need for the deductions over the next five-year period. No such carry-over to subsequent years is available for 20% charities.

This brings us to the question of choosing what charities you wish to support. Ultimately this is one of the most personal decisions you can make. You know in your spirit and soul what charities you believe to be the most worthy. Worthiness is the first criterion. Almost all charities spend some of their valuable dollars on advertising and solicitation. Other money is of course spent on staffing and overhead. Charities differ in their ability to administer funds. We are forever hearing of cases where only ten cents of the charitable dollar goes to the ultimate beneficiary. This is true even of some legitimate charities, and may differ from year to year within the same charity. Every charity has an annual report which states how much of its income goes to the cause and how much is used for other expenses. Before you make any serious contribution to a charity, speak to their fund raiser, or public relations staff. With one phone call you can learn more about the organization than you might expect. You can find out who is on the Board of Directors, what their major goals are, where they spend their dollars, and of course whether they are a 50% or a 20% charity.

For the most part any publicly or governmentally approved charity, but only some types of private foundations, are 50 percenters. All other private foundations are 20 percenters. Some organizations that look like charities aren't from Uncle Sam's point of view. Among them are organizations that lobby for change in the law. Lawyers call them 501C (4) Corporations. That means that they were organized for the purposes of changing the law and lobbying on the State or Federal level rather than for giving direct charity. Some organizations do both and have actually set up two corporations. Gifts to the one that lobbies don't qualify for a tax deduction, gifts to the other do qualify. Make sure you know the difference. Find out simply by asking.

As we've seen, you save different amounts of income tax depending on the charities you choose. If you don't pick a recognized charity (that is, recognized by Uncle Sam) you can get no tax deduction at all. But the amount of your tax saving will be affected not only by the charity you choose but also by the type of gift you give.

If money (meaning cash) is the only kind of gift you ever consider giving, reconsider. Giving shares of stock can be one of the most money-saving kinds of gift. But there are some booby traps. First of all, if the shares are in small denominations and difficult to evaluate, your executors will have more work, and that will be costly to the estate. All professional executors will tell you that they are plagued by the estate that is filled with small issues of stock. There is a good deal of checking, appraisal and evaluating to be done. The transfer of these shares from one spouse to another can sometimes take months; yet an estate cannot be wound up until these transfers are made. Sometimes two or three hundred dollars' worth of shares stops an executor from finishing his job in timely fashion. Many an heir has asked whether he could just tear up troublesome shares and throw them away. So, if you wish to make a gift during your lifetime, one good idea is not to hold on to small issues of stock that you don't expect to bloom. This is an idea to help you tidy up your estate. Another good reason to give stocks or bonds instead of cash is to avoid the capital gains tax. You already know that if you buy something for investment and then sell it at a profit that profit is called a capital gain. A capital gain has a lesser tax than ordinary income because only 40% of the gain is taxable.

Despite this tax saving people often hold on to their property even though they could turn a profit by selling. They want to avoid any type of tax. If this type of appreciated property is given to the charity no tax is paid, yet the value of your deduction is counted at the present, higher value of the appreciated property, not at your cost. See how this works:

A national preservation society which qualifies as a 50

percenter asks for money. If you gave $5,000 in cash you could deduct the $5,000 from your income tax, provided your A.G.I. was $10,000 or more. If instead you used $5,000 worth of stock which you originally bought at $1,000 you would also be avoiding the capital gains tax that you would ordinarily have to pay on the $4,000 increase. Two rules to note. If the charity you pick is a 50 percenter you can deduct only 30% of your A.G.I. if you give an appreciated property. If the charity you pick is a 20 percenter then you are allowed a deduction for only half of the market value. For example: You give to a 20% charity $5,000, consisting of bonds that have appreciated and would ordinarily have given you a taxable capital gain at sale. You are entitled only to a $2,500 deduction for the gift, and then only if the $2,500 is not more than 20% of your A.G.I.

Those of you who want to give books, records and works of art that you have created yourself can deduct only their cost. If you want to give old furniture, clothing, etc., only their present value (which may have depreciated since you bought them) can be deducted. In general you should never give investments that have depreciated to charity. This is because you will automatically lose the depreciation deduction you could have had.

Finally, here's an idea for you. If you own a country house or piece of land you might consider giving it to charity. Charities will set up a method through which you can continue to use the homestead all your life (and your children can use it for their lifetime), but the charity will actually own the property. This can help you a good deal in future estate planning if there is a conflict of residences. Remember that if you have set up two residences you may end up with double taxation through double probate. If you give the property away during your lifetime you will be deprived of using it and enjoying it. On the other hand, if you give it to charity but set up a life estate for your own use, you can both use it and give it away at the same time. This will make clear that you have only one residence and of course it will keep the value of the property out of your estate.

It is also possible to combine several interests through one strategy. For example, you can give to charity, help business, keep up investments and save taxes through the creation of a foundation, public or private. There are more private and small public foundations than you can imagine, often run by middle class families who understand something about tax planning, and have a charitable frame of mind.

It works this way. A person or family creates a trust or corporation with the help of the family attorney. This is something you cannot do yourself. The purpose of the trust or corporation must be religious, scientific, literary, educational or charitable. The government must be certain that those are the true purposes of the organization.

The creator of the trust—whether an individual or a family—controls the organization because if it is a corporation he is the only stockholder, and if it is a trust he is the only trustee. The income made by this organization is tax exempt provided it is both created and operated for the charitable purpose. The person picks the charitable purpose he likes best, and can give the money directly every year for that purpose. The charitable income tax deduction is taken when the money is given to the foundation, not when the money is paid out of the foundation. The foundation can also give money to other charities rather than make direct payments to beneficiaries. It is worth considering, as well, that you can choose a charity that helps your business. For example, a realtor might make contributions to national preservation societies; a baker could fund research regarding nutrition; makers of athletic equipment can give money to promote health organizations. The public is benefited, the business earns good will and free advertising. Remember that the amount of the gift can be very small. The foundation does not have to be a full-time job for the family.

Though you set up a true private foundation of course it will be nothing more than a 20 percenter. You might want to make your foundation a public one and therefore a 50 percenter. This can be done too. However, the trust or corporation must be organized solely for the charitable purposes that are considered public purposes by the Internal Revenue Service. It must be operated solely for these purposes and controlled in connection with an already established publicly supported organization which the foundation benefits. Choose a public organization that you favor and meet with its officers. They will actually help work out and often pay the legal cost of setting up a trust or corporation that will be controlled or operated by them. It is like the creation of a parent and subsidiary corporation where the subsidiary is completely controlled by the parent.

Another even simpler way is to have the public organization have some "significant" voice in investment policies, the making of grants, and perhaps even a common officer or trustee. In the corporate document or trust the charity that you wish to ally with can designate the specific function for which they will be using the funds that your foundation gives them. This helps you to determine exactly how you want your money spent and at the same time to satisfy the government's requirement that there be significant contribution and relationship between the public foundation and your newly created organization. Among the family assets that could be placed in such a charitable trust or corporation is stock of a solely owned company. Remember that when this transfer of stock from your business corporation to your charitable corporation is made, no gift tax is paid nor is any capital gains tax paid since this qualifies as giving to charity even though it is a charity created by you.

After death, difficulty often arises over what happens to the stock of a closed corporation. If you transfer shares in that corporation to a charitable foundation run by your own family then the value of those shares is deducted from your gross estate before taxes are paid. In this case, you are saving taxes, the family is continuing to run the company through the charitable foundation of which they are officers or trustees, a significant portion of the income is going to a charity in your name after your death, there is an ongoing foundation in your memory, and other income is being distributed to your family beneficiaries by integrating one of the income plans (to be discussed later) into the entire program. There are, however, limitations on the amount of family held stock you can give. Note that you don't have to give all the stock away but only some, thereby saving taxes and keeping your family running the business.

CHARITABLE GIVING AND INVESTMENT PROGRAMS

Today charitable giving is one of the most sophisticated areas of planning and can partially substitute for an investment program. This is particularly true for single people or childless couples who expect not to have future heirs.

The following is a smorgasbord of charitable contribution arrangements useful as both tax saving *and* investment programs:

Charitable Remainder Annuity Trust

Goal: To get a steady fixed lifetime income each year with the usual tax breaks for charitable gifts. At the end of the giver's lifetime the remaining principal will go to the charity.

Tax Savings: There is no gift tax when the annuity trust is set up; if appreciated property is used there are no capital gains. There is an income tax charitable contribution deduction at the time the trust is set up; the principal in the trust does not go into the estate and there are no estate taxes paid.

Investment Opportunities: You can give appreciated property which will be invested for you; yet, you will not without paying a capital gains tax. If instead you liquidate and reinvest the same assets without a charitable trust, you would first pay the capital gains tax.

Example: A sixty-seven-year-old retired bookkeeper has kept bonds worth $50,000 for years. She originally paid only $25,000 for them at a deep discount years ago. At this time the income from $50,000 is very important to her, but she has no intention of selling the bonds because of the capital gains tax. By setting up a charitable trust our bookkeeper receives a higher interest rate (presuming that the trust managers are good ones), gets free investment management and pays no capital gains. At the same time she gets a deduction of up to 50% of her $50,000 trust corpus which she can use over a five year period if her income is not high enough to take it all in the first year.

Charitable Remainder Unit Trust

Goal: Instead of obtaining a fixed amount of income for life you receive a fixed rate of income for life. The percentage you obtain must be worth at least 5% of the fair market value of the trust property.

Tax Savings: Same as Charitable Remainder Annuity Trust. Further, income distributions that you get every year often have a favorable tax rate. Payments are taxed first as ordinary income to the extent that it is earned by the Unit Trust and then only as capital gains to the extent that capital gains is realized by the Unit Trust. Payments made to you out of principal, because the trust did not earn enough income to meet your percentage requirement, are not subject to income taxation at all. This way if your trust is not doing well from an *income* point of view, you're getting a little break from Uncle Sam from an *income tax* point of view.

Investment Opportunities: Same as the Annuity but with one big difference. A Unit Trust helps hedge against inflation because you get a percentage of the total amount in the trust. The percentage does not vary but the amount in the trust can vary greatly as inflation increases the value of investments. Also, the percentage you receive is a percentage of the entire principal in the trust in any given year. You are not working on income only. If it is necessary to invade the principal to pay your percentage the trustees must do so.

Example: Our same bookkeeper puts her money into a Unit Trust requiring 5% return. In the first year she will receive 5% of $50,000 and she will have already obtained a hefty tax deduction of $50,000.

Charitable Remainder Net Income Unit Trust

Goal: Same as the above, except that you will be receiving income only and your trustee will not be able to invade principal to pay you your percentage rate. However, if in the future there is excess income and you got short-changed in an earlier year, your shortfall will be made up.

Tax Savings: Same as above, except that you and the trustee determine the investment policy. This way money can be increased during your retirement years. In the early years of the trust, while you are younger and have income from other sources, the income from the trust will be less. This way you will be making more money when your total income is lower (when you are older) and less money at a time that you are in a high tax bracket.

Investment Opportunities: This is the area where you do a great deal of investment planning with the charity's trust officer. You may choose to look for higher capital gains rather than income at the early stages to increase the principal. Then in later years you will seek more income. This is the best kind of trust through which to make gifts of non-income-producing or low-income-producing property since it is not necessary to invade the principal in order to distribute the percentage every year. Of course every year if the net income falls short of the agreed distribution the amount will be credited to your account and paid later on.

Example: Let's say our same bookkeeper is several years younger and doesn't need income at this time. Instead of bonds she has a piece of real estate left to her by an old aunt. It is making no income for her. If she sells it now she will have a substantial capital gain and no real investment that she would like to make. She transfers the property to a charity which makes very little income on it over the next several years. It eventually sells the property for a large profit and distributes a fixed percentage to her every year for the rest of her life after her retirement. The amount remaining goes to the charity upon her death.

Pooled Income Fund

Goal: Giving money to charity but retaining the income from the principal for yourself and of course having your tax savings. This is particularly good if you have a small contribution to make. Remember that capital growth is not given back to the donor but is kept in the trust.

Tax Savings: Same.

Investment Opportunities: This is just like a managed or a mutual fund. While the principal itself eventually goes to charity, the income goes to you. You actually buy shares in this fund which is also being contributed to by many others. Because there is more money to invest, the return is greater and the diversification of investments is outstanding. Many of these charitable funds do as well as or better than mutual funds.

Example: Our same lady has a limited amount of money that she would like to give to charity. She would like to do this tax-free and get her deduction right away. However, she does not want to lose the income that she might be getting from that capital. On the other hand, she will never use the principal itself and does want it to go to the charity upon her death.

Life Insurance

Many charitable people have very little money. They give to charities as much as they can but wish they could do more. Believe it or not they can—through life insurance. Yes, it is possible to make a significant one-time large contribution to a favored charity through the use of life insurance. If you have an insurance policy, you can give it away and obtain an income tax deduction for the cash value of the policy at the time you give it. You can also take out a new policy and name a charity the irrevocable beneficiary of the policy. You will receive an income tax deduction for your premium payments as you make them.

This is also a valuable idea for the person who wants to make an outstanding contribution to charity but can afford only a few thousand dollars a year. A person, for example, who wishes to spend $2,000 a year on charities may be considered a generous giver but will certainly never have a building named after him or her. On the other hand, $2,000 worth of premiums a year for life insurance can eventually buy an insurance policy of substance to go to charity. Once a charity is informed of such a gift, work can begin to actually create an endowment that is long remembered and appreciated.

ANOTHER KIND OF GIFT

You have a right over the property you own, that is, the right or power to decide whom you want to receive it. This is called a power of appointment. Not every country permits its citizens this power. We take it for granted; and it is granted to each and every one of us. If you give another person the right to choose for you who will get your wealth you are giving him a power that is valuable in and of itself.

A power of appointment can be created in a will, a deed, or a contract. A general power of appointment permits the recipient (donee) to name himself, his family or even his creditors as appointee (the one who will get the wealth). A special power of appointment limits the donee to appoint from among a limited list of appointees specified by the donor (the one who grants the power). When general powers of appointment are given there are complex gift and income tax consequences. Limited powers give rise to less dramatic tax results. Only by discussion with your attorney can you learn the tax result in your case. But don't ignore powers of appointment because of this. They are useful in reaching numerous goals, otherwise impossible, such as:

1. Giving a beneficiary of a trust the power to appoint the remainderman. This gives them tremendous authority and still gives you the benefit of a trust.
2. Giving a beneficiary of a trust the right to invade the trust principal, if necessary, in limited amounts, thus avoiding the problem of a stingy trustee.
3. Giving a spouse the power to appoint a new beneficiary.

8

Life Insurance

In the 20th century we accept life insurance as one of the backbones of estate planning. But in the 19th century it was considered a form of gambling, no more acceptable than five card stud. Insurance was ranked with pool halls and saloons as causing the degeneration of American culture.

Insurance has already undergone one revolution in moving from unacceptable to respectable, even essential. But the law continues to recognize the gambling aspect of insurance. When you buy life insurance you get an "inchoate right"—that is, a right that doesn't become real until sometime in the future. In plain words, when you buy life insurance you get nothing now, except the right to collect money at some future time which can't yet be known. Of course, I am talking only about death benefit life insurance and not some of the other types we will discuss later on.

Death benefit insurance means simply that you pay now for the privilege of having money paid out on your behalf at the time of your death. You are entitled to designate in the policy who will receive the money (your spouse, your children, your estate, a charity, your partner, etc.). You continue to pay according to the terms of the policy until death when your heirs finally receive the money. While this is surely a form of gambling, it's one that even the most conservative can accept.

Life insurance is an estate preserver. Some special types are estate builders. As things change all around us, life insurance remains an essential element of estate planning. Of course, the term "life insurance" is the world's greatest euphemism; it's death insurance you're buying, either as a lump sum benefit for your family or as a trust for the purpose of paying debts and taxes where an estate is not liquid. Both of these purposes of life insurance are intelligent and worthwhile, in my view. There is nothing more comforting financially after the death of a loved one than to get a lump sum of money to weather the financial storm. This is true even for those who will leave substantial estates. The money comes fast (if you pick a good company) and without undue aggravation at a time of grief.

But some people buy insurance for the wrong reasons. One is to make their children instant millionaires, and another is to force themselves to save. If leaving a large fortune to your children is your goal, proper investment and planning can much more readily accomplish it. Moreover, life insurance is expensive, and the lump sum is hit by inflation. The $40,000 policy purchased only five or six years ago is a minimal estate today. It is quite possible that companies would not even sell you a million dollars' worth of life insurance if your income didn't warrant it. If they did, payments would be so high that you would have to skimp and worry during your own lifetime.

As for forcing yourself to save, there are much better ways. Certificates of deposit and treasury bills that force you to leave in a lump sum of money are definite high yielding investments. If necessary, you can get your hands on the money quickly during your lifetime. The days when it was important to take $50, $20 or even $10 out of your paycheck every week for savings so that you could plod along toward the American dream are over. Similarly, putting away $100 a month in life insurance so that your family is assured $50,000 or $60,000 in death benefits is a high price to pay for small returns.

Life insurance companies are well aware that other investments may be more appealing—and here's where a second revolution comes in, one whose beginnings we are witnessing right now. Equitable Life Assurance Society has come up with a remarkable alternative to typical types of insurance. It was the first on the market but certainly will not be the last. The insurance pioneered by Equitable is called VLI, marketed by Evlico, Equitable subsidiary. Its generic name is *variable life insurance*. The idea is to attract people who want insurance but also want a greater potential for growth.

It works this way: The assets used to pay policy benefits are held in a separate account and invested in securities, primarily common stocks. The death benefit varies. It goes up or down depending on the investment but it never falls below the minimum face amount that you bought in the first place. This contrasts sharply with the way assets are invested with most insurance policies. Where bonds and other fixed securities are used there is no potential for growth.

Donald J. Mooney, President of Evlico, Equitable's subsidiary, says that for Europeans this is nothing new. "In Europe where consumers have long recognized the necessity of living with inflation, a significant percentage of the life insurance sold in several countries is equity-linked."

If you buy such insurance remember that in addition to selling insurance you are being sold securities. The company must be registered with the Securities and Exchange Commission and must give you a prospectus on what you are buying.

How well is this insurance doing compared to other investments? VLI, the Equitable version, is doing pretty well. In 1979 it had a return of over 29%. In 1980 it had a 49.5% return—not bad for insurance. But remember this is not to be purchased instead of other investments; it is to be purchased instead of other types of insurance. If the investment is successful it is treated together with other insurance policies for tax purposes. It will not be taxed at all if you make the beneficiary the owner of the policy. If you'd like to read more about it but do not want a sales agent to call on you, Evlico offers you a free prospectus if you write for one to 1285 Avenue of the Americas, New York, New York 10019.

Before you buy VLI, or any other insurance, let's unravel the types of life insurance on the market today. I say today because I fully expect there to be a third revolution in the field of life insurance. This will happen because of our longevity and the decline in frequency of sudden deaths in early life. Life insurance is worth the most if you have a big policy and die young, but today's trend is the other way.

TYPES OF LIFE INSURANCE

1. *Term insurance.* This is the simplest form of insurance and the cheapest. At least initially. It gives your family only a death benefit. You select the amount you want them to inherit at the time of your death. You pay a premium, normally increasing annually, determined by your age and in some cases your health and sex. The policy will automatically terminate at the end of the stated period. If you haven't died you have gambled and lost. You paid the premiums without any benefits. The policy itself has no value other than that death benefit. This is the same concept as automobile or fire insurance. If you have no fire you get nothing out of your insurance except peace of mind.

Remember that the death benefit is taxable to your estate. Many people are not aware of this, although it is a fact that we should all be taught from the cradle. It is rumored that life insurance salesmen must advise you how to avoid taxability. I hope they do because avoiding the tax is really quite simple.

Here's how. If you designate your beneficiary as the owner of the policy, then upon your death the face value of the policy will go to your beneficiary directly and not fall into your estate and be taxed. The only catch is the usual one: You can't change your mind. Because you have made the beneficiary the owner you are stuck with that beneficiary for life. If the beneficiary is your spouse, and you get a divorce, the only thing you can do is stop making payments and let the policy lapse, if you don't want to protect your ex-spouse. This catch should not deter you. Even in some bitter matrimonial disputes there are ways of agreeing to change the beneficiary or have the ex-spouse pick up the payments. Meanwhile, in the event that the marriage does last, you save a whopping estate tax.

Other features of the term policy are that the cost of the policy increases as you get older, and the renewability of the policy, the right to get a new one when the term expires, decreases with increasing age. Why is that? Because of our old gambling theory. The insurance company wants to make the odds a little better for it. If you are older you are more likely to die sooner. Therefore the premium is greater. After a while, i.e., at age sixty-five or seventy, the insurance company doesn't want to play anymore.

But don't be alarmed. The likelihood is that you won't need that huge death benefit because you will have created an estate for your spouse and children through investments and good planning. After a certain age the kids are grown and no longer dependent. When you were younger and presumably less affluent your premiums were lower since the gamble on your part was greater. In general this fits the practical needs of the average American family.

2. *Straight life* (whole life or ordinary life).   Straight life is a much more expensive method of obtaining life insurance. Insurance sales people love it. Other methods and better ones of saving money are using a bank and not an insurance company, or trying a variable life plan. There are, however, some good things about straight life insurance. One is that the policy cannot be canceled and you will be able to renew it all your life. The premiums start high and stay that way; they never increase. The policy accumulates a cash surrender value. This means that if you cancel the policy some money will come back to you. It isn't much compared to what you have paid, though insurance people may try to tell you that it is. They'll show you how much you'll pay every year as premium, compare it to the surrender value, and then compare that with term insurance to show that you got a real bargain. Look at this:

Premium $720 per year × 10 = $7,200

Cash surrender value of policy after 10 years = $5,000

Deduct $5,000 from the $7,200 and you get $2,200

Divide $2,200 by 10 and you get $220

See, you paid only $220 a year for insurance. Term insurance might even have cost more. What's wrong with this reasoning? Well, consider what you could have earned if you took your $720 a year and put it in a savings account or invested it in stock, even a few shares of blue chip utilities.

Does this mean that you should never have straight life insurance? No. Straight life does give you the confidence that you will continue to have insurance regardless of your health. It permits you to borrow against the policy, usually at very reasonable rates. If you never pay it back, the amount borrowed plus interest will be deducted from the death benefit. This can be a very heavy sum. The unpaid interest is compounded. If you don't pay at least the interest every year, it is compounded and charged against the principal paid out to you. A small loan taken out years ago can end up in a much diminished death benefit. Warning: Pay at least the interest every year so there is no compounding (don't forget that the interest is, in the year you pay it, deductible from your own income tax).

In addition to permitting you to borrow, your straight life policy has the added attraction of accumulating dividends. You may use dividends (1) to buy more insurance, (2) to maintain the death benefit if you borrowed against the policy, (3) for extra cash, (4) to invest for additional interest, or (5) to insure the cash value of the policy.

Straight life also permits you to surrender the policy and get its cash value, in the event of a rainy day. To me this seems a dubious advantage. If you have paid the high premiums required for straight life because you didn't want your policy to terminate as you grew older or less healthy, the last thing you want is to cash in your policy because you need a few extra dollars to weather a storm.

3. *Yearly renewable term insurance.* Renewable term insurance means that you pay a slightly larger premium than for term insurance, but the policy can be renewed automatically without an additional physical at the end of each term. The premium payments will increase but you will not be without insurance because of ill health. At the same time the policy can be converted from term to straight life. This gives you the advantages of renewability and convertibility. Ask your insurance salesperson about it.

You might want to consider converting this type of term policy to straight life sometime before age forty-five or so. This is the point at which straight life premiums get very high. Prior to that straight life is not quite so expensive. If you have had convertible term for years start thinking about making a change after your fortieth birthday and before your forty-fifth. You will definitely get a far smaller death benefit, if you wish to spend the same amount in premiums. But if you are enchanted by the savings element of straight life and the kids have gone on to be self-supporting individuals, you might want straight life.

4. *Split life.* This is one of the many variations on term and straight life. This particular popular variety gives you renewable term insurance plus a retirement annuity, payable generally at

age sixty-five. The renewability factor is contingent on keeping up your annuity plan. I suggest skipping to the section on annuities.

5. *Decreasing term.* Remember, in life insurance as in anything else, you get what you pay for. Decreasing term means that the amount of death benefit decreases. It is inexpensive insurance but you get less and less benefit as the years go by. For example, you take a plan with the insurance company for a ten-year policy which will pay $10,000 in the first year, $9500 in the second year, $8500 in the third year. Is it of use? Yes. You can use this kind of policy if you have a mortgage or other big debt that decreases over time. In fact this is the kind of insurance that most banks require if they give you a mortgage loan. Another good time to consider decreasing term is when you find yourself in the position of being a lender yourself, as more and more people are since they are financing the sale of their own homes. Ask the buyer to name you as beneficiary of a decreasing term insurance policy—an inexpensive method of securing their debt to you. Of course, make sure that the decreasing benefit can still cover the amount owed to you as time goes on. The death benefit may decrease more rapidly than the mortgage—so beware.

CHOOSING AND TALKING TO AN INSURANCE REPRESENTATIVE

Melvyn loves to go to lunch. He likes to go to lunch because he knows that he's better off in the friendliest possible circumstances. Melvyn is Melvyn Feldman, my insurance agent. It really isn't right to avoid Melvyn. He means no harm. Since he sells something you don't want to buy he gets bad press. Woody Allen, master comic commentator on the conditions of life pictured purgatory as an endless session locked up in a room with an insurance salesperson. How to handle an insurance salesperson is a question almost as old as the question of how to talk to your lawyer. Here are some tips.

To begin with, remember that insurance salespersons are human beings too. I am talking here of course about highly skilled professional sales people. They have great integrity and vast knowledge. They can advise you and help you. They will knock themselves out to give you extra service and comfort. They will actually be there when the death benefit is needed. But if you don't buy insurance from them they don't eat. While one of their goals is to give you good service, their major goal is selling. They can't help it, it's their business. Because of that, never believe that their only agenda is advising you. It couldn't be or they would not be in the business. They would be paid advisors.

Of the many insurance salespersons' cards you will get, some will say C.L.U. after the name. This means that this particular person has been certified as a Chartered Life Underwriter— C.L.U. Certification takes place by the American College of Life Underwriters. Certification is given only after the individual passes ten comprehensive examinations, fulfils ethical requirements and has experience in the field. The exams include life insurance, law, taxation, trusts, accounting, social and governmental insurance and economics. C.L.U. means that your salesperson has taken the time to be a professional in the field, to be thoroughly educated in it. He or she is not selling insurance while marking time until something better comes along.

Remember too that insurance representatives are backed up by vast operations. Because many insurance people are personable and personal in their discussion with you, there is a tendency to forget that some of the largest investors, land owners, conglomerates and controllers of the world's wealth are insurance companies. Use them. They are equipped with some of the most sophisticated and finest computer operations in the universe. Don't hesitate to ask for information. If there is any question you think of regarding mathematical probabilities, the amount of insurance you should have, how much premiums or a loan will cost over a period of time, ask for a computer print-out. Representatives will compare straight life insurance for you with term insurance. They will computerize the difference between a policy written on the husband as opposed to one for the wife. It's the greatest service they can do, and they can do it quickly and without cost to you.

Don't ever think you are bothering insurance salespeople. They can take it. If you don't ask one representative you will be asking someone else, or you will be buying nothing. In either case the salesperson will lose out. Besides, you may want to buy insurance some other day if not today, or you may refer someone else to him. The best thing that could happen to an insurance salesperson is to know everybody in the world. That's the major goal in life for all insurance salespeople. Remember that no matter how many questions you ask, you are not obligated to buy insurance.

If you already know what you need, go to a savings bank for insurance. Many states limit the amount that you can buy there, and you won't get much in the way of help or service, but it is cheaper.

Inquire about the services of the various insurance companies. It is not just the amount of your coverage but the ease in collecting that's important. The best insurance salesperson is one that represents many companies and is not wedded to just one. Salespeople are usually honest in telling you which is the most responsive company. After all, the worst thing that could happen to insurance salespersons other than not making a sale is making a sale with a company that doesn't deliver; if they want to keep their reputation, they will have to work overtime to make sure you get your money. There are big differences among companies in the speed of payment and, very important, in the number and complexity of the forms that have to be filled out in order to get coverage. Remember, to collect benefits, all your heirs need is the policy, a death certificate and the name and number of the salesperson. If a company asks for more, it is giving you a hard time.

If you, the insured person, gave the wrong information regarding your age, for example, your policy is not cut off, but the amount your beneficiaries receive is diminished by the higher premiums you would have had to pay at the later age. If there is a contestable error and the company lets it go for two years, it's too late for them. If the executors have a really hard time collecting it may be a case of fraud on the part of the insurance company. The average reputable companies do pay off speedily. Make sure too that your heirs know whether the insurance company pays interest on the amount it holds from the day of death to the time that payment is turned over. Ask your insurance agent about this, as well as whether a portion of the unused premium will be refunded in case you die in the middle of the month.

CHOOSING AMONG INSURANCE OPTIONS

1. *Automatic premium loans.* One useful option is the right to have the company use the cash value of a policy to pay premiums that you have forgotten to pay. This is a pretty good option for you to select, particularly if you are careless. If you are prone to leaving envelopes unopened, if you don't heed warnings, if you take long vacations or are slightly short of cash every once in a while, pick up this option. One of my favorite clients never received her premium notice because she was changing her residence from Switzerland to the United States. After years of faithful payments her policy lapsed because her trustee failed to send her mail along to her. Only after threatening to go to the state insurance department was her policy reinstated. Even that was a miracle. If she had had the automatic premium loan option the company would have been required to pay her premiums from the accumulated cash value without sending her a lapse notice.

2. *"Paid-up" insurance.* "Paid-up" insurance means that all the premiums you are required to pay from the time you take the policy to the time that you die (provided that you live to be 100 or less) are paid. It really is a prepayment program. People elect this because they fear that they will not have the money to make the payments after their retirement. They are worried about having fixed expenses when they are old. For most people however it's a bad idea. Unless you have done almost no planning in your lifetime, you will need to have the policy as a death benefit less and less as you grow older. If it should really happen that you can't afford to keep your insurance up, that will probably be in old age, the time when it is needed least, not most. Meanwhile you will have been paying for very expensive insurance at the highest possible premium rates very early in life when you need the money to build your estate. Once the policy is paid up the interest accumulates with deadly slowness. Because of this there are very few paid-up policies around. Many of them are old. If you do have a paid-up policy the best thing to do with it during this inflationary time is cash it in and put the proceeds away in a certificate of deposit or treasury bill at the highest possible interest rates.

3. *Retirement income policies.* Retirement income policies

are an all too expensive method of getting an annuity for yourself. In fact, if that's what you're interested in, skip right to the chapter on retirement plans and read about better things for you and your family.

4. *Modified life.* For the person who wishes expensive straight life insurance but can't afford it, modified life insurance is both good news and bad news. A modified life policy permits you to pay a small amount of premiums—that's the good news. However, as years go on you will be paying a disproportionately larger amount toward the end of the policy—that's the bad news. Actually you're gambling on yourself becoming richer. Since I don't like a straight life policy, I'm not in favor of modified life insurance either.

5. *Disability waiver.* With a disability waiver, for a small extra amount the company will continue making payments if you become disabled. This is usually a good option because your key element is to make sure nothing happens that forces you to cancel your policy at a time when you would not wish to. Involuntary cancellation is the only real tragedy that takes place with respect to insurance. In investigating disability waivers ask the salesperson at what age, if any, the disability coverage terminates, what the term *disability* itself means to the company, whether you pay separately for the disability, and whether it matters how the disability arose (illness, accident, etc.).

6. *Double indemnity.* For a small additional charge many companies will include a double indemnity clause in your policy. This means that you get more money if you die as a result of an accident rather than because of an illness. Why should you get, want or even deserve more money if you die accidentally instead of through natural causes? You will have provided for your family in precisely the same way, their needs will be exactly the same, the rest of your estate will be identical—and yet people are fascinated by this little gimmick called double indemnity. What it really means is that the insurance company gambles with you. Accidental deaths are actually quite infrequent. For a small amount you can get twice the death benefit if you should die in that fashion. If you feel it's worth a gamble and you enjoy that kind of thing, by all means go ahead. Make sure, though, that

it's a cheap thrill. Ask the salesperson exactly what the extra cost is.

HOW MUCH INSURANCE?

To calculate the amount of insurance that you will need is a trick worthy of Merlin. Those of you who love math and forms will have a ball. The most comprehensive calculation method, and the most down to earth that I have seen, is found in Jane Bryant Quinn's *Everyone's Money Book.*

For a simpler method, try the following. Prepare a needs budget for your family if you were gone. Put down what it actually costs your family to live. Include extraordinary expenses that will surely arise such as repair of major equipment, if equipment is part of your everyday life (i.e., farmers and their families), or a college education.

Next, take the number of years you would like to provide for your family without their having to dip into other capital and without your spouse having to increase his or her earnings. At least ten years of financial security through insurance is usually appropriate. Take the yearly budget, multiply it by ten, add a 15% inflation factor, add a one-time cost for education, equipment or other extraordinary but expectable expenses. Subtract other income from all sources such as other investments, Social Security, spouse's earnings. The result will give you a rough idea of how much of a nest egg you need to replace your earnings for a ten-year period.

Next, use a 10% a year return on investment and estimate how much increase you need. If you need an *extra* $10,000 a year for ten years, over and above other resources, to make up for your loss of earnings, then you buy $100,000 worth of insurance. At the end of ten years only the income thrown off by this lump sum will have been used up and your family will be left with a tidy sum for continued investment. If emergencies have occurred through the decade then at least they will have a fund to invade.

Your calculations might show that family needs are so great that it is impossible to pay for enough insurance to yield a satisfactory income. Take a second approach. Purchase enough insurance so that if the principal plus interest is divided by ten, and one tenth is used each year, the family could continue to live in the style to which they have been accustomed. Of course, at the end of the ten-year period no nest egg would be left. By then, however, the family would have made other adjustments for carrying on.

Once you have arrived at the amount you would like the family to have as a death benefit, do your shopping for the cheapest possible insurance. Take out the policy and move on to the next phase of your estate planning through life insurance. That is the use of life insurance for estate tax payments.

LIFE INSURANCE TO PAY ESTATE TAXES

A final and often essential use of life insurance is to pay your estate taxes. This is certainly not recommended for everyone. It is necessary only for families with non-liquid estates. But for them it can mean the difference between financial security and total disaster. Consider the farming family or the family whose major income comes from a butcher shop or dry cleaning establishment. I once knew a family with a small business whose major asset was a camera of a sort very rare in the United States. When the camera was purchased it cost the family $50,000, but it was worth nearly half a million dollars five years later. Taking special photography was the business of this family and everyone participated. Their livelihood and life style were based upon the ownership of the camera. However, the legal ownership was in the hands of a closed corporation in which the father owned all the stock. In a case like this it can easily happen that the only way to pay estate taxes is to sell the stock in the business. The business though had only one major asset—the camera itself. The family could never afford to repurchase this valuable piece of equipment once it was sold for tax purposes. This is a truly illiquid estate.

For this kind of situation life insurance trusts for the purposes of paying taxes are ideal. Remember first that setting up a life insurance trust will not affect income tax. No income tax will be saved and no extra will be spent. On the other hand, by setting up a life insurance trust the death benefit will not fall into your estate and there will be no estate taxes on it. As usual, you will have to give up your ownership or control over the policy. The amount of the policy should match a rough calculation of how much estate taxes you may have to pay. This way, you will not be taxed on the very money that you have put away (in the form of the face value of the policy) for the purpose of paying taxes. When the policy is put in a trust, of course, there is gift tax. But the tax is based only on the value of the policy when the transfer is made, not on the eventual death benefit.

Also the usual $10,000 per year, per person gift tax exemption applies; if the policy has a value of more than $10,000 at the time it is transferred, the first $10,000 will not be taxed.

You may wonder why you can't just give your spouse an extra insurance policy to pay the taxes with. Why do you have to create a trust? That's a very good question, but there is an answer.

We are talking about the goal of helping heirs pay taxes by using insurance proceeds. If once the policy has been transferred to them outright your heirs die before you do, the value of the policy will be taxed in their estate and will not be available for use to pay your estate taxes. Next and even more important is that a trust can give the trustee the power to purchase assets from your estate upon your death or to make loans to your estate from the face value of the policy. With the sale or loan, your estate has the cash to pay taxes. Remember the trust cannot have the explicit power to pay estate taxes. Why not? Because the trust can't be used to pay your debts (taxes are a debt) to Uncle Sam or you are in danger of having the trust fund counted in your estate. Instead, authorize the trustee (who can be your spouse, your attorney, your accountant, etc.) to use the proceeds and invade principal for loans to your estate or the purchase of assets from your estate. This will create liquidity and give the estate the wherewithal to pay off Uncle Sam.

For example, farmers who own land and have everything tied up in it can create a trust with life insurance as the funding element. The trustee can be their spouse or next of kin. The trustee will be authorized to use the insurance proceeds to make loans or to purchase a portion of the land. Now the land belongs to the trust. The beneficiary of the trust is designated as the spouse or primary heir. Therefore, the spouse or kin are beneficiaries of the land. Now you have left the land itself to the people you wish to benefit, yet you have created some cash in the estate to pay Uncle Sam without selling the land to an outsider.

Those of you who are interested in using life insurance as a method of providing money to pay estate taxes, remember the following rules:

1. If the trustee is *obligated* by the terms of your trust to use the insurance to pay taxes, the amount of the policy is included in the estate. This is not good.
2. If the trustee is *permitted* to use the proceeds to pay the taxes, only the amount used is included in the estate. This is better but still not good.
3. If the trustee is merely permitted to purchase estate assets at fair market value or lend the money to the estate then the amount is not included even if the trustee uses the power. This is good. Make sure you pick your trustee carefully. Choose someone who will know what it means to obey your wishes without their being written out in the insurance policy or trust document.

9

INVESTMENTS

MONEYTHINK FOR THE INVESTOR

Sometimes I think that having $10,000 saved is the worst thing in the world. It's not enough to make a major investment, but it's too much to leave in low-interest-paying savings accounts. Like Diogenes looking for an honest man, there seem to be hundreds of thousands of Americans looking for the perfect investment. If you are one of them, you're in good company because no one else can find it either. There is good reason for this—all of which has to do with Moneythink.

New or small investors want to make money in the worst way, and that's the way they usually do it: in the worst way. They begin by "asking around." They ask people like lawyers, successful friends, brokers and anyone else they can get their hands on. E.F. Hutton, a stock brokerage house, launched a brilliant TV campaign showing people "hushing up" to eavesdrop on what was being said between a broker and client. The ad agency knew the secret of what makes the investor tick—he wants someone to tell him what to do! Nowhere in the field of financial planning is your baby money-self so apparent as in investments. Most people are looking for advice—more specifically, they are looking to be told by the true adult

135

(broker, financial planner, friend) exactly what to do and when to do it so that it all comes out with a profit at the end.

It doesn't work that way. The more you think it does, the less investing you'll do. What's worse, you may continue to invest but always at a loss. To begin to invest properly, the cardinal rule is trust yourself. If you have married the right person, picked the right job, learned to cross the street when the light is green, you can trust yourself to make investments.

More important, you can forgive yourself if you make a mistake—which you will do, but you will also make mistakes if you do nothing more than listen to others. At the very beginning of this book in discussing estate planning I said, "Never play another person's game." That goes double for investing. For example, if you are a low risk person and make a high risk investment on which you lose, you'll be obsessed with that loss forever.

If you're still hungry for advice, try to follow my hard-learned rules for successful investment:

1. *Don't believe the world's greatest lie; it will only keep you poor.* The world's greatest lie is that anyone can make $1,000,000 overnight. This lie is created by people with something to sell you. I've looked through hundreds of portfolios showing the income and assets of all types of people. Those with assets (excluding their residences) over $2,000,000 show solid, slow investments—real estate, blue-chip stocks (the stocks of leading companies), and bonds. Very little income or assets were derived from speculative stocks or low quality bonds. In fact, when the rich involve themselves in get-rich-quick schemes, they often do so to take a loss. It gives them a *chance* of winning, but if they lose they usually do it to trade off against capital gains.

2. *Don't fool yourself into thinking you have money to invest when you don't.* One reason that people are so uncomfortable with their "extra" $10,000 is that it really isn't extra money. It is money they can't really afford to lose. But investment money is money you could lose freely and never look back. You may get a twinge—even millionaires do when they lose—but you won't have a real financial setback.

Often young couples who have held back their expenses and saved a little money itch to put that money in some magic place and watch it grow. When I ask if they have bought their own home yet, or co-op or condominium, they usually say no. It is a mistake to pre-invest. If you haven't bought your homestead yet, if you haven't saved at least ten to twenty percent of your yearly income, you don't have money to invest.

3. *Don't think your money isn't invested.* Just because money is in a mutual fund, or Treasury bills and not in individual stocks, individual bonds, syndicates or tax shelters doesn't mean it's not invested. Money placed in high interest Treasury bills with a bank is money invested. As long as it is not being spent on overhead or new luxuries like cars and vacations, you have invested your money. You might want to invest it better, but don't lose sleep on the belief that you're not doing anything at all.

4. *If you have limited funds to invest, don't diversify.* The small investor often reminds me of myself as a child at the toy counter. Give me a lot of little things instead of one big one. For a small investor that's wrong. Remember, diversification is essential if you invest a lot or frequently. But if you have one small pot and want to try, what you need is in depth knowledge. Whether it's stocks, bonds, options, syndications or real estate. You have to know what you're doing. You can't possibly know everything about all types of investments. The greatest experts don't. They specialize.

5. *Learn to take yes for an answer.* Small investors lose money because they're greedy. It's a bitter experience to get a good tip in the stock market, buy one or two thousand dollars' worth of shares, fail to sell on time and then watch the price plummet down again. If you have a high-risk investment, take your profits when you find them. If you have a long-term, high-quality, low-risk investment you can wait a little and not just grab the first few dollars of profit. Distinguish between the two and you'll sell right.

6. *Don't play if you can't stand to lose.* If after all the Moneythink that we suggest, you know that losing money will cause you endless depression, don't invest in any high-risk venture. Putting your extra money in Treasury bills, in managed funds and other conservative investments is enough. One can actually live a whole life—and live well—without having elaborate investment stories to tell at cocktail parties. Just relax.

To uncover the money investor in you, go back to our first principle of Moneythink. Were your parents adolescents during the Depression? If so, they have had the experience of not being able to earn money, even though they were willing to work. They also have had the experience of seeing capital investments disappear. The probable result is that they taught you to value earnings above investments. If this is true, try to loosen up. Start small, as if you were learning to ski. Don't expect to win a gold medal on your first shot, if you were taught at home to fear heights.

Some of you will have very specific childhood memories of money. In some cases, your parents invested and you saw the effect of losses or gains in the home. This will color your views greatly. If you think about them, you can easily get in touch with your own money personality. But I cannot emphasize too strongly that for most of us, there was *no* investment teaching. Most of us have been brought up in investment ignorance. Our parents did not invest and we don't. If you are starting from scratch, don't feel alone. With the exception of the few who have inherited wealth, everyone else is in the same boat.

You can learn, you can even have fun with money. I will not give you extensive investment advice which, as they say in more sophisticated texts, is "beyond the scope of this material." But I will give you a couple of ideas for your $10,000.

Here are my criteria for investing small amounts:

1. It has to be an investment that will get you royal treatment if you have $10,000, more or less, to invest.

2. It has to be an investment in which you could put more if you have it.

3. It must be an investment giving a chance of making at least 20% profit.

4. Finally, it must be fun to learn and study so you'll become knowledgeable about it.

COLLECTING FOR INVESTMENT

Many types of investments meet the criteria above. But one that is sweeping the country has special estate planning pitfalls. Whether by means of crafts, antiques, collectibles, paintings or the more traditional items of silver, jewelry or other precious metals, accumulating wealth through things is all the rage. Even *The Financial Planner,* a special magazine for people in the field of giving investment guidance, has devoted an entire issue to collectibles.

Because everything is so expensive and yet we must live—meaning that we have to furnish our homes, buy clothes and perhaps jewelry—many people are trying to kill two birds with one stone: living well and making investments at the same time. Rather than buying a reproduction, they put money they would ordinarily save into an original painting in hopes that the increase in value will be far greater than savings bank interest. By and large, this is true. As long as you're not fooled by phony collectibles you probably will make a bigger profit buying and owning the right items than in other forms of investment that require similar cash outlays. It's possible to do much better in real estate, but you are required to deposit several thousand dollars and incur obligations, Collectibles can be bought anytime you have extra money.

Before you try collectibles as investments, learn to think like an investor. Know who you are as a money person before you collect. Instead of asking the old question—what would I do with a million dollars?—ask what you would do with five hundred dollars and see what it is that you would really like to buy? List purchases you have already made that are worth more than $1,000. Truthfully write down your reactions to each one. Were they satisfying? Were they useful in your home or office? Did you feel elated? Did the elation last? Most important, is it an item that you want to know more about so that you can become an expert?

If you are going to invest in collectibles, you are going to have to think about maintenance and storage, in order to guard their value. Can you realistically own large paintings that may need humidifiers? How would you feel if you had to put your collection in a vault? Can you afford the insurance? And the theft protection?

Why did you like the item? Is it because it cost a lot and made you feel wealthy? Or because you bought it in a spiffy place and were grateful that they would let you in the door? If you answer yes to these two, you may not be ready to actually invest in *things* which require you to get the cheapest price and maybe even do some bargaining. One of the most successful collectors I know used to scout flea markets wearing black knee socks and sneakers and a dumpy old coat. But she sure got great buys. If your thrill comes from being treated deferentially because you can afford an overpriced item, you do not have the mentality for investing in things. Soul search and Moneythink. Just because you like to shop does not mean that these kinds of investments are for you.

But if they are, take your shopping energy and your consumer hunger and do some constructive investing. You won't be alone. Success is dictated by following three rules. First, buy what you like, so that you will cherish it even if its value does not increase. Second, concentrate on one or two types of items, so that you become an expert. And third, buy the most expensive item of its type that you can afford. If you can't afford to buy the best vases, then collect porcelain spoons or something less expensive. Buy the best of the lot.

Watch out for phony collectibles. Some companies are creating false markets for their goods by advertising them in limited editions. In fact, if they don't have beauty and value, their artificial scarcity won't bring their prices up. Junk is junk. There's no excuse for you to be ignorant. There are hundreds of appraisers, scores of collectors' magazines, and numerous books that teach the value of collectibles and what they have sold for in the past.

The most important step in determining whether you can make your investment future in things is to sell something. If you can't sell something you can't make money. You can still have fun collecting, of course, but you won't be acting like an investor. No matter how much your rugs, advertising signs, or textiles have increased in value, they will be nothing more than an estate tax headache if you haven't sold some and used the money to improve your collection, to make other investments or just to enjoy extra luxuries. You would be surprised how often people are great at buying and bad at selling. Some people can get the best purchase price, but can't make a decent sale.

If this describes you, start your Moneythink. Why can't you give up the item? Do you feel that you will not be loved if you insist upon a high price? Are you greedy and always think you're underpricing? Are you hesitant and believe the market will go up?

To sell right, go to auctions and see what similar items are being sold for. Talk to dealers and see what prices they offer you outside the auctions. Go to retail and wholesale establishments, if any exist for your items. Or go to flea markets, galleries, specialty shops. Compare price, but don't be ignorant. Don't use what you paid for the item as the criterion; use what the item is being sold for today. Remember, too, that for certain items the great days are over. Don't regret not having made your sale five years ago, and don't judge your success by old prices.

Think of yourself as an investor. Remember, you too must consider. . .

Tax and Estate Matters for Collectors

What people who are accumulating wealth through collections don't realize is that they are also building a mighty estate problem and a big liquidity problem during their lifetime. Another problem is evaluation of the items left by you in a will. What is the value of your collections for estate tax purposes? You know by now that the I.R.S. will use the highest possible value, while your heirs will want the lowest.

Tangibles—our legal word for personal property, including art, antiques and collections, jewelry, clothing and memorabilia—used to be given brisk treatment. Attorneys thought that they would have relatively little dollar value and would be distributed on the basis of sentiment. Today many people, particularly young people, use their money to collect, so a more respectful treatment is in order.

Letters precatory, again. A will can be used to leave collectibles to whomever you please. All you must do is designate your beneficiary and what collectibles you have in mind. Go back to the rules regarding wills and you will see how this is done. Don't forget, if you are specific about the items and the items are not there at the time of death the beneficiary will get nothing. If you are vague about the items the executor will be responsible for purchasing a replacement item. If my will says that I leave *my* collection of bottle caps and there are none left when I die, the beneficiary gets nothing. If it says I leave *a* collection of bottle caps to my best friend's son Tom, the executor (who may know nothing about bottle caps) must go out and find a set to give to the boy.

Evaluation of tangibles. The value of tangibles is their fair market value; that is, what a willing buyer would pay and what a willing seller would take. Often the Internal Revenue Service will take your word for it when you give an evaluation. Once they challenge your evaluation, however, you have to give evidence for it. It is not easy because no sale has really been made. There are professional appraisers who advertise in all law journals and in many daily newspapers. For a price, they will give you an appraisal. The appraisals differ from one insurance appraiser to another.

The I.R.S. knows this. They understand that the most reputable appraisers know only a range of prices and even they can never predict an actual sales price. The result is that the Service usually insists that value be based on the best use of the property, if a piece of property has more than one use. For example, as a collectible a plate may be worth $100, as a plate it could substitute for a cheap item. The Service will accept the $100 valuation, seeing the plate in its role as collectible rather than dinnerware.

If you use a paid appraiser make sure that you know what it costs before an appraisal is made. Appraisers generally work in one of two ways. They may charge a percentage of the value of the items. This is the worst possible approach for you since you are not interested in a high evaluation but a low evaluation. A percentage gives the appraiser an incentive to appraise higher. This is fine if you have insurance in mind but terrible if you have taxes in mind. A better idea is to have an appraiser work on an hourly basis. This way you can control the cost by giving more or fewer items to appraise.

Even more important than the immediate cost of the appraiser is the type of appraisal they give. An appraisal will not be accepted by the I.R.S. unless it contains very detailed information suitable for scrutiny by a court. If the I.R.S. is serious about giving you trouble they will get their own appraisers. In such a case, you should insist that the Service, before imposing their appraisal, show why they are rejecting yours.

Appraisals. The appraisal should have the credentials of the appraiser showing that the appraiser clearly qualifies as an authority. The basis for the values should be carefully worked out and put in writing. This can be done in paragraph form. The various bases used include auction catalogs, dealers' catalogs, exhibitions with prices quoted, the credentials of the artist if known, comparative sales by other artists or by the same artist of other works, the state of the art market at the moment, a photograph of the piece, a certificate of authentication if any, the cost and date of acquisition by you, and any other factors that the appraiser relied on in making a judgment. The appraisal should be dated and signed.

The tax court, if your case ever gets that far, tends to be extremely realistic. The judges often recognize the "white elephant" nature of a piece. For example, an enormous piece may be very difficult to sell. Who's got room? The tax courts have toned down the Service's evaluation when pieces were large or out of fashion, and certainly have always been curious about what other pieces by the same artist have commanded in the past.

Nothing will serve you better than to make notes every time you buy a piece. A true collector does this anyway. Every time you go to a country auction or craft fair or browse through catalogs, make a notation of the date that a piece was offered for sale if that piece is one that you are interested in or by an artist whose work you have already bought. By keeping a little diary you not only have fun and gain a better command of what you are buying, but you become a more informed taxpayer. Do you know exactly the price of a craft work that you bought at a fair six years ago? Today you may know that the piece has risen threefold in value and you may feel happy about it. But I doubt that you know to the dollar what you paid. By keeping a running list you are doing yourself a big favor.

For unusual items and some not so unusual (such as boats), the courts from time to time have accepted reproduction cost as an alternative to looking at the fair market value. Keep this in mind if you have a special piece of property that you really are not sure how to evaluate. Remember too that the old evaluations for insurance purposes don't mean everything but they are some additional evidence of true value.

TAKING STOCK

Before finishing my advice to you, I decided to take a pilgrimage to L.F. Rothschild & Company, the revered brokerage house. There I found guru Stephen Stark, a partner in the firm.

I pinned him down with the big question: What is the one piece of advice that you would give any investor? As you will soon see he gave a lot more than one piece. What was the most important thing to remember? "Don't fall in love with a security —securities do not always come back—be adaptable." In other words, don't stand on that same street corner. I told him the beggar story, and he acknowledged that that was the whole problem. Don't stagnate.

He also said that people can and should control their investments. There is no reason to follow blindly the advice of brokers although their advice is invaluable. Apply common sense. Remember that at today's rates money doubles in about eight years. For the time being you can use this as a rule of thumb to judge investments. If you are investing for a trust the same criteria can be used as in investing for an individual account. What are your goals, what are the goals of the beneficiaries? Stark gave the example of a trust fund for a seventy-eight year old widow whose death would cause the remainder to go to charity. Here he would concentrate on income production to every extent possible. On the other hand, if the beneficiary was a twenty-five year old with a trust that would go directly to him when he reached the age of thirty-five, Stark would concentrate on growth so that when the remainder was transferred at age thirty-five it was as large as possible. If you do use an investment broker to help you as trustee, remember that you have the final say, but you should find one that can give you guidance, not just take direction from you alone.

How to talk to your broker? First and foremost don't lie. There is no reason to make your assets seem greater. If the broker is not interested in you because you are too small you are better off finding out right away. Admit what your goals are. If you are investing your only $10,000, say so. The decisions will be different and you will be much happier in the long run. After you've spoken enough, listen. Be interested in what the broker has to say and read the literature he provides. This is time consuming, but it will pay off. Make sure that the program your broker has outlined makes sense to you. Good brokers, Stark says, do follow-ups which they initiate. He says to remember that brokers are part of a service industry. They are not selling a product. The service is ongoing even if you have not bought anything for a while.

Finally, try to follow this piece of advice which I go along with Stark in putting in block letters: DON'T LOOK BACK-WARDS—LOOK FORWARD.

10

Planning for People: Business Persons

Many people who own and run their own business must occasionally wonder why they stay at it. Often they could do better elsewhere. And then the personnel problems, the mounting bills, the overhead, the inflation, the accounts receivable. But they keep it up, and if they continue, they'll die with the business still in their hands. Most will want that business to continue to care for their families even though they're not around. Since they themselves are the business this won't be easy. But if they give no thought to it at all, it will be impossible.

For such people, there are only three alternatives: They can sell the business during their lifetime, make a contract for its sale upon their death, or leave it in their will. If they do the last, there is much to consider.

THE BUSINESS PERSON'S WILL

It comes as a surprise to many, but an executor has little or no authority to keep a business going after the death of the proprietor. The usual will gives the executor nothing more than the power to sell the business for cash and distribute the

146

proceeds among the beneficiaries. In fact, because there is pressure on the executor to wind up an estate, many small businesses are actually sold to a low bidder. Some very simple things can help you do better. Merely putting in a will that an executor has power to continue running a business for a longer period of time helps. It can even be directed that the cost of operating the business be paid out of the other assets of the estate. A business can be placed in trust to be run by the chosen trustee, so that after the estate is completed and probated the business goes on. The beneficiaries of the trust (your grandchildren or children) will ultimately inherit the business. Meanwhile, the trustee—who may be a professional, your partner, or surviving spouse—manages the business. A part of the trustee's fees constitutes a salary for running the business.

What trustees need is a complete list of their powers, including perhaps the power to incorporate if they deem it wise. And all this should be spelled out in the will. Meanwhile you work with the chosen trustee as much as possible so that he or she can learn to run the business as you would wish. This means that the business person's will must be very specific. If you wish the trustee to buy and sell, accumulate inventory, buy real estate, appoint other fiduciaries, expand or keep the size of the enterprise relatively the same, this should and can be specified in a will.

On the other hand, you may wish the business to be run by your surviving spouse only. It may not be necessary to create a trust. If you have included your spouse throughout your business life, you can rely on him or her to take over the business when the time comes. This is the simplest and most direct way of getting your biggest asset to the right parties—your spouse and kids. Yet it is used so infrequently that some lawyers and clients forget that it is an option. Strange as it sounds, a proprietor thinks of giving the business to his immediate heirs only as a last resort. Why? Sexism and ego.

Businesses today, even the smaller ones, are generally run by men. They are accustomed to being the patriarch of the family. Through the years even the more enlightened ones have sheltered their wives from participation in the business for a variety of reasons: old fashioned traditionalism, a desire to protect the spouse from the inevitable and sometimes frightening ups and downs of the family fortune, sometimes a canny desire to keep the spouse in the dark about what's really going on so that in case of a separation or divorce she knows as little as possible. The patriarch also believes that the female of the species cannot properly run a business, or would run it into the ground if given charge.

This feeling is often enhanced by the wife. She will place the sole burden of financial security upon the husband, saying she knows nothing about this kind of thing, or "you go visit the lawyer, these things make me nervous." The motivation for this is generally the wife's overwhelming desire to please the husband and give him the feeling of power that she knows he needs, and that he thinks he deserves for his fidelity and hard work.

This is all well and good between a couple who have a spoken or unspoken agreement that the wife will stay out of the picture and the husband will earn the bread. What becomes difficult, costly and sometimes simply a downright shame is the situation where the only children of the marriage are female. I have often seen fathers ignore completely the possibility that their daughters might run the business. I often see mothers who run a business ignore their daughters in favor of sons.

In fact, many of my clients spend a good deal of time in my office talking to me about what I think of their sons-in-law. These people, who are excellent in business and who do not hesitate to select me (a woman, in many cases the age of their own daughters) as their attorney and financial adviser, refuse even to consider their female off-spring when it comes to taking over the business. They would rather leave management to a comparative stranger (a son-in-law or nephew) and build in elaborate controls over him in order to protect their daughters whom they truly wish to inherit. They never accept the possibility that a more direct route would be to permit the daughter to control the business.

Odd too is the frequency with which fathers complain about their sons' refusal to follow in their footsteps. Many men with several sons and daughters expect their sons to like what they like but never dream that the daughters might more closely share their tastes. Countless times I have met women in middle age who are opening their own businesses for the first time.

Talking to them, I have learned that their parents had had their own business but that the daughter, while inheriting some money, had been legally "pushed out" of control. Fathers go through terrible anxiety trying to make sure that the daughter who will be helpless without any management powers will still be financially secure. These female entrepreneurs often start their businesses from scratch when they would have made fine candidates to carry on their father's tradition if they had only been permitted.

I often witness heartbreaking scenes after the death of the breadwinner when the estate is being probated and wound up. The grieving spouse may come to my office together with her daughter. The daughter is alert, knowledgeable and financially oriented. The son who has been "left the business" is careless or just not interested and justifiably angry at being saddled with this responsibility when he would much prefer to have a job, teach, be an artist or writer. But at birth he was already elected as the candidate for business manager and the daughter at her birth had the role of protected helpless child sewn up.

Will you be able to shake loose your prejudices about your children? Will you dismiss this part of the book as pro-feminist baloney?

Of course, times are changing, though very slowly. Male business people constantly meet competent women these days. They are getting the idea. Also, keeping a good business going has become harder than starting up a business in the first place. Men can no longer deceive themselves that once they have created an empire their sons will not destroy it, even if they are careless or uncaring. Inflation makes strange ideologies. I am finding fathers who do leave their daughters the business, saying "Women should not be in business but she is different." So be it. Consider whether your daughter is different before you turn somersaults leaving male relatives and even sons-in-law in control.

Considering Business Legal Form

Give some thought to the legal form that the business will take. It's not too late to turn a sole proprietorship into a corporation, a partnership into a sole proprietorship or a corporation into a partnership. For the most part these critical business decisions will be made during your lifetime and for reasons of lifetime planning, not death planning.

When we focus on wills we find that the business should be left in the form in which it is easiest to operate and with which all of the employees, managers, financiers, and customers are acquainted. There are some special points to consider which are relevant only to the estate plan. For example, if you do plan to leave your business in trust rather than outright, remember that a corporation causes certain complexities. In many states the law forbids a trustee to accumulate income. Yet a wise corporate decision may require that profits be kept in the business and not distributed. This can put the business administrator into conflict with the trustee. If they are both the same person this can cause downright schizophrenia. The trustee knows that he is responsible for distributing as much income to the beneficiary as he is able. In certain trusts the beneficiary is taxed on the income of the trust whether or not the distribution is actually made. If the earnings are retained by the corporation and never distributed, it is possible that the beneficiary will have income tax and no income. On the other hand, if retained earnings accumulate in the corporation and are then paid out all at once, the trust might have a large income in that year. To prevent these kinds of problems the will itself can state that earnings can be retained by the business and paid out over a scheduled period of time. Only you know your own business and only you know what is practical.

Handing Over the Helm

Most business people have already taken care of their business before making a will. They give some thought to handing over the helm to relatives, employees, or purchasers of the business. This means that a well worked out plan for transferring control is necessary. The plan must include the procedure for payment to the business head, avoidance of taxes to the extent possible, and the smooth operation of the business while the transfer is taking place. There are several methods of transferring during your lifetime so that the business is not owned by you at the time of your death. One of the major reasons for doing this is to avoid the estate tax that will occur if you die owning your business. Remember the transfer during your lifetime also has tax implications and costs. It is useful to have some idea of how much tax you would have to pay if your estate were augmented by the value of your business and how much you save by transfer during your lifetime.

BUSINESS EVALUATION

You may also need some idea as to how to evaluate your business. I understand that you may not want to evaluate your business, and that you can't put a value on what you have worked for all your life, including the benefits, sentiments and pains that go beyond the dollar. But consider that I've included a chapter on evaluating artistic and written work. If Michelangelo can do it so can you. You are not evaluating the business to measure your own personal worth or how good a business person you are, nor to regret that you did not stick to that high-paying job twenty years ago. Remember that for tax purposes the best result is the lowest value.

It is very difficult to evaluate a small business. There are many intangible factors. You as a person are one of the values of the company, sometimes its biggest asset. With corporations whose stocks are not publicly traded (these are called closed or close corporations) evaluation is relatively easy. But with partnerships and single proprietorships it really is difficult. Even Uncle Sam does not have a precise formula but has a list of factors to be looked at in determining the value of the business.

The difficulty of evaluating a business at a time when an actual arm's length sale has not taken place has created experts who sell their services in the art of business evaluation. What they do is find a company that is publicly traded which runs a business like the one they are evaluating and look at the value of its shares. It is not easy. In a way it is like Plato finding the perfect form in the universe. There is a perfect chair but we never can see it—we can only see the chairs that exist. There is a perfect sum that properly evaluates a business, but we cannot know it, we can only guess at it and be as accurate and close as possible.

Evaluating the Helm

It's possible that you have already established "helm-worth" by signing a restrictive agreement with other shareholders or partners that places a monetary value on your share of the business. This is frequently done with closely held corporations. Because these closed corporations and partnerships are often family run affairs or are owned and run by partners who are practically "married" to each other, it is important that outsiders not get a chance to interfere with the business. While technically these small businesses may have a corporate form, in practice they are run no more formally than a single proprietorship. Frequently a contract is signed between the partners and family members restricting the sale of the stock to outsiders. These restricted stockholder or partnership agreements are important documents in determining the value of shares. Their purpose is not only to restrict sale to outsiders but to provide a buy-out plan in the event one of the business people wants out or a compensation plan for the surviving spouse in the event that one of the businesspersons passes on. Usual restrictions include:

1. Absolute prohibition against transfer; no one is allowed to sell, give away or leave his or her stock. (Be aware that this is allowed in most states but if this absolute restriction is for an unlimited period of time it may be invalid.)
2. Provisions requiring that all give consent before there is a transfer to a stranger.
3. The right of first refusal—the others must be given the chance to buy out your share before you transfer it.
4. An option to purchase—a formula for fixing the price of your share in case you desire to sell so that the others can buy first.
5. A buy/sell agreement—the estate of the businessperson is required to sell back the shares to the survivors at a certain price.

You can see that by the terms of such agreements the businesspeople themselves set a value on their business interest. The government is very interested in what you say your business is worth. This means that every time you make a loan, an income tax return, or a buy/sell agreement you are giving your view of what your business is worth, and the government will use this as evidence for you or against you in determining the value of your business for estate, income and gift tax purposes.

Small Business with Restricted Stock

Putting restrictions on the sale of business shares through these kinds of agreements has an interesting income tax effect, which in turn sets the stage for estate planning. There are cases that began in 1918, during the robber baron days (one of them is what lawyers call the old Tex-Penn Oil Co. case), and continue on to the present which hold that if shares in a closed corporation are restricted with respect to their sale they have no value. Therefore transfer of the shares themselves (not the business but the shares representing the business) is not a sale of anything of value. Since there is no sale there is no taxable capital gain, no taxable event. This leaves business people free to transfer and retransfer restricted shares among themselves and their families. If the shares are restricted under an agreement, even transferring the helm during your lifetime so that you have gotten rid of your interest can be done without a taxable event taking place at the time you make the transfer.

Let's say that you did not give over the helm during lifetime and your estate does end up owning your interest in the business. The effect of an agreement restricting the sale of shares upon the value of the business for estate tax purposes remains hard to predict. The Internal Revenue Service in Treasury Regulation Section 20, 2031–2(h) says:

> (h) *Securities subject to an option or contract to purchase.* Another person may hold an option or a contract to purchase securities owned by a decedent at the time of his death. The effect, if any, that is given to the option or contract price in determining the value of the securities for estate tax purposes depends upon the circumstances of the particular case. Little weight will be accorded a price contained in an option or contract under which the decedent is free to dispose of the underlying securities at any price he chooses during his lifetime. Such is the effect, for example, of an agreement on the part of a shareholder to purchase whatever shares of stock the decedent may own at the time of his death. Even if the decedent is not free to dispose of the underlying securities at other than the option or contract price, such price will be

disregarded in determining the value of the securities unless it is determined under the circumstances of the particular case that the agreement represents a bona fide business arrangement and not a device to pass the decedent's shares to the natural objects of his bounty for less than an adequate and full consideration in money or money's worth.

I have put in this rare quote from the law for two reasons. First, it is one of the few actually written in English, and second, it is very important. The regulation says that the restrictions, if voluntary on the part of all the shareholders, may not fix the value for estate purposes, but are merely evidence as to what the value is. The ruling also warns that every agreement is scrutinized to determine whether a real business arrangement is involved or whether the agreement is only one to pass on the helm to the business person's heirs.

Since there is so much uncertainty as to whether you and your partners can determine the value of your own business through these agreements the best I can do is give you some hints. For the best chance of having the government accept your estimated evaluation make an agreement that provides the following:

1. The estate *must* sell the shares.
2. Either the price is absolutely fixed in the agreement or a complete formula is provided so that the absolute value of the shares can be determined.
3. The agreement is for the purpose of a buy out, not for the purpose of transferring shares to your heirs at less than their true value.
4. The obligation to sell is binding during the lifetime of the business person as well.

Agreements that the government won't accept as valid for evaluation purposes are ones in which:

1. The sale price applies only for a lifetime sale and not for an estate sale.
2. The rest of the surviving business people have only a right of first refusal and the estate remains free to sell elsewhere.
3. The agreement is made for the purpose of transferring the helm to beneficiaries at a low price.

Clearly, there's a problem here. You want to make these

agreements just so that you can transfer your business shares to your heirs with the lowest possible tax and therefore at the lowest possible value. But if that's your purpose the government will disregard your evaluation determination. This sounds hard to balance. The government often considers the very personal relationships between the parties. The I.R.S. looks behind the buy/sell agreement to your motives. Since they can't see your motives they look at who is getting the shares and for what price. They need to be convinced of the propriety of your actions before they will accept your evaluation.

If the I.R.S. accepts the evaluation for estate tax purposes it doesn't mean that it's accepted for gift tax purposes. If shares of restricted stock are given as gifts the gift tax will not be based upon the evaluation in the contract even if an estate tax would have been. It may be higher. The reason for the distinction is that when someone dies the mandatory sale takes place then and there. It is a true obligation. On the other hand, when a gift is given, there is no binding obligation for the person who is getting the gift to sell at the time he receives it. In the future the contract could be amended to eliminate certain restrictions. The value in the agreement will be some evidence of its gift tax evaluation but nothing more than that.

In the event that your own evaluation isn't accepted the I.R.S. has a list of other factors that it will look at.

The fair market value of the shares or interest in a business—this means what a willing seller would take and what a willing buyer would pay under normal market conditions—is most important. Once again, this is very subjective. If the market is depressed, if there are special circumstances, the Service may adjust the fair market value accordingly. For example, if a bank forced a sale of the shares this would not be a normal circumstance. For most of you there will have been no prior sale of part of the business interest and nothing for the Service to look at. So the I.R.S. looks at other factors.

One is earnings, meaning future earnings expected of the business. How to determine future earnings? Why look at the past, of course! Take the balance sheet and scrutinize the earnings history over five or more years prior to the date of evaluation. See if there are any earning trends; be more sophisticated than just averaging the past five years or so. See whether there has been growth or decline in earnings over the period of time. See whether losses in any past years had to do with special events. Make adjustments for non-recurring factors like a widespread recession; make adjustments for special bonuses or salaries to officers or extra dividends to shareholders that diminished earnings at a time when there was actually great profit.

Next apply a multiplier factor. For example, if earnings are $50,000 a year a potential buyer would expect to pay a multiple of that amount. The multiple depends on good bargaining and good negotiations, and a good deal upon how steady or volatile the business is. Is it a new business or an old business?

Have dividends been paid and if so how much? This figure is used in the same way earnings are used. If the dividend is significant one selects a multiplier factor that a willing buyer might pay.

Another factor is book value—the assets of the company less its liabilities. Once this figure is determined, it is divided by the number of shares in the business and a value or book value per share is attained. The problem is that there can be dispute over what should be listed as assets, and how assets and liabilities should be evaluated.

Another is the lack of marketability. Don't forget that we wouldn't be looking at factors other than fair market value if there was a free market for the shares.

Good will is probably the hardest thing to evaluate. People rarely understand what good will means. It does not mean how much your clients love you. The I.R.S. doesn't inquire about that. They find a good will factor when they notice that you are making more money than you are entitled to make given your tangible assets and the type of business that you are in. For example, take a lawyer who has a tax business which is a sole proprietorship and who earns $30,000 a year. Since this is actually a low amount for a tax lawyer this person would have very little good will: if anything, he has negative good will. He is earning less than he should be in comparison with the average tax attorney in this country with the same number of years in business. This applies as well to a dry cleaner or a shoe maker. If on the basis of its size and the community it serves a business should earn $30,000 a year but instead is earning $50,000, there can be only one reason. Since the Service does not believe in sheer luck, this factor is called good will. It comes into play only if there is a significant difference between what is being earned and what could reasonably be expected under all the circumstances.

Finally, there's you. Since evaluation may be taking place upon the death of the key man, the Service considers this loss as a factor in evaluating the share.

For the most part once these factors have been considered they are thrown into "the pot" and the court makes a decision favoring or not favoring the taxpayer. Very infrequently are pinpoint mathematical evaluations made.

Minority Interest Holders

The Service knows that a minority business interest holder has given up control and it understands that the inability to have control diminishes the value of your shares. The Service calls this giving a discount for minority interests.

In general, if you are a minority interest holder you know it. It doesn't really mean 50% or less. If more than 50% is needed to make important decisions, then a minority shareholder may have even more than 50%. The most significant decision that you can't control if you are a minority shareholder is the decision to liquidate and dissolve the corporation. Take a look at your agreement to see how much of a vote is needed for that decision. The amount of the discount that you get is based upon expert testimony. As much as 50% has been given and in other cases 35% and in still others 20%. You can see that the use of a business evaluator can be well worth the cost.

THE HELM WITH IT!

Once the helm has been evaluated you may want to consider methods of transferring your business during your own lifetime. Of course this has the advantage of giving you cash for retirement, letting you watch and see how the business is being run, setting you up as a consultant to your business which would give you a good feeling of control and taking the value of the business out of your estate so it will not be taxed. On the other hand, transfers during your lifetime have the disadvantage of resulting in a taxable gain, reducing the income derived from the business, and perhaps worst of all "putting you out to pasture" too early. Methods of transferring small businesses, partnerships and corporations are very complicated and should only be done with very expert estate planning and tax counsel. Still you want to at least try to keep up with the concepts and methods, and attempt to minimize the negative aspects of lifetime transfers and maximize the positive aspects.

The many methods of transfer fall into only two categories. Selling your interest in the business or giving it away. In the first category are buy-and-sell arrangements, useful for all types of small business, including single proprietorships, partnerships and corporations. Recapitalizations are methods of exchanging stock and are useful for corporations.

A buy-sell agreement is purely a matter of negotiation between you and your potential buyer. The value of the business and the terms of payments are dictated by the marketplace and the talents of your attorney. Watch for the following major clauses:

1. Sale price.
2. Consulting clauses in which you will receive a salary or retain a portion of the business after the sale.
3. Postmortem rights, how much your family will get should you die before the transfer is complete.
4. The actual time of transfer, an important point for tax purposes since it dictates the date on which you obtain a capital gain for income tax purposes.
5. Security, if there is a pay-out is there enough collateral to insure that the bargain will be kept.

Another way to transfer the corporate helm is to give the common stock of the closed corporation to those family members or those of the younger generation that you wish to take over. Instead of leaving stock to your heirs in a will or selling the stock to them, the device of recapitalization takes place during your lifetime, but does not involve a sale of stock in exchange for money. It can be done without gift tax or income tax consequences to you if planned carefully. Of course, since you are not in ownership or control of the common stock at your death (you've given it away previously) there is no estate tax either. Not only have you avoided tax, but you have also avoided the larger capital gain that would result if you transferred later on. In effect you have "frozen" the value of the common stock as far as you are concerned as of the date it is transferred. This is because while your company may grow and the common stock may have greater value, you will not own it. Instead it will be owned by the younger generation that will not be interested in selling or transferring the stock for many years.

In order to get all of these benefits the recapitalization must be done under strict rules. Certainly you will be getting advice from your lawyer and accountant. This is another highly technical area that you cannot handle alone. You will have enough difficulty handing over the helm while keeping the members of your family happy. First, children may not be interested in taking over a business; on the other hand, they may resent placing the control of the business in anyone else's hands. Parents are often stymied as to what to do. Second, the president of a closely held corporation may start to hand over the helm in his or her 50s or 60s, but not really wish to retire as yet. There must be a balancing of good tax planning and personal goals and interests. Finally, the children or those others who are taking over may not yet have a grasp of how to run the business. The parents must also insure themselves of continued income from the profits of the business since this remains their major livelihood.

A proper corporate recapitalization takes all of this into consideration. Through recapitalization the parents or those in present control of a closed corporation exchange their common stock for preferred stock which carries with it a fixed rate dividend. This means that the corporation's builders (you) retain a right to participate in future earnings and profits. Meanwhile, the common stock is transferred to the children or whomever is about to take over the helm. The value of the preferred stock must be equal to that of the common stock so that there is no gift or income tax resulting from the exchange.

In order to effect an exchange without any tax consequences the exchange must be for a valid business purpose. Some of these purposes include transferring management, providing incentives to younger generation family members to become active in the business, and even reducing estate taxes upon the death of the principal stockholder if it can be shown that payment of estate taxes can cause the liquidation of business assets and diminish or harm the business. In any case recapitalization requires a plan which must appear on corporate records and be filed with the corporate tax return.

Remember that for a pure recapitalization to take place without tax problems there should merely be an exchange of stock. If there is other property being given or exchanged as well, often called "boot" very delicate planning must be done in order to avoid taxation. In many cases taxes cannot be avoided.

If you can't bear the thought of losing voting control of the corporation, the preferred stock can retain voting control. The problem is that because you still have control there may be estate taxes since you have not relinquished all your rights. Watch out if you possess 20% of the voting power of all classes of stock during the three-year period prior to death. This can result in estate taxation of the value of the preferred shares. The value of the common stock may also be included since the voter may actually have control over the income from non-voting common stock.

Partnerships

If you are at the helm of a partnership rather than a corporation there is also a way to freeze the partnership interest. This is done when one partner gets a limited interest in the partnership profits but has no responsibility for the losses. His interest must be protected from risk if the partnership is liquidated. The other partner (presumably the younger generation) contributes a small amount of capital or gives services in exchange for a partnership interest. That partnership interest has full participation, and bears the risk of loss. Again, there must be careful planning to make sure that there are no tax consequences.

Installment Sales

If methods of giving control which do not include the actual payment of money are unacceptable to you, you can try the device of installment sales. The owner of stock or a partnership interest sells the stock or interest to his or her children or whomever is about to take over, on an installment sale basis. The seller is actually financing the transaction and gets back both cash and a note showing that there is a debt that is to be paid over time. The asset is transferred and its value is frozen as of the time of the sale. Future appreciation of the asset (stock or partnership interest) is transferred to the purchaser. Meanwhile, capital gains, while they will have to be paid, are deferred until the installment sale price is paid.

Private Annuities

A related method of transferring assets and still making a living is the use of the private annuity. A private annuity can be given by anyone who is not in the regular business of selling annuities, like a child or other relative of one who is the principal of an ongoing business. Here the rights and control of the business are transferred in return for a promise to pay a fixed amount monthly, weekly, or yearly for the remainder of the life of the transferor. The property will be transferred and therefore out of the estate of the transferor, future appreciation will accrue to the younger generation, and capital gains will not be realized until the annuity is paid and money is actually received.

There are disadvantages. For example, if the annuity is unsecured and the business fails it will never be paid. If the transferor suffers an early death not much will have been paid under the annuity.

11

Planning for People: Couples

What do people who are going to get married, or begin to live together, or get a divorce have in common? They are all affecting their estates and their right to hold and own property. Marriage is a three-party contract: the bride, the groom and the State. The State comes in because tax laws, property laws, real estate and inheritance laws, even laws regarding testifying, are affected by the relationship between people. Most estate-planning books assume a happy marriage, ending in widowhood. Today, it is unrealistic to concentrate solely on happy, long-married couples. Without a recognition that people have all kinds of relationships, a good deal of estate planning, tax planning and property planning makes no sense. Where the law deals only with married couples or the parent-child relationship I have indicated this as the book goes along. Otherwise, everything said applies in general to all readers. In this chapter I make a special effort to provide additional material for those in transition (about to be married or divorced) or in that special status not yet officially legally recognized—living together.

For those about to marry or those recently married I discuss the antenuptial agreement—a contract that can be signed that affects support, ownership and estates' rights during marriage. For those living together I discuss the methods of protecting individual interests or owning property as if you were a married couple, whichever you prefer. For those about to be divorced I explore the greatest tax pitfalls of transferring or dividing property. The emphasis is on financial planning and not on any of the other aspects of the relationship, including children, visitation, emotional difficulties, rights in a divorce court or through negotiation.

MARRYING: ANTENUPTIAL AGREEMENTS

The law has a poetic and telling phrase for antenuptial agreements—we say they have a "chilling effect on the personal relationships of the parties." Still with all the "chill" in the air over finances these days, and all the fears caused by alimony, galimony, and palimony, antenuptial agreements are having a heyday. Mind you, the word is *ante*, meaning coming before or prior to, not *anti* meaning against or adverse to. These agreements are those which traditionally couples have signed prior to a marriage in order to define the financial arrangements they will have throughout the years. But antenuptial agreements can be signed during marriage as well.

Antenuptial agreements are very old (actually biblical). It is only the content of modern agreements (who does the chores, the housework, how to handle the two paycheck family) that is new. The antenuptial agreement was designed by the wealthy to protect themselves. Like so many things in estate planning they are useful for us all, but most of us do not know about them. In France many couples sign an antenuptial agreement prior to their marriage. The French have standard agreements provided routinely by attorneys. Several cantons in Switzerland also require these agreements, while others still have the wife's money becoming her husband's automatically upon marriage. Holland too has a form of antenuptial agreement, dealing particularly with inheritance between spouses.

In America antenuptial agreements were used mostly by wealthy families with daughters. There were two reasons, one social, the other historical. Historically, until the Married Women's Property Act of 1848, a woman's property, upon marriage, was transferred to her husband. If she stayed unwed all her life she was perfectly entitled to hold money, use it, run a business, manage investments and more. If she married she surrendered her independence: The law no longer held her fit to handle the finances. The scoundrel who married a woman for her money knew what he was doing. He didn't even have to wait until her death to inherit. When they married, her money became his and any business that she managed became his too. If she was an heiress the husband would be in charge of her wealth immediately upon her inheritance of it. Naturally the wealthy worried that their children would be courted and married solely for their money. Fears of intrigue, possibilities of murder, or of commitment to a mental institution tortured the minds of the wealthy. They wanted to devise a way that would make certain that their children were not being married for their money.

Enter the antenuptial agreement. This agreement is a contract signed by both parties and notarized. In most states it is acknowledged as if it were a deed. It need not be filed with the court. The contract relates exactly how the parties will hold property during the course of their marriage. It also frequently waives any rights of inheritance that a partner may have. To cap it off, there can be and frequently is a release of any spousal or marital share in the other's estate. This means that when one spouse dies the other doesn't inherit anything at all unless that spouse has been left money or some specific items in a will.

This supersedes the law which in almost every state requires you to leave some of your wealth to a spouse who survives, unless there has been a divorce or a formal separation. In some states the estate of a deceased is even permitted to carry on a divorce proceeding that has been commenced in order to prevent the surviving spouse from inheriting. But if there has been no formal proceeding, a spouse is entitled to inherit no matter what the deceased wanted.

I am reminded of a fascinating case where a gentleman married for the second time. He had a will leaving everything to his first wife, who died before him. He never made a new will. He made a second match with a miserable creature who truly had no interest in him whatsoever. Shortly after the second marriage they separated. He fell ill and her contribution to his illness was that of visiting him almost on a daily basis at the hospital and taunting him. Her behavior was so appalling that his doctor and physical therapist actually had her ousted from the hospital. Shortly thereafter he died leaving only the old will.

He never brought any separation or divorce proceedings against the second wife. Technically they lived together up until the time he left for the hospital. The question was, would she automatically be entitled to a third of his estate? An antenuptial agreement signed by her prior to their marriage would have made the answer simple. Such agreements can accomplish what your will can't—that is, you can disinherit your spouse provided he or she voluntarily lets you! Alas, it was never signed and remains to this day only a possibility in his attorney's file cabinet, useless to his sons who must fight her claim in other ways.

This brings us to the next useful role of the antenuptial agreement: protecting children of a first marriage in the event of a second marriage. Those of you who are newly divorced may or may not be heartened to know that you are eight times more likely to marry than someone who has never been married at all. People who have married once generally like the institution of marriage, even if they didn't like their cellmate. Because there are so many second marriages, many of them very successful, antenuptial agreements are being reconsidered and are certainly becoming more popular.

Second marriages, particularly later in life, often do not have the purpose of making the couple an economic unit, striving together for a lifetime of financial upward mobility. Rather, both partners are usually settled into their financial life styles; they want to preserve what they have achieved and to protect their children. They are aware that the second marriage may not work out; if that happens, they don't want to add financial pain to the emotional pain.

The antenuptial agreement is ideal. It waives any rights which each spouse must under state law give to the other in their estate; yet it permits either spouse to *voluntarily* leave to the other as much as he or she wishes. If there is an ongoing business or other important income producer, the agreement can state who shall run the business or handle the investments and who shall receive the income or proceeds from it. The agreement can state that funds from a certain source belong to both parties equally or in different proportions. The parties can even agree on how they will spend certain sums throughout the course of the marriage.

Recently another element has been added to the list of what can be agreed upon in antenuptial agreements. In many states it is legal for both parties to an upcoming marriage to agree on what will happen to their finances in the event they should divorce. This is a rather pessimistic approach to a new marriage; still, it can be very helpful, especially when one party has already been through a nasty and expensive divorce proceeding. There was a time (and it is still true in some states) when providing for the division of property and for support in the event of a divorce was against public policy. The theory was that this would encourage divorce and make it too easy. What has actually happened is that people are getting divorced more frequently despite the length and cost of divorce proceedings.

It is certainly not easy for a newly-married couple to determine how they would like the finances to be distributed in the event of divorce or separation. But many people do know. Most important, it is not necessary that the contract cover everything. For example, if there is one major business or one particular trust fund or an upcoming inheritance or perhaps jewelry or certain furniture being brought into the marriage, the contract can be addressed only to these assets. If there is a significant investment or business brought into the marriage by one party, the agreement can specifically state that the other has no right to control that particular asset or any profits derived from it.

Another possible clause is a waiver of support. More and more women working means less and less alimony and maintenance for women. Many couples agree to waive their rights of support (a man has a right from a woman these days) in the antenuptial agreement. This means that both parties will have an incentive throughout the marriage to accumulate their own wealth and to follow their own careers since they have waived their right to be dependent for the rest of their lives on their spouse in the event there should be a divorce. Such waivers must be fair when made, or they can be set aside.

These agreements certainly require counsel. In fact, one of many ways of setting them aside is to claim that one of the signing parties did not understand the terms and did not realize what he or she was doing. If there is counsel on only one side it is very easy to show that the party without a lawyer was not represented. The party may have understood it perfectly but in later years may want out and claim ignorance. In some cases the claim is perfectly true. One client of mine was himself a lawyer, but he worked in the Judge Advocate's office, and knew no more about this aspect of law than any "layperson." The wife had been represented by a high-powered attorney, and the husband had signed an agreement allotting an exorbitant amount of money to the wife in the event of divorce. Instead of waiving rights, she was demanding rights in the agreement.

Another requirement, other than being well represented, is that of full disclosure of assets and income. The law wants to prevent people from giving up rights to money they don't even know exists.

LIVING TOGETHER: P.O.S.S.L.Q.'s AND OTHERS

What are P.O.S.S.L.Q.'s? They are the census bureau's acronym for "persons of the opposite sex sharing the same living quarters." Since none of the existing terms—lovers, cohabitees, or whatever—were acceptable to all concerned, the bureau created its own term to cover what has become an increasingly common state of affairs. Of course, not all non-blood-related adults living together are of the opposite sex; however, since estate planning for same-sex couples is no different from estate planning for P.O.S.S.L.Q.'s, I treat them all here in this chapter.

But the suggestions you find here are not only for persons who are mated in some way. Often roommates in the old-fashioned preppy sense of the word, or sisters living together, or more distant relatives who are financially interdependent need to make joint estate plans. Their situation is not like that of married couples, to whom the law gives certain automatic rights and tax deductions, or of close relatives who may be next of kin under the laws of intestacy. Distant relatives or those not related by blood may very well have to protect themselves if they have made financial plans together for years without any thought to what would happen if one died or if for any other reasons they split.

To protect the rights of P.O.S.S.L.Q.'s or others living together, consider the three methods of (1) wills, (2) contracts, (3) joint ownership. Let's look at them one at a time.

Wills. A will is a will is a will. Everything you have read about wills so far in this book generally holds true for people in special relationships. Obviously, however, the marital deductions which Uncle Sam wishes to encourage will not apply to property left to a member of an unwed couple. That's just the point of them. Uncle Sam still wants to encourage the nuclear family and tries to do it by giving tax incentives.

For people without these protections, tragedies can occur. People living together over long periods of time rarely concern themselves with protecting each other's rights. Because they see themselves as a couple, each somehow believes the other will have a special right to inherit. Not so at all.

Of all the people who need wills, unwed couples need them most. No state has recognized the validity of these relationships in its laws of intestacy. No statute places a member of an unwed duo on the family tree. It is likely that a distant cousin, someone you exchange cards or fruit baskets with at Christmas, will have greater rights than the person you live with. Don't die intestate, having made no provision for this person in your will.

Many people believe in the automatic existence of the common-law marriage just because they live together. For the most part however, states do not recognize this. If they do, they require minimally that the arrangement be one in which the parties "openly and notoriously" announce to the world that they are man and wife. They want evidence such as the wife's taking the husband's name, the couple's owning property together or being otherwise interrelated financially, if possible having children. In fact, a common-law state generally expects the couple to act more like man and wife than do most validly married couples.

Today's unwed couples have no intention of fooling their neighbors by pretending they are married. To qualify a couple for common-law marriage it is also usually required that neither party be married to anyone else while living together. You will be interested to know that New York, for example, has not had common-law marriage since April 1, 1930. Unwed couples there have to have been together prior to that time to be considered validly married through common law association.

Remember, there is a vast difference between living together as cohabitees and being a party to a common-law marriage. A common-law marriage is a valid marriage. It is just as legal as having a ceremony, getting a license, passing out the hors d'oeuvre, and having the first dance together. Today, bit by bit and piece by piece—starting with the Marvin case in California, in which a woman who had lived with the famous actor Lee Marvin sued for "palimony," and continuing to the present— rights are slowly developing between unwed people living together. The law is not basing their rights only upon proof of a valid marriage. Instead, the rights are based on an unspoken contract between the parties.

But P.O.S.S.L.Q.'s should not rely on the rights of cohabitees that seem to be developing under our divorce laws. It's too risky. For the most part only valid marriages are recognized. When it comes to inheritance, P.O.S.S.L.Q.'s have no rights whatsoever in each other's estates. Of course, you can always contest a probate proceeding, but you'll probably lose.

While statutes do nothing for you, a will can make all the difference. You are entitled to leave anything to your partner (as long as you leave one third of your estate to your spouse if you are married to someone else). If both parties are unmarried, there is no problem at all. Make out a simple will, leaving whatever you choose to your cohabitee. If things go wrong, the will can be changed in an instant. In fact, as with any will, it can be secret and your beneficiary need not even know of its existence.

Some people who live together are more concerned about financial arrangements than those who are married. To insure that the inheritance they wish will proceed easily, they have recourse to such devices as a joint, mutual or reciprocal will. There are even contracts to make wills. Lawyers hate these because they tie the hands of the persons making the will and forbid easy change in the future. One thing that attorneys delight in is that wills can be made and remade as life goes on.

These special wills have the opposite effect.

A joint will is a single document signed by two people as their will; it is very useful when two people are co-owners of the same property and they want to protect the survivor's right. Mutual wills are separate wills, but the provisions are similar, often mirror images of each other. In reciprocal wills two parties name each other as beneficiaries. Any of these wills can be accompanied by a simple agreement that the will won't be changed in the future without the written consent of both parties. If one changes the will, the other still has a contract under which to sue the estate. While this is limiting, it is also very protective. Once a will is made, leaving you a certain amount of cash or property, you're protected even if the relationship falls apart. People living together in later years, when estate rights are very important, or those who are contributing significant amounts to the other cohabitee might consider these special will programs. What you are doing is creating the kind of protection that Uncle Sam gives to spouses by making sure that a specified proportion of your estate will be your partner's no matter how the relationship fares. The contracts are not recommended for validly married people because the inheritance will not qualify for the marital deduction.

All the other aspects of planning remain the same, and they are explained in the rest of this book.

Contracts. Another popular method of protecting rights between P.O.S.S.L.Q.'s is a contract. The idea of the contract is similar to that of the antenuptial agreement for people newly married or about to get married. The parties agree on how their property will be held while the relationship is going on and how it will be divided if and when the relationship breaks up. The true legal effect of these contracts is still in dispute. I could not personally advise anyone to rely solely on a contract even if it were formally written, contained lots of legalese and was signed and notarized. In fact, P.O.S.S.L.Q.'s have been as successful in obtaining rights through oral agreements as through written agreements when a court found it fair to award rights. Even though almost every women's magazine on the stands today contains articles regarding these contracts, there is no indication from the courts that they will be upheld and enforced if one of the parties refuses to abide by the terms. Why is this so? Again, it's a matter of public policy. Almost every state makes the sale of sex illegal; the courts will not sanction or enforce deals made where sex is the "consideration." A contract between two unmarried parties living together, regarding how they will own property, may be judged unenforceable because it encourages unwed relationships.

A startling example of this took place several years ago in New York, which illustrates how the courts still look at unwed couples. The New York Family Court Act provides relief for battered spouses. The object of the statute is to bring intra-family offenses (beatings, harrassments, menacing and reckless endangerment) to the Family Court and not to the Criminal Court. Many studies in England and in the United States have shown that most crimes take place between people who know each other, and even more between members of the same family. Battered women were afraid to go to the Criminal Courts when they were injured by their husbands. The police were unresponsive to their complaints; often they would tell the woman to go home and cook a good meal, whereupon the battering husband would frequently renew his efforts to injure his mate. Finally, many women kept quiet because the man was the only breadwinner in the family and they would lose support if he were arrested.

To remedy this problem the Family Court was given special jurisdiction. The judges had special experience with family problems and there were support systems unknown to the criminal court. Of course if the injuries were too severe the matter would be transferred to the criminal court.

What does this have to do with people living together? Simply this: The Family Court found that many people who used its services were living together, had children, were economically interdependent, but were not validly married. They were ghetto families or families that did not have the financial means to seek private help or private counseling. After much conflicting case law, the highest court in New York State finally decided that the jurisdiction of the Family Court was *not* available to unwed couples even though they fit perfectly into the scheme and even though there were children involved. New York's highest court said that by extending such help to unwed couples the courts would be recognizing a "meretricious" relationship. It took an act of New York's legislature to amend the law and include "persons related by consanguinity or affinity." It sounds like a new acronym is in the making.

So far, contracts between unwed partners have not proven a reliable means of assuring that what is promised in the agreement will be honored by the courts. Unless you have the money to pay for lengthy litigation, I would stay away from these contracts. Instead, I would look into the third and final device for protection, which is joint ownership.

Joint Ownership. Owning property together is as old as the Middle Ages, if not older. When husbands and wives own real estate, they are automatically considered to have the special rights of joint ownership. This means that one of the owners cannot sell, give away or bequeath the property or use it as collateral for a loan without the knowledge and consent of the other person. One half of it can't be left in a will to a former wife or a child or friend, so that you end up being partner with someone you dislike. Joint ownership can have the "right of survivorship." No matter what a will says, if one person dies the surviving joint owner has the automatic right to inherit the whole piece of property. Frequently deeds to real estate provide for joint ownership with right of survivorship.

Stocks, bonds, bank accounts, co-ops, condominiums, certificates of deposit and almost anything that you can think of other than tangible personal property can be owned jointly with right of survivorship. This gives unwed people the best protection around. If you are a joint owner the law does not look at the other relationships between the parties. It couldn't care less if the parties were living together or hardly knew each other. The law upholds the rights of joint owners without question. They are entitled to everything from an accounting to each other, in case there is income being produced by the property, to full disclosure if one party is foolish enough to try "secretly" to use his or her share as collateral for a loan.

You may not want to be so tied down with respect to ownership of property. Maybe you would like to give away, sell, or be free to leave your half to someone else. Or perhaps both of you would like to be more independent and free. You can have that too; but of course you get less security. You can own property instead as "tenants-in-common" (this has nothing to do with landlord-tenant law). This means that every bank account, share of stock, bond, real estate co-op, etc., will have both your names on it, but instead of saying "joint tenants" it will say "tenants-in-common." Each of you does own half of the property, but you are free to sell your half, give it away, use it as collateral, or leave it in a will. There is no right of survivorship. Your mate can end up owning only half the property with some stranger. As I said, less security, more flexibility.

An Important Word of Caution

No matter how you may feel about your relationship the law does not treat you the same as married couples in dozens of important ways. For example, if you jointly own income producing property each of you must declare it separately (you are not entitled to file joint income tax returns.) If you have disproportionate income you may have achieved security through joint ownership, but will suffer from bad income tax planning. Remember too that while a husband and wife can make unlimited gifts to each other without a gift tax, you can't. So if you give your P.O.S.S.L.Q. half a house, a gift tax will be imposed unless the value is under $10,000. As always, plan for the best tax savings and balance security with freedom.

DIVORCING

It may be a little unusual, but I think that it's important to include a section on estate-planning for couples who are getting a divorce. Without recognizing that more than one out of four couples divorces, no estate-planning book can be complete. Oddly, some of my most fascinating and gratifying cases have been matrimonials in which the parties were wise enough to get down to tax planning as part of their separation agreements. When the opposing counsel was a qualified and sincere lawyer, the savings for the soon-to-be non-couple have been extraordinary.

Today almost any five-year-old child knows that alimony

(called in some states support and maintenance) is taxable to the person who receives the money and deductible from the gross income of the person who gives the money. To qualify as alimony the payments must be periodic and either spread over more than ten years or contingent (meaning that payment stops in the event of death or remarriage or the like). On the other hand, child support is not included in the taxable income of the person receiving it nor is it deductible by the one who provides it. If the support is not allocated specifically as alimony or child support it will be treated as alimony. Remember, no inclusion or deductions take place unless the payments are made pursuant to a court order or separation agreement. Money given informally is neither taxable nor deductible.

Things are not so simple, however, when it comes to transferring property from one spouse to the other in the course of getting a divorce. Property transfers, like child support, are not income to the recipient, nor deductible by the transferor. Instead, the transfer of property in exchange for the discharge of marital obligations is a taxable event like a sale of property. For example, if a wife had the right to ownership of certain property and waived those rights in a separation agreement in return for other property (say, the husband's share of the marital home), the husband is actually making what Uncle Sam defines as a sale. The transfer can result in a capital gain.

A simple paragraph in a separation agreement in which the husband gives the wife the marital home plus a $50,000 lump sum in return for her waiving other marital rights has the same effect as a sale of the house by the husband on that date to a stranger. That means that if the husband had a capital gain he could be taxed even though no actual dollars came back to him. The value of the transferred property is calculated upon its fair market value at the time of transfer, and not of course upon its sale price, since no real sale was made.

Many a husband or wife who has transferred property to a spouse in the course of a divorce proceeding gets a big surprise when hit with a capital gains tax. The lawyer also gets a big surprise when hit with a malpractice suit for not informing the client of the possibility of the tax. The only one who is not hurt is the donee, because giving up your marital rights is not a taxable event.

If the parties exchange property of equal value as a result of equally dividing their joint or community property, there is no taxable event. This means that if there are two parcels of land of equal value and the parties want to transfer their half shares to each other so that each owns one parcel separate from the other, they can do this without paying any taxes. But short of these equal divisions, separating parties must take care in order to avoid capital gains tax.

If property is given to one of the spouses without any waiver of marital obligations, the transfer is considered a gift and a gift tax is imposed. This is so even if no gift was ever intended. Remember, the gift tax is paid by the giver. But if the giver gets a divorce within two years after signing an agreement and transferring money, the I.R.S. will not consider the transfer a gift and no gift tax is paid. But, ironically, should the giver die within three years of transfer and before a divorce, the transfer to the spouse will be considered a gift *causa mortis* ("in contemplation of death") and be included in the estate for estate tax purposes.

If a house remains jointly owned and one party gets possession of it, the other's contribution to mortgage and upkeep above 50% is considered alimony to the spouse occupying the house.

Marital Transfer Tax

Marital transfer tax is one of the most complicated areas of federal and state law. Here is one place where you should definitely talk to an attorney and an accountant. Again, do so with knowledge and a basis for your discussions, since the matter is complex even for the professionals. Here are some guidelines for you:

1. If the property is all yours and your spouse has no claim on it and you are making a transfer to him or her, it will be treated as a sale. You will be considered to have income, in the year that you make the transfer, equal to the gain that you realized when you transferred the property. Since you actually didn't make a sale and no money changed hands, the gain will be reckoned as the difference between the value of the property when you bought it and its value when you gave it away. Here is what we

can call a fake gain—one that you never really see and yet must pay taxes on. In fact, if the property is subject to depreciation recapture this may not even be a capital gain, but may be treated just as ordinary income. If the fair market value is less than you paid for the property, you can take a loss.

2. Once again, the recipient, the spouse who gets the property, has no tax consequences.

3. If there is no question that both spouses do have a right to the property (i.e., if the state community property law or other marital law gives each spouse a right to property regardless of who bought it), then transferring it from one spouse to the other will not be a taxable event and will not have any gain or loss associated with it. Remember, though, that in community property states, spouses are entitled each to one-half of the property; if there is a division of the property giving a spouse more than one-half, that extra share above the half may be taxed as if it was a sale.

4. Often in times of divorce one spouse will buy out the other spouse's share of the marital home. When that happens, the spouse who sold his or her share does have a gain or a loss as if he or she had sold the house on the open market.

5. The same applies if there is a right in a family business that one spouse has and sells to the other for cash. This happens often these days. One state after the other is recognizing that women who have never earned money still contributed to the growth of a family business. As a result, statutes are compensating the non-working spouse. But, of course, once there is a divorce it is unrealistic for the spouse to continue to have any part of an ongoing business. So divorce settlements often include buy-out of the wife's interest in the family business. The wife is actually selling her share in that business. It is very interesting to note that if the buy-out is made by the husband with his separate property, this is considered a true sale. If, on the other hand, he only gave her some marital property as part of the buy-out arrangement, this is not considered a sale, but only an exchange of property.

6. Interesting too is that if a wife or husband does have a marital right, she or he will be giving a gift by giving it up. These days, with women working, many agreements state that the wife is self-supporting and waives her rights to obtain support or

maintenance from the husband. If she does this without getting anything in return, she may be giving him a gift. This, of course, raises another question: Since today a husband could get alimony from his spouse, if he gives up his right to do so, is he making an even exchange with her? Is he giving her a gift?

7. In 1977 the I.R.S. did find that a wife who gave up her right to get money from her husband was making a gift to him and *she* had to pay a gift tax. In order to make sure that people don't go through lengthy divorces unnecessarily, the I.R.S. has held that if property is transferred under the terms of the separation agreement and there is a divorce after two years, it will presume that there was good value in exchange for anything given up and that it wasn't a gift. That way, gift taxes are avoided altogether.

This only happens if a divorce is finalized within two years after the signing of a separation agreement. What it means is that if you sign a separation agreement you better not reconcile unless you rip up the agreement and void it. Even then, the I.R.S. may find a way to show that a true transfer was made during that period and that a gift was completed. In that case, ripping up the agreement may constitute a gift back, and now the other spouse may have to pay gift taxes!

Divorce Trusts

During the course of your separation agreement you may give your spouse a claim against your estate. It is valid to provide that support; alimony or maintenance (whatever it is called in your state) can continue to be paid to a spouse even after the death of the paying spouse. This creates a claim against the paying spouse's estate which is *deductible* from the gross estate in determining estate taxes. This is true too with respect to the value of property transferred in trust under an alimony/galimony trust.

In an alimony/galimony trust, which is created in the separation agreement itself, one spouse can transfer property to a trust for the benefit of the other spouse, naming someone else as trustee. This is attractive because the soon to be ex-spouse can be given income only, with the principal going to other beneficiaries. This works well when there are large income producing assets that should not be sold or given away outright. The trust can be created instead of or in addition to paying alimony or support.

The recipient spouse (the beneficiary of the trust) pays income tax on the amounts distributed (even if the income is derived from tax-free investments). The settlor (the spouse who created and funded the trust) is not taxed on the income from the trust, nor does he get a tax deduction for the income distributed to the recipient spouse. The settlor-spouse can keep certain powers and even name himself as the remainderman if his soon to be ex-spouse dies first. Meanwhile, the supported spouse has the trust fund as security for payment, which may let him or her sleep better than would a mere contractual obligation from the soon to be former spouse.

What happens when the recipient-spouse dies? The monies in the trust do not fall into the estate of the recipient when he or she dies, provided he or she gave up support rights equal to the value of the property in the trust. For example, a wife who gives up her right to be supported in return for being the beneficiary of a trust will not have the amount of money in that trust counted in her estate when she dies. In determining whether it is best to get a trust set up for you or to get alimony, don't worry about estate taxes.

What happens when the settlor-spouse dies? The settlor's estate is reduced by the value of the recipient's interest in the trust. This is calculated by use of actuarial tables showing how long the surviving recipient may be expected to live. Only the remainder is included in the settlor's gross estate.

MONEYTHINK WRAP-UP

For the most part money transferred to a spouse with no strings attached (i.e., in a trust) is not part of your estate if given away pursuant to an antenuptial or separation agreement. The property is not in your control. If you do make a transfer to your spouse pursuant to a divorce decree or separation agreement, and then you die within three years, the government will look to see whether what you transferred was given for good value in return. If it was not, it will be considered a gift *causa mortis* and included in your gross estate.

Often, a separation agreement provides for life insurance owned by the dependent spouse, but paid for by the insured. Don't forget that premium payments in that case are taxable alimony. On the other hand, if you buy your life insurance policy for your spouse and you remain the owner of that policy, the I.R.S. may argue that it is part of your estate when you die. Most executors have been successful in fighting that assumption and getting the amount of the life insurance benefit deducted from the estate if the decedent was obligated by court order or separation agreement. Also, as long as you are not divorced from your spouse but only separated, money that you must provide for your spouse under the terms of a separation agreement will be considered part of the marital deduction and will qualify for deductibility from the gross estate.

This is a very complicated area, which is unfamiliar even to many attorneys and accountants. The best advice is:

1. Know that there are tax consequences of transferring property to your spouse while you are married, while you are separated, and because of a divorce.

2. Know that many of these transfers are considered to be the same as a sale by the I.R.S. and you will end up having to pay income tax on the difference between the value of the property when you bought it and the market value of the property when you transferred it.

3. If you give away any of your rights such as support, estate rights, or property, without getting anything in return, you are giving your spouse a gift and may have to pay a gift tax.

4. If you give anything to your spouse because of a separation agreement and die within three years, and prior to a divorce, it could be considered a gift *causa mortis* and included in your estate for estate tax purposes.

5. Consider making an alimony/galimony trust, giving your spouse money in trust instead of outright, and then leaving the remainder of it to your children upon your spouse's death. This money will generally not be counted in your spouse's estate and no estate tax will be paid on it when the beneficiary spouse dies.

6. Get a lawyer and an accountant.

12

Planning for People: Artists and Crafts People

There shouldn't have to be separate planning for those in that special profession, the arts, or in that ancient profession, the crafts. But there does. Every good estate attorney worth his paint and brush treats his artist clients specially. But it's your duty too, Mr. or Ms. Author, Artist, Sculptor, Weaver or Potter, to play Moneythink and admit that you owe it to yourself and your profession to see the business side of your art. Don't be hostile toward money matters; find those internal barriers. Remember, you were a money baby too. Are you blocking because the matters seem irrelevant and a waste of time and creative energy, or because the money person is forcing the artist to place a price on something that we all know cannot be evaluated? It may even be that you don't believe you can grasp technicalities and would rather avoid them.

The result is notorious throughout the artistic and legal communities. The artist does one of two things: either makes no plans and very little money, or what may be worse, hires lawyers or "financial planners" and gives over all his or her wealth to these people to handle, not always for his own real benefit.

Fortunately, however, more and more artists and crafts people are recognizing that by not putting a value on their work they are diminishing, not enhancing its worth. The idea that

180

artists who seek just compensation for their work are less talented, or too crass to have the true artistic gift, is a myth largely invented by patrons to get prices down and keep artists hungry.

Recently, the area of estates law and tax law for artists has become very well developed. The bottom line still leaves many question marks regarding the evaluation of a work of art for tax purposes. This is to be expected, and will always be the case. I am happy to say that we still cannot computerize the value of a painting.

Happily for estate planning, we can answer the following question: What is a copyright anyway? What is it worth? Will works of art be taxed in an artist's estate if they aren't sold prior to death? Can the artist simply give away his or her works to a family member and save gift taxes? How much income does the artist have to declare when a work is sold? If an estate is tied up in sculpting equipment and enormous sculptural works, how will estate taxes be paid? If the artist is an author what is the value of notes, journals, scribblings, and even a library? How are works evaluated? Should an artist incorporate? Should an artist include special will clauses? Let's take a look at some of these questions and more.

THE ARTIST'S WILL

An artist's beneficiaries are the same as anyone else's. There may be some special need to name charities, such as museums or educational institutions, as beneficiaries of specific works of art, but other than that, the same considerations regarding marital deductions and charitable deductions will apply. What is unique is that the artist may have assets that differ from those of the average citizen. Aside from any other kinds of "normal" holdings like stocks, bonds, real estate, and jewelry, the artist will own two other types of assets: works of art created by him and not yet sold, and copyrights. Often the work of art will have a copyright attached to it. As you will see, the work of art is a separate piece of property from a copyright. However, to get the best sales deal the works of art—anything from books to textiles—and the copyright attached to them often must be sold together.

The will of the artist has as its first goal the appointment of a special executor. This executor must not only have all of the qualities discussed elsewhere in this book but also be very familiar with the artist's work and, even more important, with its marketability. The executor should be a good salesperson. If the artist plans to have his or her work sold, or if all works are to be kept by the family or given to charity, the executor should be sensitive to the needs of the artist and have worked intimately with him or her. Appointing a literary or artistic executor is not enough. Many artists do this without making the person a formal executor in their wills. The result is that the attorney, next of kin, bank, or accountant that is made the formal executor has the last word over the literary or artistic executor. If you use co-executors, one a lawyer type and the other an artistic marketing type, make them truly co-executors so that they have equal say. Include in your will what happens in case of an impasse.

If you own copyrights no doubt you also know that copyrights expire or terminate. Assets that terminate may not be eligible for a marital deduction. If you want to leave the copyrights to your spouse and get the benefit of the marital deduction, you can do so, but only through some careful planning. Ask your attorney about this, because thousands of dollars can be saved by good planning in this area alone.

If you are the kind of artist who gets royalties, make sure that your will states specifically whom you wish to receive the income of the royalties and whom you wish to receive other assets surrounding the royalties. Be specific. A trust can be set up that is funded by royalties as they come in. If you use a paid trustee, and you should, put your trustee on a cash receipt basis. This means that only when the royalties come in will he be paid. If royalties do not come in for any reason, even though there may be an entitlement to them, the trustee cannot use trust money to pay himself.

Finally, make sure that you have a clause in your will that gives the executors the kind of powers you want them to have. Give them specific directions if you think they can be carried out, or give them leeway and discretionary powers if that is what's needed. If you are going to make a mistake, make one by giving too much power to your executors. There is nothing worse than to tie the hands of an executor who knows that if only he could transfer property to a charity or to a family foundation thousands would be saved in taxes, and your artistic works would be preserved.

A special problem for artists and authors is illiquidity. Royalties are paid over time, copyrights are legal fictions, and works of art have to be sold in order to be turned into cash; yet estate taxes must be paid. The artist's estate is frequently the most illiquid type. If there are no stocks, bonds, cash, or other assets that can be sold, prevent your works of art from being sold for tax purposes by providing a life insurance trust for the purpose of paying taxes.

COPYRIGHT

This is not a book on copyrights. Many have been written, and it is a good idea for you to read some. Protecting your work, filing the copyright, are all covered in excellent books such as *What the General Practitioner Should Know about Trademarks and Copyrights,* by Arthur H. Seidel, published by the American Law Institute. Also ASCAP and other artist's trade unions provide their people with information. You are always welcome to write to the Copyright Office, Washington, D.C. and ask for material prepared by the Government Printing Office. Service is prompt.

The copyright itself, of course, is a "legal fiction"; that is, a right created by our law. More accurately, a copyright is a bundle of rights. This bundle includes the right not to be copied, the right to publicly perform and display the work, the exclusive right to reproduce, the right to receive payments for the use of the work to which the copyright is attached, the right to sue if there is an infringement (a polite word for stealing with or without intention) of the work.

Artists infrequently realize that they get a common-law copyright merely by creating the work. The work can also be published (offered to the public and sold with the appropriate copyright notice and registered in the copyright office in Washington, D.C.). Many of you undoubtedly have such copyrights already. If you don't, see a copyright attorney for registration. The copyright will permit you to sue not only to stop the infringer, but to impound and destroy all the illegal infringements, get special damages, including the infringer's profit, and get costs and counsel fees. These are important to artists as well as authors.

Copyrights last for fifty years after the life of the creator. Joint works last for fifty years after the life of the last surviving creator. Works for hire have copyrights which last for seventy-five years from the date of publication or one hundred years from the date of creation, whichever is shorter. If you are creating works in later life and hope to leave a legacy for as long as possible, consider working with a younger collaborator. The copyright will last fifty years from the time of the collaborator's death, not yours, and you might be able to make a very favorable arrangement for the work.

To be a joint work two or more artists must have created a piece and intended it as a joint work. Joint works are owned as tenants in common (each artist has an equal share in the work and its copyright). If this is not your intent, have a contract prepared. When a joint owner dies, his estate will inherit his share, not the co-artist.

Works created before January 1, 1978, have a shorter term that can be renewed for up to forty-seven years by the creator, or by the beneficiary or executor.

Owning a copyright is not like owning real estate or equipment. The Internal Revenue Code does not consider a copyright, or a literary, musical or artistic composition, or a letter or memorandum created through a taxpayer's personal efforts, as being a capital asset. The code defines such assets as work—just like the work I do, or a steelworker does or a cabdriver—so that when you make a sale of these things you receive ordinary income tax treatment rather than special capital gains treatment.

Because this mystical, magical copyright is not a capital asset, an artist can be heavily taxed when selling his works. Consider, together with your accountant or attorney, the possibility of giving your work to a relative, paying the gift tax, and then having the work of art appreciate in the relative's possession. When the beneficiary sells the work, capital gains treatment may very well be more available. I say "may" because tax treatment differs in various circumstances surrounding the transaction.

PRICING

Now's the time to engage in Moneythink, so you can think straight about the market value of your works. For lots of sound business reasons, the priceless must be priced. Separate this exercise in market evaluation from the work of judging the artistic-spiritual value of the work. The artists I've worked with that really can't face a financial evaluation and even become angry about it finally learn that they fear an evaluation will diminish their chance for immortality.

For complete planning, three things must be evaluated: (1) the work, (2) the royalties, (3) the copyright. Even the I.R.S. is sensitive enough to conclude that "in the field of works of art . . appraising and authenticating is not an exact science." So bemused is the I.R.S. about this knotty issue that it has created an art advisory panel of twelve rotating museum directors, curators, and art dealers. This panel of experts in any given year has adjusted approximately 75% of all appraisals it has reviewed.

Evaluators consider the value of comparable works, the selling price of works already sold, appraisers' reports, the reputation as well as the potential of the artist, training and rarity. These are only some of the factors considered. In fact anything that sheds light on value is acceptable for presentation in evaluating.

For example, if a large number of works were to be placed on the market all at one time after an artist's death, the I.R.S. recognizes that this flood would depress the price, and that is a factor in bringing down the value of the works for estate tax purposes. Naturally, if an arrangement has been made with galleries or patrons to buy the art at a given price on the death of the artist, that price will hold since an actual sale is being made.

If you have royalties coming to you, these are usually easier to evaluate, because you know how much they have been in the past. Perhaps they are based on amounts sold that cannot be projected except by looking backwards to see what has already been paid. That is exactly the kind of information the I.R.S. wants to see. With copyrights, too, keep track of what you *have* earned from them; that shows what you *will* earn from them. Since a copyright lasts for fifty years after the death of the artist, under normal circumstances the copyright has a value of three to seven times its yearly earning capacity. This is nothing more than an estimate and any other factors for evaluation are acceptable. Again, look to the experts here—the estate-planning attorney who deals with artists and writers, the accountant with a specialty.

INCORPORATING

There are many things that artists and writers can do to increase their wealth during their lifetime.

Let's consider the age-old question: Should I be a corporation? A corporation is another legal fiction. It is actually the creation of an entity separate from the person who created it. Like a trust, it is another legal clone. The creation is accomplished by fulfilling certain statutory requirements, slightly different in every state. Most attorneys can form a corporation for you, but your best bet is to choose one who will be working alongside you and who understands your business and the art world.

Once a corporation is formed, you can use it in several ways. When you transfer creative works to the corporation, it becomes the owner of the art. Work that you do after the corporation is in existence is created by you as an employee of the corporation for hire. The result is that the special seventy-five-to-one-hundred-year (whichever is shorter) copyright period discussed above applies. This is generally better than your lifetime plus fifty years. More important, when you are paid, you get a salary. The salary is taxed as ordinary income, which is deducted by the corporation from its profits.

Your salary should not be based on sales in any one year. Artist's sales are too erratic. You can be heavily taxed in one year, while perhaps you are truly starving in the next. Instead, distribute salary over time. You can do this as the employee of the corporation, even though you own all the stock in it. If you don't need quite so much money, forego salary; let it remain as a corporate profit, which may be taxed at a lower rate than your personal income tax.

Once the corporation is formed, you could use it to your advantage in various other ways. If your family has stock, dividends can be paid to them by the corporation. Two hundred dollars per person is tax exempt in any given year.

Best of all, you will become entitled to the better pension planning provisions for corporations. Read the Retirement Chapter for ideas. Moreover, as an employee you are entitled to fringe benefits, such as all your insurance, including health and dental insurance, even to a group legal service if you wish.

You also get the benefits of paying estate taxes in installments and even freezing the value of your works in the ways suggested for the stock in closed corporations.

Corporations also let you make a gift of stock tax-free. Whereas you can't give away your works of art free of gift tax unless they happen to be valued at precisely $10,000, stock values can be fractioned off to precise amounts. You can give up to $10,000 worth of stock in any calendar year to any person without a gift tax.

Another corporate benefit is that liabilities such as money owed to creditors, or slander and libel suits (a problem for movie makers and authors), are the responsibility of the corporation, not of the individual artist, since he or she does not own the work. Since people are getting more litigation-conscious, this is often a useful protection.

If you are a new artist, don't expect to get credit in the name of your corporation alone. Just like a new business, you will have to sign documents that make you personally liable. This is because banks and other lenders know that if they move against the corporation, you may already have removed all of the corporation's money through salaries that you drew. In order to make sure that there is a fund to collect from, they may ask for your signature.

Whether a corporation is the right thing from all points of view, particularly in the art field, is a question best answered by a lawyer who frequently handles such matters. Remember that works of art can be used as a trust corpus. If you are going to be your own trustee, you cannot keep control over the funds, in your case the works of art, in the trust and still get all of the tax benefits and savings. If you do insist, as many artists do, on controlling the way your work will be exhibited, that may be enough to ruin your tax breaks. This differs with different kinds of works and different kinds of trusts, so once again check with your attorney.

In any case, trusts can have all the good benefits of keeping income at a low tax rate, and helping you manage your property in an organized way, either by yourself or with expert help. You can test how your property is being handled during your lifetime while you have control; you can even keep income taxes at your child's rate if you set up one of the children's trusts that I write about. Of course, once the property including the art is out of your control it's not even counted in your estate for eventual estate tax purposes. It is also possible that whereas when you sell your work the proceeds are defined and taxed as ordinary income, sale by a trust may mean there is only a capital gain tax to pay. Artists and authors receiving royalties can set up trusts using these as the corpus. A discretionary (sprinkling trust) can be just the thing when an artist has beneficiaries with differing needs.

One of the worst money problems that artists have is erratic income. One way to help is to have deferred income, whether it's royalties or proceeds from the sale of a work. For example, an author could agree with his publisher that royalties over a certain amount would be deferred to another year.

Under E.R.T.A. you can give a work of art or a copyright to charity and get a charitable deduction. Prior to E.R.T.A. no deduction for a work of art would be allowed unless both the work and copyright were donated.

13

How to Talk to your Lawyer, Trust Officer, and Accountant

Several years ago I was asked by the National Organization of Women to participate in seminars they were giving free to people with matrimonial problems. I expected that the group would be made up of poor women without lawyers, caught up in matrimonial battles that they could not understand. The sessions were held on 19th Street in Manhattan, in a small building with a self-operating elevator. I conducted the clinic for about two years on Wednesday evenings. Sometimes the elevator door was locked and it was impossible to get up to the meeting room. Once we all sat on the steps while I gave my advice. Another time we couldn't get through the door at all and held our clinic in the freezing city streets. I was doing this as a professional volunteer; I thought the women were doing it to get free legal advice about how to handle their problems with their husbands.

I was wrong. Well over 50% of the women already had lawyers. One of them, married to a wealthy doctor, had paid a counsel fee of $18,000. Most of the others had paid respectable fees to lawyers who were well-known New York City practitioners. These women weren't asking me how to handle their husbands but how to deal with their lawyers!

I am well aware of the difficulty that a lawyer brings into the client's life, particularly on personal and emotional matters like estates, financial planning, wills, income tax and divorces. At first I was shocked to find that when I asked intelligent women, "At what stage are you in your case?" almost none of them knew the answer. Very few understood what divorce law was about or what they could expect.

Years later, when I became heavily involved in trusts and estate-planning work, I expected that the tune would change. Matrimonial lawyers have special problems because of the highly emotional nature of the work. I figured that the lack of communication between clients and lawyers was due to that, and surely in a different area of law things would change. Wrong again!

At the New School for Social Research, where I often lecture on the topics covered in this book, I again found that the students were not seeking inexpensive or free advice. They were all quite willing to have private counsel, privately paid for a good job well done. The problem was that none of them could find anyone they had enough confidence in to employ. I began to have personal discussions with students and clinic members and then with others regarding their relationship with attorneys. I found that in general attorneys are hated as a group. Most people consider lawyers necessary evils. Many consider them unnecessary evils and do their best to avoid attorneys altogether. Some people would prefer to lose money rather than try to save money and have to deal with counsel.

People complained to me that lawyers do not answer questions, are sharp with their clients, and sometimes even yell at them; that as clients they cannot understand the legalese used in documents and that lawyers are no help since they talk the same lingo; that they place utmost faith and trust in lawyers and find that they are too slow and don't complete the work quickly; that they can't reach them on the phone; and finally that clients get passed off to other lawyers in the same firm with whom they have no personal relationship.

Let's deal with these problems. In the financial planning field we talk about planning teams. The team generally consists of the attorney, the accountant, and an insurance agent. If you can't speak with the members of this team, you're not going to sleep well at night. Let's make an effort, then, to learn how to talk to your professional planning team.

LAWYERS

The first step in talking to a lawyer is finding one. There are many ways. Lawyers still do not advertise on a regular basis. It is my opinion that the best ones do not. I have every respect for legal clinics that advertise heavily, but I cannot suggest them as alternatives to traditional law firms when it comes to financial and estate planning. In fact, they will probably reject complicated financial planning and tax planning tasks, although they do offer their services for simple wills. Attorneys are best found through word of mouth. That's the hardest but the most successful method. Ask people you know; it may take quite some time to find someone satisfied with his or her lawyer. A word of caution: "Don't be too negative." Most of us are not satisfied with our brokers, hairdressers, or others who give personal service. When it comes to an ongoing service, relationships form, change, and break. Just because someone has something negative to say about an attorney doesn't mean that you won't find him or her a good bet for you. Get a few names together. If word of mouth is not successful, call the Bar Association for referrals. Remember that there is no guarantee that attorneys referred by the Bar Association are particularly outstanding. They have simply paid their dues to the Association and gotten their names on the list. Most Bar Associations will give you a few names, and you will often get a discount for the initial consultation if the referral is through the Bar Association.

If word of mouth and Bar Association didn't pan out, try calling a law school in your area. Not all but some academics have active practices in the fields in which they teach. So if it is taxes that you are interested in, you might call the tax department to see if any of their professors have a practice. Many don't but are very familiar with colleagues who are full-time practitioners and will give you a name. Finally you can look in the Yellow Pages. There is no reason for a lawyer to list himself in the Yellow Pages under a specialty if he or she doesn't really specialize. Even though the Yellow Pages are a form of advertising and anyone can claim a specialty, lawyers will generally list themselves under the topic in which they work most.

Once you have names, make phone calls. You can tell some things over the phone. Of course you can tell whether the attorney will speak to you in the first place or whether a consultation appointment must be made. In general, a lawyer will speak only briefly to someone who is not making an appointment. This is purely practical. It is impossible to do everything in a day if one is continually on the phone speaking without compensation to people who simply want to have your ear. Also, it is really impossible to give any advice even on simple matters without getting all the facts. The advice can be harmful, as if a doctor were prescribing medicine to a patient he has never seen or examined. You can get an idea what the cost of an initial consultation is, its length, and what can be expected from it. If you know all this, you are ahead of the game. Once you have your consultation, don't be afraid to take notes and ask whether you can make a follow-up phone call if you think of something. Generally, if you are about to become a client, follow-up phone calls will be just fine.

As in any good consumer guide, there are some rules you should follow to make the best of the attorney/client relationship. They are:

1. *Organize your thoughts*. It wastes valuable time to leave out any of the details of your case. And remember, incorrect or misleading information can have serious consequences.

2. *Talk about fees*. Even if it's difficult for you to talk about money, in the long run it's more difficult not to talk about it—especially if you're hit with unexpected legal fees. The best time to bring the subject up is right at the start, during the consultation.

Your lawyer may bill by the hour or charge a flat fee, an open retainer or a contingency fee. Lawyers who bill by the hour set an hourly rate for the value of their services and then charge you according to the amount of time they spend on your case. The major drawback of this system is that you don't know how much your case will cost until it's over.

Lawyers charging flat fees tell you in advance the cost of their services, no matter how much time they spend on your case. If it's a straightforward matter and takes very little time, this system can work against you, since flat fees are generally set high. However, most lawyers charge a small flat fee for routine matters such as drawing up a will or reviewing a lease.

A far more sensible approach to fees, and the one used by most lawyers, is the open retainer. Under this system, you pay an initial fee, which the lawyer believes will cover the total cost of his or her services under ordinary circumstances. If something extraordinary happens and the lawyer has to put in a lot of extra time, you will be asked to pay extra charges based upon the lawyer's hourly rate.

Contingency fees are paid only if you win your case. A lawyer who takes your case on a contingency basis receives a substantial percentage of the money the court awards you. If you lose your case, your lawyer also loses and gets nothing for his or her time. Because of this risk, contingency fees are used mostly in negligence cases.

3. *Ask for a retainer letter.* Once you decide that a lawyer is right for you, ask for a retainer letter. This letter should list the services the lawyer will and will not perform. It should specify the fee as well as any extra costs (charges for making long-distance telephone calls and duplicating materials, for instance) that you'll have to pay. In addition, most retainers list the services the lawyer is prohibited from performing without consulting you. If any of these items is not included in your retainer letter, ask your lawyer about it.

4. *Realize that you can control your own legal fate.* Tell your lawyer right at the start that you want to know what's happening at each stage of your case. Remember that you're not asking for anything special—just the service you're paying for.

5. *Talk to your lawyer in writing.* Writing a letter is slower than picking up the phone, but it's often the most effective way to deal with your lawyer. Whenever you think of an important detail that doesn't need your lawyer's immediate attention, put it in writing. Your letter will become part of your permanent file—a telephone call may not. In addition, it's a good idea to keep a diary of your case. As soon as you realize that you have a legal problem on your hands, record any relevant incident, conversation or expense. Your lawyer can use this documentation as the basis for your case.

6. *Take notes*. Talking to your lawyer can mean a barrage of facts, dates, figures and legal advice. With so much happening at once, it's easy to forget an important detail unless you take notes.

7. *Demand plain English*. Tell your lawyer that jargon is a poor excuse for communication and that you want him or her to use language you can understand.

8. *Talk to your lawyer's secretary*. Take your questions about schedules, mailings and other nonlegal matters to your lawyer's secretary instead of to your lawyer. You'll probably get the information you need more quickly this way.

9. *Don't hold back information*. It is important to tell your lawyer *all* the details of your case—even those you think are small or insignificant. Holding back information can only work against you.

10. *Don't tell your lawyer how to run your case*. You hired your lawyer because he or she understands legal rulings and can apply them to your situation. Keep in mind that no matter how similar your case may seem to those you may read about, no two cases are alike.

11. *Don't call your lawyer all the time*. Lawyers, like most people, don't like to be nagged. If you waste your lawyer's time on unimportant phone calls, you'll have trouble getting through when you need to. If your question concerns something that can wait, put it in a letter.

12. *Don't be afraid to shop around for a second opinion*. To get a second opinion, simply tell another lawyer that you want him or her to review your case. The lawyer will read significant documents, unravel the proceedings for you, explain what has taken place and may also tell you what steps he or she would take next. It's then up to you to weigh the facts and make a decision. The charge for this service varies, depending on your case and on the lawyer you choose for the second opinion; be prepared to pay about the same amount as you would for a consultation. Telling your lawyer about the second opinion is up to you. If you choose not to, you can be sure that the second-opinion lawyer will keep the information confidential.

When you have no other choice, simply tell your lawyer that you feel your legal interests are best served by someone else. (The law does not require you to give reasons.) He or she will give you your complete file and, as a courtesy, may talk to your new lawyer about the case. In return, you must pay any outstanding fees.

When you get down to what is really bothering people about their lawyers, you often find that it isn't so much the lawyers but the law that is objectionable. People understand that doctors cannot perform miracles and that health is not entirely in control of the doctor. On the other hand, with lawyers people expect much more control over events. People think that the law is very certain and that if you push button A you will get result B. They are surprised to find that there are so many choices, none of which is 100% perfect, and that there is always some exposure to risk. For example, even after a great plan for investment or tax savings has been devised, the Internal Revenue Service can make a new ruling and ruin the whole thing. Instead of giving up on feeling in control and secure, remember again that there is no magic, that even the finest lawyers always have something to learn. Change your expectations so that you will get the best plan and not the perfect plan. This will help you sleep and make you far less disgruntled by the whole process.

Remember, too, that the law is very slow. Months and months are given by statute for procedures that are merely paperwork; often the reason is that many bureaucrats, accountants and lawyers have to review documents. Don't expect speed. While accountants have deadlines, lawyer's deadlines are often changeable. Expect this and you will have much less anxiety.

TRUST OFFICERS

Talk to your trust officer with confidence and assertion. Your trust officer is in a much different relationship to you than your attorney. Of course, a will or trust can name a lawyer as trust officer. But here I am talking only about the person's role as trust officer, someone who has the duty and right to make investments and to distribute income to you. Someone who has often to decide between types of beneficiaries—whether to do something that is good for the income beneficiary or the one who will eventually inherit the lump sum that is left over. People can feel trapped by their trust officers. The trust officer was named by someone else in a trust or will and often can't be changed. The trust officer can resign, leaving no one in control. A person named as a co-trustee with a professional may often feel inadequate next to the trust officer's superior knowledge and experience. If the trust officer is with a large institution like a bank or trust company, you may have to fight the bureaucracy if you want to have an oral dialogue and not just wait for written annual reports.

In fact, this whole book has sprinkled through it ways of talking to your trust officer. If you know something about tax savings, there is nothing wrong with saying so. If you know something about investments, there is nothing wrong with saying so. The trust officer need not take your advice; that too would be a breach of responsibility. But a knowledgeable beneficiary will be listened to. Open up an oral or written dialogue. If your trust officer is really ignoring your wishes, put everything in writing. Remember that a trust officer may be removed under certain circumstances. There is no question that this can be a lengthy and unpleasant proceeding, requiring accountings. If there is true negligence, or outright thievery, it must be done. If it is merely a matter of difference in judgment, the trust officer will win. It is his judgment that counts as long as it is consistent with what a prudent person would do.

Speaking of prudent people, you won't be surprised to learn that the law has a rule called the prudent man rule; which adds a note of conservatism to the duties of trustees. A trustee who does not act in a reasonable, moderate and prudent fashion can be heavily penalized for the consequences. In fact, let's say a trustee takes too much risk and makes money for you. This can still be a breach of the prudent man rule, even though the result was a success! In the future you may not want successes that are so risky.

On the other hand, a trustee who has consistently lost money for you may bear no responsibility if he or she acted prudently. The result is that many times money is left in low-interest-bearing but safe accounts in savings banks. Some clients tell me that they could do better themselves just by transferring the account to certificates of deposit. There is today no burden on the trustee to get the best possible interest or return. That is not the mandate to the trustee. Instead, acting prudently is the criterion. This is something that all beneficiaries have to live with.

If you are female and expect that you will have a tougher time talking to lawyers, accountants, and trustees, you are right. For the most part times change slowly and there is an element of superiority that professional men feel towards women clients. Some are outright sexists and believe in their souls that women are less able to understand, are foolish, can't handle money, and are best treated with a pat on the hand and no information. They also see women as weaker and incapable of challenging them if they do something wrong. Accompanying this very frequently is a resentment that a woman is benefiting from the hard work of her husband while she contributed nothing to the growth of his wealth. These people really do see the woman who did not earn dollars as a parasite. That doesn't mean that they are unwilling to take her money for their services, and it certainly doesn't mean that they will say this to her face. Widowhood to many male attorneys is still seen as a boon where the wife cashes in on the dead husband's fortune. Other professionals are struggling to change their feelings, and some of course really don't feel that way. I would like to say that women lawyers, accountants, and trustees are really the same as men, because it sounds fairer. But in my experience it is not true. Women who hold these offices and participate in these professions *are* different. They are generally more respectful of their clients, both men and women, try to communicate better, and are far less patronizing. This does not mean that they are smarter, know tax law better, or will save you any more money. That varies considerably from professional to professional. It does mean that as a group they have less of a know-it-all attitude.

Many of you will not be able to pick your lawyer, accountant, or trustee—a trust or will or the family business will dictate who that person is. If you find the kind of sexism that I am talking about, once again your only recourse is knowledge. Even there, you may very likely be made fun of for reading too much or taking too many courses. Do it anyway. That is not true fun-making; it is a panic reaction from professionals who fear that you will know something and be able not only to expose them for ignorance but to bring them down from their professional pedestals to the level of human beings. Good luck.

ACCOUNTANTS

The most important thing about talking to accountants is to remember to talk to them in the first place! Accountants are often the forgotten professionals of financial planning. Their significance cannot be overstated. Yet most accountants tell me that the public considers them necessary evils. My experience is that they are wrong. They are hardly considered as evil as lawyers although they certainly are necessary. In fact, while few people have a lawyer, executor, trustee or estate planner, almost everyone has an accountant, if for no other reason than to help file a tax return once a year.

As with most service professionals, it is not easy to find an accountant. The best method is still word of mouth. The best person to ask for a suggestion is a business associate that you respect. Business people have the same goals that you have from a financial point of view. A friend or relative may be someone you get along with but not someone who has the same Moneythink as you. It goes without saying that you should ask someone who has nothing to sell. An excellent source for finding an accountant is your lawyer. We all work with professionals we respect. It's easier for you to come to an attorney who has an excellent ongoing relationship with an accountant. But if you have an accountant that you like and trust, a lawyer should never impose his or her own choice on you.

If you have no business associate or attorney that is helpful, call your local banker. Banks will frequently recommend three accountants from a list of approved names. These are people they are familiar with and have worked with, and to that degree they have some stake in the matter. Nevertheless, their guidance is usually excellent despite the fact that there is business mutuality. On the other hand, going to a State Accounting Society is not helpful. You will get a list of accountants but no guarantee of their performance.

In selecting an accountant avoid a relative. There are too many conflicts. I have found the same with lawyers. Remember that to do the best work for you an accountant must know everything about your finances. If you have any reservations about this, whether because the accountant is a friend or relative or because you feel uncomfortable, choose somebody else.

The good thing about accountants is that you can usually "test the waters" without paying a fee. Speak to your accountant. See if the chemistry is right. Have a preliminary meeting at his or her office to see the type of operation. Come alone or with your spouse if you will be working together.

The specialists at the accounting firm of Bloom Hochberg & Co., P.C., gave me handy tips on how to judge an accountant during the first and second meetings. They have the following words of wisdom: (1) Don't confuse a bookkeeper and an accountant. An accountant should have a junior member of the firm doing the actual bookkeeping work. It is cheaper for you and it shows that the accountant has better things to do. (2) Avoid a fence sitter. Any good accountant will guide you in your choice. (3) Beware of a super specialist. He may have tunnel vision. (4) If on your first meeting an accountant can't charge you up with ideas for at least four hours he is asleep. (5) See if the accountant is taking an initiative in helping you plan—for example Bloom Hochberg & Co., P.C., sent out brochures to explain to their clients the All Savers Account that became popular in the Fall of 1981. They didn't wait to receive phone calls, they made them. (6) Don't judge an accounting firm by its size. An accountant is a living, breathing individual. A big firm is made up of them. An individual practitioner may be just what you're looking for.

After initial judgment and initial consultations there usually will be a meeting where the accountant browses through some of your books and records. Bring your tax returns to the consultation—two or three years worth. Include personal returns, corporate returns, existing wills, schedule of assets, insurance policies, and trust instruments. Be prepared to reveal personal information regarding your age, your dependents and your hopes for the future. If you're serious about having an accountant review all of these documents there may be a charge. If it is just for the accountant to get a picture, a practiced eye can look through a tax return in a very short time and see if you're taking advantage of everything you're entitled to.

Accountants generally charge on an hourly basis. They charge far less for bookkeeping services than for their accounting services. Many people who go to new and dynamic firms get scared because the hourly rates seem so much higher than what they have been paying for years. Think to yourself, is my present accountant doing only bookkeeping work? If so, compare the charge to the bookkeeping charges of the accounting firm, not to their planning and more creative work. Most accounting firms will charge varying rates depending on the status of the person working for you. You will pay less for the time of a junior than for a senior partner. You can only learn from experience whether an accounting firm is deploying its personnel correctly to get the most for your money. Remember the bookkeeping part of the fees is substantially cheaper than the pure accounting work.

Beware of the accountant or firm that gives you a cheap price just to get a foot in the door. How do you know? Ask for an estimate of charges for the next two or three years. See if they have grossly undercharged just to get your business at the beginning intending to give you a big increase after a while.

14
RETIREMENT

I have heard that in Alaska, when Eskimos get old, they quietly leave the village, stand in the middle of a floating block of ice, and drift off to sea forever. Personally, this gives me the chills. I would rather see the Eskimo moving to Florida or Arizona or taking that long-wanted trip to Europe in old age.

I'll bet that more of you are interested in this book for retirement planning than for any other purpose. And you should be. When we are faced with Social Security as our only retirement plan, we are faced with meager comfort indeed.

There is good news and there is bad news. And they are both the same news. We are all going to live longer. With any luck we will not have to "die in the saddle," but will be able to retire gracefully, with the anticipation of living the good life. The best kind of retirement gives you the chance to do everything you wished to do when you were younger. It can work today better than ever. Apart from good health, a successful retirement is perhaps our greatest life goal. Ultimately, the financial aspects of retirement are up to you.

Money can't buy happiness, but having enough of it to live with dignity beats being poor. This becomes even more true at retirement. Every aspect of life, including health and physical condition, is affected by sufficiency and security of income after labors are over. True, longevity may not be purchasable, but at the same time it's evident that hard-working poor people don't live longer than the wealthy. Longevity increases with general well-being, and general well-being increases with financial security.

As with most other things that deal with planning, the public is being offered an alphabet soup of terms. Keogh, I.R.A., stock options, annuities, perks, and more. What is this stuff? Almost all of us already have some kind of pension plan or some kind of benefit from employment, and yet few of us understand it. Clients have often made appointments with me two or three weeks before their retirement to have me interpret the terms of their pension plans, profit sharing plans, and other retirement benefits. For the first time they are calculating the amount they will actually get upon retirement. In all the years—sometimes twenty or thirty years of service—they have not kept track. Doctors and lawyers are not immune. They too wear retirement blinkers. They may have well-developed pension funds filtered through professional corporations, and yet be stymied if you asked them directly how much is in their plan.

You don't have to be a Moneythink expert to know what's going on. It can be painful to look at retirement, to face aging. Excuses come easily—it's too boring, too expensive, too complex to focus on retirement. But sooner or later (make it sooner) you must.

FOCUS ON RETIREMENT

Retirement means many things to many people, including anything from "free at last" to "being put out to pasture." The concept of freedom differs from person to person, and the response to not working also differs. Because of the emotions associated with retirement, few people focus early enough in life on the financial meaning of retirement and what that is really all about. It is quite simple. *Financial retirement means the ability to live independent of uncertain income.* By *uncertain income* I mean money earned from a job or from investments that might not pan out. Money earned may come from running a business as well as from being directly paid a salary.

Some people are born retired. They have inherited enough wealth so that they never have to rely on uncertain income.

They may work and they may risk investments. Often they do. But they need not. Financial retirement has nothing to do with age. It can be obtained from the cradle. Most of us strive a good portion of our lives to reach financial retirement. It is possible to reach the goal at age thirty, forty, fifty, sixty, or never. People who are in need of uncertain income but who have no jobs are not retired. They are merely out of work. People who could enjoy their normal life style without ever earning one penny more and who are still working are financially retired.

How do you become independent of uncertain income if you have not inherited money? There is only one way—create a fund of money that is secure so that you can be certain that it will yield a specific amount of income sufficient to maintain your life style. When you have done that, you have reached your financial retirement goal.

There are three ways to do this. One is to get lucky, win the lottery, and have a great big pool of money to invest in risk-free fashion. I think we all harbor that fantasy. It is not a dangerous fantasy, but it can become one when it replaces good practical planning.

The other two ways to create the fund are more in our control though not as exciting. They are: (1) Save money by not spending all that you earn as life goes on; and (2) defer taking all that you earn, and have this money put away for you instead of getting it directly in the form of salary. Most of us know what it means to deliberately not spend money for the purposes of saving. The second method—simply not accepting all you could earn—we also do every day. For example, our Social Security system really takes a part of our earned income. It is simply not received when earned, the idea being that we will receive it when we reach financial retirement.

We all know that ways of retiring include saving through not spending and deferring income in one way or another so that the money is not in our hands to spend right now. Every single corporate retirement package, every individual independent I.R.A. and Keogh Plan, every union pension fund is based on these two simple concepts. Every decision you make regarding retirement planning should be simplified into an analysis of the following questions: (1) Am I better off receiving and spending the money today? (2) Will the money be as risk-free as possible so that I really get it when I need financial retirement? (3) If I invested the money safely today, would I get more or less than I will by not accepting it in the first place? (4) Is Uncle Sam giving me tax benefits if I take the money now or if I wait?

Every I.R.A. decision, every decision regarding taking a new job and which job to take must force you to focus on those four questions. The answers in any individual case are very simple and will utterly avoid confusion—or avoid utter confusion, as the case may be.

Even question #4, Uncle Sam and taxes, can be answered very simply. In order to make it worth your while to save through not spending or not accepting income, Uncle Sam has provided numerous methods of postponing income tax on money that you save or don't accept, if it's done for retirement planning purposes only. This means that you will be receiving money on paper. You will not be able to spend it, you will not be taxed in the year earned but only years later, when you receive it. For most of us this is a marvel. For some of us it is not. Some of us will actually be in a higher income tax bracket in the future than in the present. If that is possible for you, Uncle Sam is doing you no favors. Part of the Uncle Sam benefit program is that income earned on the money not spent or not accepted through the years is also not taxable in the year earned. Instead, income tax on income earned is postponed until the date of retirement. This should permit you to develop a large reserve of money that was not taxed when it was earned and was not taxed as it accumulated income through investment. It will of course be taxed finally, but this should be at a time when you have no other income (in plain English, when you are retired and not working); for most people, the tax will be lower. As we go through each type of retirement possibility, we will see the tax effect, the savings effect, the investment effect, and always the trade-offs.

Everything that we will deal with here is applicable to everyone. But ultimately your retirement life will be consistent with your work life from a financial point of view. If you have always made less than your neighbor, then you probably will retire on less. There are only three exceptions, and the last one is a fake. The first exception is created by those who deprive themselves consistently during their working years so that they can save money. The great risk here is that one may not live to enjoy the benefits. That decision is personal and not financial.

The second and closely related exception is that of the individual whose job does not pay well but has fabulous retirement benefits. Many civil servants have a retirement package that is out of proportion to their weekly salaries. During their working years they may have a tight money situation and find their first real freedom at retirement. This too depends in part on your desire to enjoy and your need for future security.

The final way of living better after retirement, which I've called "fake," is to have what is now called a second career. This means that you have a pension or other retirement plan from your first job and augment your retirement through a second job, perhaps in an unrelated field, when you retire from your first job. Psychologically, this is wonderful. Many people love to work and should always work. Going into a new field seems to them like play and brings excitement into their lives when they are in their mid-sixties and could use a little. It's a fine idea, and I applaud every agency, private and public, that is developing the second career concept and helping people find a new road. But this has nothing to do with retirement planning. Retirement planning means that you do not *need* uncertain income. If your financial health depends on yet another job after retirement from your first, you have not reached a retirement goal.

As with any other kind of financial planning, different plans suit different people. The individual retirement accounts are of no interest to a corporate person. On the other hand, the profit-sharing plans of large corporations are of no interest to a professional working on his own.

RETIREMENT PLANS

Retirement money does not materialize out of thin air. Only by saving can you have retirement income. But today, saving means something very different from what it meant in the past. It used to mean that you actually took out some money from your weekly paycheck and socked it away—literally in a sock, if that's what you wished. In twenty or thirty years you had accumulated a cash fund which you would use frugally and slowly through your remaining years. This was always the worst way to do things—but now it is downright impossible. You will be paying income tax on the money in the year that you earned

it, but you will not be using it until years later when everything
you buy with it costs ten times as much as when you were earning
it. If you put it in a bank or in any other way gained interest from
the savings, that income too would be taxed heavily every year.
This means that for a lot of deprivation in your youth you would
be getting very little compensation as you got older.

The whole idea of a real RETIREMENT PLAN is to use
money in the way that has the best tax advantage for you. For
example, a corporate executive might rather have stock in his
corporation held for him until he retires than to get extra cash in
his paycheck every week. If he received the money outright
every week, it would be taxed as income, and then as he invested
it the income on that would be taxed. If instead the company
holds stock incentives for him, he will always have this reserve,
but it won't be taxed until he actually uses it in later years.

The government has taken the same idea for the individual
who has no employer, or for the individual who is working for
someone who has set up no pension plan or for someone who
wants to augment an employer plan. The government calls it
I.R.A. if you have an employer and Keogh if you are
self-employed. You can deduct the amount you save from your
income and pay no income tax on it in the year that you saved.
Through the years, as the savings accumulate income, that
income is not taxed either. Only when you withdraw the money
at the age of fifty-nine and a half or over does taxation begin. I
hope at that time you will have retired, and so the taxes will be
much lower than in your earning years. If you don't want to
retire so soon, you certainly don't have to. You can defer using
the money for even more years until you are seriously ready to
take that around-the-world cruise.

Keeping the tax goals in mind, let's explore various
retirement planning devices.

I.R.A.

If you do not have any pension plan from an employer or
the government, you can create your own pension by
contributing to an individual retirement account (I.R.A.) up to
$2,000 or an amount equal to 100% of your earnings, whichever
is less. You can deduct this sum dollar for dollar from your

adjusted gross income before you pay income tax in the year that you make the contribution.

If you're lucky enough to have an employer who makes a contribution to a pension plan for you, you can still set up your own I.R.A. You can also make voluntary contributions to the employer's plan if it is a so-called "qualified employer plan" which permits such contributions. To be entitled to contribute directly to the employer's plan you must not designate the contribution as non-deductible for income tax purposes. If you make no designation, deductibility is presumed.

You can have your own I.R.A. and also contribute to your employer's plan but only to the combined tune of $2,000 or 100% of earnings, whichever is less.

If you have a spouse who is not working at all and you file a joint return with your spouse, you can set up an I.R.A. pension fund for the spouse and get a deduction from your income tax of $2,250 or an amount equal to your compensation for that taxable year, whichever is less. When you set up the accounts they need not be evenly divided. One can have as little as $250 and the other as much as $2,000.

Don't forget, once you have reached the age of seventy and a half you will get no deductions for contributions you make. So make your contributions early. Remember also that you can't use an employer's plan for a spousal contribution.

If at least five years prior to a divorce your ex-spouse set up an I.R.A. and for at least three of those years contributed to the account for you, you can continue to make contributions, even after a divorce. How much? The lesser of $1,125 or the sum of your yearly compensation and alimony, support or maintenance includable in your gross income for income tax purposes.

You can make your contribution anytime within your taxable year and even after, up to your final extension date. So if you get an extension through August 15, which is possible, you could make a contribution to your own pension plan as late as four months after the usual April 15 filing.

Keogh

If you are self-employed and have no boss-benefactor to set up a pension plan, you can set up your own and make contributions every year which are deductible from your gross income. Contributions are limited to an amount equal to the lesser of $15,000 or 15% of your earned income up to $200,000. If you overfund a Keogh in any given year you can withdraw the surplus before the deadline for filing your income tax return.

Like someone with an employer plan, if you have a Keogh you can have an I.R.A. too.

The money we are talking about can be placed in a bank account, in certificates of deposit, or in an investment program with a brokerage house which will buy stocks and bonds for your Keogh. The types of purchases that can be made are practically infinite; they include everything from horse farms to stock, and from stock options to real estate but no collectibles. The important thing is that to avoid being taxed on the income that you make from these contributions, you cannot take any of the money until you are fifty-nine and a half years old, become disabled or die. When you retire and pull out your money you will be taxed, but only at your tax rate at that time. If you terminate a Keogh the distribution will not be considered premature.

If you hold shares in a Subchapter "S" corporation (a corporation with ten or fewer shareholders that have elected to take special tax treatment) you can also create a qualified pension plan. All the Keogh rules regarding amount of contributions, and tax savings apply.

S.E.P.

Simplified Employee Pension plans are created for employees by an employer under which both can contribute to an I.R.A. for the employee. Since the new tax law (E.R.T.A.) permits employee contributions to an existing employer's plan, the S.E.P. has become less popular. S.E.P. is a type of hybrid between I.R.A. and Keogh. Deductible contributions can be made of the lesser of $15,000 or 15% of compensation by the employer on behalf of the employee. The employee includes the contribution in his gross income, then takes an equivalent deduction; so no tax is paid. The employee can also contribute the lesser of $2,000 or 100% of compensation.

Deferred Compensation

The most straightforward way of earning money to use later is not to get the money right away. This simple idea of having whoever owes you the money, like your employer, keep it for you without paying it to you is called deferred compensation. Corporations often set up a special deferred compensation program for their employees. It is very simple, certainly simpler than any kind of pension plan. You *are* compensated in an amount that is not paid to you in the year you earn it. Instead it is paid out later on and therefore taxed to you when you get it, not when you earn it. How much money do you get? That depends upon your employer's formula.

Many companies use a phantom stock plan. That means they take the yearly deferred earnings and convert them into an equivalent amount of corporate stock. The stock is not actually issued. Later, when payment is made, the amount equals the value of the stock at the time of payment. The employer has invested your deferred compensation for you in stock that never exists and is never actually bought, so that the growth of your earnings has something specific by which it can be measured.

Sometimes a corporation actually makes an investment in other securities and the executive will get the appreciation in value of the acquired securities and the interest on the dividend income in later years. The employee becomes the creditor of the employer. If he goes bankrupt you will never collect your deferred compensation. Make sure that you really will be getting a better tax break in years to come than you do now. As I've already said, the whole idea of waiting for your money is to benefit by being taxed at a time when you are in a lower income tax bracket. If you expect to be in the same or a higher bracket later on, get your money now and don't take the risk. Don't forget, you are also relying on your employer's investment judgment and not your own.

If you die prior to payment, your beneficiaries will have to pay income tax. If they are in a high bracket, this may not be a good idea. Consider making your children beneficiaries of deferred income rather than your spouse, if your spouse is already well provided for.

Annuity

An annuity is merely a plan by which you are guaranteed an income for your lifetime. The principal is never used up and you need never face the day when your income has dried up. If you have no annuity, but instead have a fixed amount of cash you may outlive your money. With an annuity the insurance company takes the risk of your longevity. The gamble is the reverse of insurance, where you get the most for dying the earliest. With an annuity you get more by outliving your normal lifespan as measured by the actuarial tables.

Annuities can be joint, first paying to you and then to your spouse for life. Annuities can be for a specified time so that if you die earlier than expected your beneficiary keeps collecting until the term is over. In choosing annuities compare them as you do life insurance for cost, service and fringe benefits. Also check on the withdrawal policy in case you need the lump sum back.

Annuities can be purchased for the first time at retirement. You pay a lump sum and get a monthly income. Annuities can also be deferred, bought early in life and collected at retirement. Your contribution to the annuity is not tax deductible, but the interest that accumulates is not taxed until withdrawn.

Corporate Retirement Plans

There used to be a T.V. game show called "Let's Make a Deal." The game was to offer a contestant either a certain amount of money or the secret contents of a box. The excitement was fantastic. Should one take the money or the box? The audience would scream: "Take the box, take the money, take the box, take both!" After the choice was announced, the suspense really made your heart pound. If the money was selected, everyone hoped that there would be a bunch of carrots or a leek in the box. If the box was accepted, and turned out to be tiny, everyone hoped that inside there might be an automobile key. In every case the excitement was heightened by the element of risk. I was so fascinated by this game that I decided to play it with my mother.

I went to a local women's store and bought some handkerchiefs and gloves and put them in a box, and then I took a five-dollar bill and asked my mother which she wanted. But my mother hated the game. She didn't want me to spend five dollars, nor did she want to find out what was in the box. She spoiled the game because she did the one thing that was unexpected. She refused to play.

For a week the box lay, sealed with Scotch tape, alone and silent but conspicuous on our kitchen counter. Every day I would beg, "Please play the game. Do you want the box or the five dollars?" Every day she would say, "I don't like such games. If you spent a lot of money on things for me, I will be very angry." I had a terrible dilemma. If she thought I spent money on her, she wouldn't play the game. If she wouldn't play the game, the box would never be opened. Every day I eyed that box and, even though I knew what was in it, I was eager to see the contents again. How could she be so incurious? How could she require such certainty? Finally I gave up.

I said to her, "There is less in the box than five dollars' worth of items." She looked at me and repeated, "There's less than five dollars' worth of items in the box?" I said, "Yes." "In that case," she said, "I'll take the five dollars."

Her refusal to make a choice until she knew the facts was probably the best lesson I have ever learned. Don't make financial choices until you know all the facts, even if knowing the facts spoils the game that others are trying to play. To help you spoil the game, take a look at the following, which explains the types of retirement benefits in store for you in a corporation.

1. *Profit sharing.* A percentage of corporate profits goes into a profit sharing fund and is divided among employees according to various formulas. Some companies base it on merit, others on years of service, and some on a combination of both. In some companies, not every employee is covered. The yearly amount obtained depends on the profit earned by the company. The amount can be extremely small if profits are low. In companies where executives get very high salaries on a yearly basis, the little guy might end up with almost nothing because not much is being left in the company as profit.

A plan is either qualified or unqualified. The difference corresponds to differences in tax treatment. An unqualified plan permits discrimination, and can be haphazard as to when money will be withdrawn or distributed. Employer contribution is deductible by the employer when the employee is taxed on the money. The employee pays tax (ordinary income, not capital gains) when he or she is entitled to take out the money.

If it's qualified it must be in writing and the employee is not taxed on the money put into the fund until retirement. The employer takes a tax deduction for the amount when it's put in. The formula for a qualified plan must be definite and state when the money will be distributed, how many years of service are needed, and at what age the money can be withdrawn. No employees within any group can be discriminated against.

When you finally withdraw, you will be taxed. If a plan permits you to withdraw while still employed, you will have ordinary income tax to pay. If you withdraw money from a plan to which you have contributed, there will be no tax if you do not withdraw more than you contributed, since you already paid tax on that when you earned it. If you are no longer employed, but instead get your money when you retire, then the money you contributed comes back tax free and the income derived from it is taxed as ordinary income in the year you receive it. Your employer's contribution and the interest earned on that is taxed as ordinary income or as capital gains, depending on what's best for you, provided it was paid in prior to 1974. Money paid in after that date is only taxed as ordinary income. In both cases you can average out tax payments over the years. Of course, you can take out your money in stages, and then it will be taxed as ordinary income as you withdraw it. Or you can take out all of your money at once and place it in an I.R.A. account within sixty days of withdrawal. This is good if you do not need it right away, since once you have retired you will not be covered by any ongoing pension. You are entitled to use the individual retirement account previously discussed for more years of postponing income tax. If you die prior to retirement, your beneficiary takes the proceeds. There will be the same ordinary income tax that you would have had, except that there is a $5,000 income tax exemption. If your beneficiaries take the money in a lump sum, then they too can use the ten-year income-averaging procedure. If they do that, estate tax will be paid. If the ten-year income-averaging procedure is not used, no estate taxes will be paid.

There has been much talk about the word "vesting." You are vested on the date at which you are absolutely entitled to money in the profit sharing plan. You may be partially or fully vested (entitled). Read each plan carefully, because they differ. For example, some plans allow for full vesting (entitlement to all the funds set aside for you in the plan) after five years of employment, so that 20% of the funds is vested in each of the five years. Another plan may permit partial vesting after two years but only give you 10% vesting each year. That means you will not be fully vested for ten years. If you should leave prior to full vesting, you generally will get the portion that was vested and forfeit the non-vested portion.

In comparing profit sharing plans, watch for fringe benefits. The most important one is loans: At what rate, how much, and when can a loan be taken? Is disability or other kind of insurance also included, and how much? If there is a policy, can it be converted if you leave the company?

A quick way to figure out whether you are better off with more salary or a plan is as follows: Pretend you would get a salary $10,000 higher from one company over the salary of another, but that the second company has a profit sharing plan. Multiply the $10,000 by the most common interest rate prevailing at the time you are doing your math, for every year until age sixty-five. Before doing the multiplication, take that $10,000 and reduce it by the amount called for by your tax bracket. Then take the same $10,000 (don't reduce it, since you will not be taxed) and take a look at what the profit sharing plan of the company has been earning in interest over the past three to five years. Do the same math. If the figures are close, look at the performance of the investment planners and the performance of the company. See how often in the past five to ten years the company has not been able to make a contribution to the employees' profit sharing. Notice whether the bulk of the investment made is in the company itself. This doesn't give you much leeway if something happens to the company.

2. *Pension plan.* Pension plans are similar to profit sharing plans except that the amount of money you get is measured by a definite formula based on actuarial tables, not on the profitability of the company. The amount of growth does not vary with the fortunes of the company. The pension is usually definite and calculable. It depends upon the salary you earn and the number of years you have been in service. Age too is generally in the formula. Compare formulas for each job. There are several options attached to pension plans. They may be taken in a lump sum or in installments. If you die prior to

obtaining your final installment, an annuity can continue to support beneficiaries. In pension plans, unlike profit sharing plans, you are often not vested until you retire. This means that if you die or quit you may get back only the money that you put in and there will be no graduated vesting program.

3. *Savings plan.* Some companies will match the money you are willing to place in savings. This money is also tax free when contributed, if placed immediately into the savings plan. Types of investments differ and can include investing in the company itself as well as in outside funds. Here, too, your investment is managed and it is wise to compare the performance of the investment manager with, say, the performance of a large, well-advertised mutual fund.

4. *Stock bonuses.* Stock bonuses can be a glory or a dangerous thing. You receive company stock instead of the usual cash bonus. Often the stock is transferred to you without cost as additional compensation or is offered to you at a favorable purchase rate. In either case there is ordinary income and you will have to pay immediate income tax, even though the stock does not yield cash to you immediately.

5. *Stock options.* A stock option is far different from a stock bonus. An option merely means a choice or a right to buy; regardless of what the present price is, the buying price will be fixed when the option is granted. The option permits you to buy the stock at a fixed price within a certain period of time. Options themselves are valuable and, as with real estate, options are often sold or traded. Many people buy and sell the stock options through brokers, making money not on the buying and selling of the stock but on the buying and selling of the option. If you leave a company that grants options before your option period has expired and you haven't picked up your option, it is usually forfeited. Sometimes there are restrictions on the stock that you purchase. For example, it cannot be sold to an outsider, or it must be sold back to the company, or upon the death of the stockholder the company must redeem it. Always compare the restrictions that the companies place on the stock as well as the value of the stock at the time that you are checking into the value of the stock option. These stocks certainly involve an element of risk. They are not the guaranteed money that the pension plan is. If you exercise your option and the value of the stock goes down, you are in the same boat as any other buyer of stocks. If

you haven't exercised your option and the value goes down, you simply don't exercise it, but you haven't received any kind of benefit. You can negotiate a sliding-scale price, so that if the value falls, the stock option price is also reduced.

Be aware of the difference between stock options that are tax shelters, and those that are not. Look for a stock plan that involves no tax to you when you receive the option or when the option is exercised. Our recent Economic Recovery Tax Act has created a category of stock options called the Incentive Stock Option. If your company's plan qualifies you will have no tax when the option is given and no tax when you exercise the option to buy the stock. You will have a capital gains tax when you finally sell the stock for a profit. To qualify for the new Incentive Stock Option with favorable tax treatment (1) you must hold the option for at least two years; (2) after exercising it hold the stock for at least one year; (3) your employer must meet the technical rules for Incentive Stock Options.

What you're interested in is a plan under which you will be taxed only *after* you sell your stock and make your profit. Some plans work out so that you actually have to pay a tax when you are handed the option, since it too is something of value. This is not so good, since you may never exercise that option and you may get nothing out of it but a tax. The difference in tax treatment depends on (1) a comparison of the stock price and the market price of stock and (2) when in the course of your employment you are entitled to exercise your option. The rules are extremely technical and differ with various types of plans. The question to ask your personnel officer is, "Will I be taxed when the option is granted, when it is exercised, or only when I sell my stock, if I ever do buy it?"

Stock options that don't have good tax treatment do have another value. Since the time in which you can exercise the option is irrelevant, it permits you to "play the market" with your company stock. If you have an option to buy stock at $10 a share and there is no restriction as to when you can exercise that option, you could buy at $10 and sell the next day at $12. You will pay a double tax. First, on the value of the option itself, since it gave you the right to buy at cheaper than market price; second on the gain you make when you finally do sell. If it was a tax-sheltered plan you would be taxed only once, when you sold and made your profit. However, you would be restricted in time as to when you could make your sale, and so you might miss the best time to make a profit.

If you die before exercising an option, one of two things may happen. As already mentioned, there may be no right in an estate to exercise an option; it may fail and terminate at death. In that case, of course, there are no estate taxes nor is there any benefit from the option. If it does not terminate on death, then the estate must evaluate the stock option and pay taxes on it even if it doesn't exercise the option. Since this is silly, stock options are generally exercised and an estate tax is paid. Again, watch for a liquidity problem. Just as with the estate that is illiquid and needs money to pay taxes, your estate may need money to exercise good options. Use your life insurance trust for that purpose as well as for tax payment purposes if part of your estate is heavily involved with stock options for which your beneficiaries will need cash.

Check with your personnel officers to see whether loans can be arranged for the purchase and exercise of the stock option. If you don't have the cash to exercise your option, it does you very little good. When comparing stock option packages, don't forget to find out not only whether loans can be made, but also at what rate and on what collateral, so that a good package can be used to advantage. At the same time find out whether the stock option itself is salable. Just as on the stock market, you might want to sell your right to buy cheap. This way you never actually buy the stock but you do make a profit by selling your right to buy. In most cases you can't make this sale because the companies want to restrict ownership of stock, but certainly check it out. A stock option turns into what is called a stock warrant if it is negotiable to an outsider.

Incorporation for Independent Professionals

One might well ask how a self-employed professional can ever afford to retire. The answer is that we can all have retirement plans but we must build them ourselves. We will not be given choices between different employer packages. We will be given choices between different packages that we select from what is available to the independent professional.

Let's take a look at that word "independent" for a moment. The truth is that very little is available to the true independent.

We are no longer pioneers working singly on the frontier. The best that an individual professional can do is an I.R.A. or Keogh type plan. You are simply going to have to get partners; it doesn't matter whether they are for working purposes or planning purposes. But you will be much better off if you don't go it alone.

Minimally, if you have an association of several doctors, lawyers, or accountants which has continuity (it will continue despite the death of one of the parties), centralized management, free transferability (the interest can be transferred to a nonmember without the approval of the others—not restricted), limited liability (that means that no one of you will be personally responsible for the debts of the association), you will be entitled to develop your own group pension plan and group insurance. If you don't meet these criteria, you will come up against the I.R.S. and have a problem. To clinch the success of your association, simply incorporate. The now popular professional corporation has been recognized in the majority of states. Those that don't have general recognition do permit such incorporation for practitioners of medicine, dentistry, and law.

This corporation permits you to have qualified pension plans, profit sharing plans, and all the life insurance benefits of any corporation. Look back to the retirement devices. You can have those things too. The problem is to have sufficient cash flow to fund them. That's where your expert professional pension planner comes in.

A word to those of you who are really very young. I suggest that you invest a few hundred dollars in an interview and discussion with professional pension planners, even though you have no partners and no one to join with. This may help you to decide how quickly you should associate yourself when it becomes worthwhile to do so. I will tell you this: At some point, if you are a success at all, it is not only worthwhile but essential to do so in order to develop your retirement program. Don't be a dinosaur; don't practice alone for financial planning.

15

The Forgotten Miss P.

It seems that I have forgotten Miss P. It really is not my fault; everybody forgets Miss P. I might have actually completed this book without ever mentioning her, had I not seen her through the window of a restaurant. I have not seen her for years, but she looked exactly as I remembered her. Miss P. was the secretary of a lawyer whom I knew long ago. He was a very famous and wealthy attorney who made his fortune in the heyday of sole practice. Like most entrepreneurs, he had almost no vision of office management. Things were taken care of haphazardly. He tried to do his own bookkeeping and accounting when he could. He saved as much money as possible on overhead; he kept the same furniture for fifty years until he retired at the age of eighty. Among the furniture that he kept without updating was Miss P.

Miss P. was more than a secretary. She brought his coffee, bought his wife gifts, ran his office, soothed his clients, and did just about everything else. Once a year Miss P. got a raise. She never knew from year to year if she would get one or how much. Sometimes she received a bonus at Christmas, sometimes not, depending on what the lawyer's needs were and whether his wife wanted a mink coat that year or a vacation in Europe. Miss P. had no set vacation schedule or sick days. There was no union and never would be. In fifty years of working together, she called him Mr. Lawyer and he called her Miss P. She was the "girl" in the office. Miss P. never left.

I didn't know Miss P. very well. But I do remember some years ago her saying to me, when she learned of my expertise in financial planning, that she often lay awake at night worrying about what would happen to her when she or Mr. Lawyer retired. I realized that she was confiding that she had no pension plan whatsoever. There was no agreement; there was no arrangement at all. Perhaps she could manage on Social Security and what she saved or invested from the small salary she had been paid throughout her lifetime. Retirement planning or estate planning had never been discussed. She feared speaking to Mr. Lawyer about it, and he of course cared only for his own plan and not hers. I heard that Mr. Lawyer had retired. I am very happy to see that Miss P. looks well and has enough money to eat in a New York City restaurant. But frankly I don't know how she manages.

While other friends are talking about their annuity plans, pension plans, trusts for the benefit of the employee, and other job securities, as far as I know Miss P. has nothing to talk about at all. I remember that from time to time she invested in the stock market; maybe that saved her. I am certain that Mr. Lawyer did nothing for her upon his retirement. He certainly had no legal obligation to do so, since there was no contract and no agreement. His obligation would have been moral only, and with a man like Mr. Lawyer that would have meant nothing.

But even with more generous and sensitive bosses, where there is no legal obligation there may be no payment. An elderly doctor, lawyer, accountant or businessman of any type who retires may simply not be able to make any quick, last-minute employee retirement arrangements. They may have no money to do so; they may retire because of illness, failure, or old age. The trusted, dedicated employee may look to the beloved boss's relatives to help.

Everybody forgets Miss P. Fortunately, there are fewer Miss P.'s left. More and more women—there are few men who have permitted themselves to be exploited as the Miss P.'s of this world—are aware of their rights and their needs. They may belong to a union or they may reject the job that does not give them the retirement security they need. The result is that many employers now know that they must give some thought to offering a benefit package to their employees.

We have considered these packages several places in the

book. This is all very well. But we forget that there still are some Miss P.'s left. There are many dedicated workers who feel that their lives and their stability are keyed to remaining in their long-time jobs. They fear rocking the boat by demanding employee benefit packages because they worry about being fired. They work for idiosyncratic bosses who feel that because they have a job to offer they need not offer benefits. They, perhaps in middle age, worry about being out in the cold with no job whatsoever. Finally, they convince themselves that eventually their boss will pay up for years of dedication by offering at least a livable retirement benefit. They never bring it up, they worry about it often, and they usually end up neglected.

I have a thought for the Miss P.'s of this world. I cannot say that I have a solution for them. But I do have a thought. Of course I could give them a pep talk on speaking up and demanding their rights. I could tell them that there are many jobs out there even for middle-aged women, and perhaps *especially* for middle-aged women, if they only would look. I could tell them not to stand for all of this. By and large, many would listen. I know this because I know that Miss P.'s are becoming rarer and rarer. When I make speeches on financial planning, I find my audience filled with young, alert, assertive women who would never let themselves be in Miss P.'s situation. I am not worried about them, nor am I worried about the many middle-aged or older women who are making their demands known. But I am worried about the few Miss P.'s, no matter how their numbers have dwindled.

So now I am talking only to you Miss P., because I know that if I tell you to make demands, all that will happen is that you will read this chapter, get more worried, and still do nothing. The major reason that you will do nothing is that you are probably correct in sensing that your boss will not accommodate you. If you have lulled a boss into a sense of not having to support any retirement benefit plan for you, and you have done so over a period of many years, it is very possible that this boss will give you your walking papers if you make such a demand. He may believe that times have not changed. He may feel that he can get a new secretary (bookkeeper, file clerk, or whatever your job) for a lower salary with fewer demands. I believe that he will have a rude awakening and you will get a phone call of the "who's sorry now" variety when his interviewing is over. However, I know, Miss P., that you do not want to take that chance.

I also know one other thing about you and that is that you generally have enough money to live on. Because you are a good financial planner from a budgeting point of view, and because you have never been used to living on a lot of money, you generally save and even sometimes invest. You are one of the few people with surplus income. Statistics show that you may have more surplus in proportion to your income than a young executive making $50,000 a year with a fancy car, two fancy homes, and a big vacation-entertainment budget. What indulgent young ones consider necessities are luxuries to you and so there are always a few cents extra around.

If you have no pension plan or retirement plan, if you are certain that you will lose your job if your demands are too great, if your boss has already indicated or refused or you know he will refuse to do better for you, and only if these factors exist, I suggest the following safeguard for your future: *deferred compensation.*

Deferred compensation is the payment of salary or any other compensation for work done or services rendered in a year at some time in the future. Its purpose is to create a source of income in future years and at a time when income tax will be lower. An employee who chooses deferred compensation is assured that the maximum income tax rate will not be greater than the amount he or she would have paid if it were present compensation. An employee pays income tax in the tax year when the income is credited to his or her account or set apart for him or her; not in the year earned. Therefore, a boss can keep money set aside until a later year in order for the employee to get a deferred tax benefit. If the employee is actually guaranteed the money in a particular year, even though it isn't received then, that may itself be considered enough to impose a tax. To make sure that the government doesn't think you get the right to the money too early, all you need is a contract from your employer, saying that you have earned a certain amount of money but that it will not be paid to you until later and that the money is not being held in trust for you or in escrow for you.

First make a contract in writing with your employer. It should contain the following: (1) a designation of the time and manner that payment will eventually be made; (2) a statement that there is no annuity contract or other asset already set aside to pay the money; (3) the investment device which will be used to measure the appreciation in the salary from the time it could have been given to the employee to the time that it will be actually paid; (4) a declaration that payment will be made only upon termination of employment, retirement, emergency, or death and that in an emergency it can only be paid as a result of hardship arising from items beyond the control of the employee (like illness).

Don't let the boss tell you that deferred compensation is too complicated or that he doesn't know much about it. The type of sole practitioner that we are talking about probably has made deferred compensation plans for himself. Perhaps he took a bonus in the following year when he thought his overall taxes would be less, rather than paying himself his bonus in the year it was actually earned.

In order to fight inflation the compensation will be paid to you at a later date at a specific interest rate. The Internal Revenue Service has already approved the crediting of interest. A simple technique is to defer compensation payment, while agreeing upon an interest factor which follows the prime rate, or the cost of living index over a base level year. A very fancy thing to do, which I do not suggest for Miss P.'s, but which you should know about, is called phantom stock. This means that the increase in compensation is geared not to an interest rate or increase in the cost of living but to the increase in the value of the boss's business. You will be highly motivated because you are actually investing your salary in your boss's business in anticipation of getting it back plus an increase based on his good fortune. Many bosses look upon this as an incentive or motivation plan for the employee. Unfortunately the Miss P.'s of this world are usually so motivated already, and such good workers that no such incentive is needed. And yet bosses, especially the old dinosaur types that I have described, like deferred compensation. This is because they can use the money and not pay it in the year that work is done for them. This gives them a better cash flow. Of course, they can't take an income tax deduction for payment to you until the year you are actually paid, but this really takes very little from them. Your boss will also have to make a deferred compensation plan for anyone else on your same level, but since there is no one else on your level, this should be a very easy requirement. The only risk is that the boss may not be able to meet his obligations when the time comes because he has not saved the money and put it away for the employee. There are ways of safeguarding against this:

Don't forget to protect your salary and interest from your boss's creditors. A common solution is to have the employer transfer stock, if it is a closed corporation, or some other collateral to protect the employee. If there is none, try an insurance policy used to protect the employee. The Internal Revenue Service has already approved this. It is even possible for a third party like a bonding company to guarantee that the employer will perform.

In the contract you should include who your beneficiary will be, in case you die prior to the time you receive your deferred compensation. The amount of it will be counted in your estate for estate tax purposes. Of course, not all Miss P.'s are Miss P.'s, some are Mrs. P.'s. If you do have a spouse, I suggest that you do not make the deferred compensation part of the marital share. This is because you will pay income tax on the deferred compensation in the year it is received even if that is the year of your death and it is received by your estate. The income tax you pay can be used as a credit against the estate tax. So if you believe you may have a big enough estate for tax purposes, and you have beneficiaries other than your spouse, make sure your deferred compensation is in the nonmarital portion of your bequests.

Finally, try to negotiate! Ask your boss to contribute to the deferred compensation plan. Read the *entire* retirement section to see what other devices are possible. Consider an I.R.A. or Simplified Retirement Plan. Don't just wait and hope. Good luck.

APPENDIX I

Financial Planning Data Sheets

Life Insurance Schedule
(List all policies)

Company   Face Amount   Owned by   Beneficiary   Cash Value

Retirement Benefits for Corporate Employees

Type	Estimated Value	Designated Beneficiary
Pension Plan		
Profit-sharing Plan		
Thrift Plan		
Deferred Compen- sation		
Salary Continuation		
Health, Accident, etc.		
Self-employed Re- tirement Fund		
Other		

225

Retirement Benefits for Self-Employed

Type	Estimated Value	Depository	Designated Beneficiary
IRA			
Keogh			
Professional Corporation			

Other Benefits

Type	Estimated Value	Designated Beneficiary
Social Security		
Veteran's Pension		
Veteran's Death Benefits		
Disability Benefits		
Other		

Business Interests
Description

Name of Business
Form of Business
Fiscal Year
Parties or Shareholders
Number of Shares or
  Interest Held by You
Shareholders Agreement,
  if any
Partnership Agreement,
  if any

Information to Bring to a Consultation with
Your Lawyer or Accountant
Family Data

	Name	Age	Health	Marital Status
Self				
Spouse				
Children				
Dependents				
Other than above				
*Distribu-tees				

*Others who take by intestate succession that you do *not* consider dependents.

Names and Addresses of Key
Professionals

Attorney
Accountant
Broker
Trustee
Executor

Personal Assets

Asset	Husband	Wife	Joint	Description	Value
Bank Account					
Treasury Bills					
All Saver Certificates					
Principal Residence (less mortgage if any)				co-op condo real estate	
Summer Residence (less mortgage if any)				co-op condo real estate	
Other Real Estate					
Stocks					
Mutual Fund Shares					
Patents					
Copyright					
Trademark					
Royalties					
Significant Personal Property (over $500)					
Bonds					
Mortgages					
Savings Accounts					
Personal Effects					
Power of Appointment					
Interest in Trusts					
Potential Inheritance					

Tax Shelters
How Secured
Miscellaneous
 (explain)

Subtotals
TOTAL

List Significant Debts—Over 1% of Your Monthly Earnings

Husband	Wife	Joint	Amount to Whom Owed	Date Due

APPENDIX II

Reaganization in a Nutshell

You already know that there is a new federal tax law passed in 1981 that became effective in 1982. Because it was so emphasized by President Reagan I have coined the phrase Reaganized to represent the changes in our laws.

To grasp exactly what happened you have to know a little bit about what the situation was in the first place. Here is an outline of the changes that were made as it effects our discussion. There were significant other changes dealing with investments in real estate and oil, income tax changes that do not concern us here and many others. For our purposes take a look at the following:

Post Reaganization

The amount of estate taxes have been substantially reduced because the amount of money deducted from the adjusted gross estate before arriving at the taxable estate has been greatly increased. Here are the deductions beginning in 1982 and ending in 1987. Next to them is a figure which represents the credit which you can take off your taxable estate which is equivalent to the amount which you deduct

The Way We Were

The exemption prior to Reaganization was $175,625 or a credit of $47,000.

from your adjusted gross estate. Either mathematical
method yields the same result.

Year	Credit	Deduction Equivalent
1982	$ 62,800	$225,000
1983	79,300	275,000
1984	96,300	325,000
1985	121,800	400,000
1986	155,800	500,000
1987	192,800	600,000

Result: By 1987 there will be no estate or gift tax on transfers of $600,000 or less.

Post Reaganization
Any amount that you give to your spouse is deducted from the adjusted gross estate before the estate tax is figured.

The Way We Were
Only one-half of your adjusted gross estate or $250,000, whichever is greater was deducted.

Result: You can give your spouse all of your estate without federal estate taxes (there are restrictions in how to give it, which we will discuss later).

Post Reaganization
Gifts to spouses have no gift tax.

The Way We Were
There was a limited amount of gifts that you could give to your spouse tax free—only the first $100,000 was tax free, the next $200,000 worth of gifts had a tax imposed on 50%. Gifts over $200,000 had gift tax imposed with no exemptions.

Result: More money can be transferred to a spouse gift tax free during your lifetime.

Post Reaganization
Each spouse is considered to be a half owner of jointly held property provided there is a

The Way We Were
Jointly held property was presumed to be wholly owned by the one who died first, and to

right of survivorship no matter who paid for the property.

rebut this presumption it was important to show who made payments.

Result: There is no change for people who are not married to each other and have joint property; but transfers between spouses are simplified from a tax point of view.

Post Reaganization
The estate and gift tax rate are decreasing for larger estates until by 1985 the maximum tax rate will be 50% for combined estate and gift transfers of over $2,500,000.

The Way We Were
The old rate was 70% for taxable transfers in excess of $5,000,000.

Result: Gift and estate taxes are decreasing for the wealthy.

Post Reaganization
Income tax rates are decreased so that 50% is the maximum tax on earned income, 20% is the maximum tax on capital gains.

The Way We Were
The maximum income tax was 70% and 28% on capital gains.

Result: Income taxes are reduced for the wealthy and the upper middle class.

Post Reaganization
Gifts of $10,000 per year, per person can be given by an individual gift tax free.

The Way We Were
Gifts of $3,000 per year, per person could be given gift tax free.

Result: Much larger gifts can be given on a yearly basis to children or other beneficiaries without paying a gift tax.

Post Reaganization
Gifts made for the purposes of paying tuition or medical expenses are completely gift tax free regardless of whether they exceed the $10,000 a year amount.

The Way We Were
No such thing in old law.

Result: Greater gifts can be given for hospital coverage for older donees or college coverage for younger donees.

Post Reaganization
Gift tax returns are paid annually.

The Way We Were
Gift tax returns are paid quarterly.

Result: Accountants are very happy.

Post Reaganization
Gifts made within three years of death do not have to be counted in the gross estate.

The Way We Were
Gifts made within three years of death had to be calculated in the gross estate to determine if taxes were to be paid.

Result: Takes the headache out of lifetime gift giving even in old age.

Post Reaganization
The rule that certain property like farms was evaluated for estate tax purposes at their use not at their best use continues and the rules loosened up.

The Way We Were
The best use rule existed but the requirements were tighter.

Result: Very important for families who have most of their wealth in farms.

Post Reaganization
The orphans deduction is abolished.

The Way We Were
There was a $5,000 deduction from the gross estate for each child surviving the person making the will if upon the death of that person the child would be left an orphan.

Result: There is a minor loss for those estates that are over $600,000 where there may be orphans upon the testator's death. *This law is something new under the sun. If you already have a will, have it reviewed.*

APPENDIX III
Estate and Gift Tax Schedule
(For estates pre 1982)

Table A

Unified Rate Schedule			
Column A *Taxable amount over*	*Column B* *Taxable amount not over*	*Column C* *Tax on amount in column A*	*Column D* Rate of tax on *excess over amount in column A*
			(Percent)
0	$10,000	0	18
$10,000	20,000	$1,800	20
20,000	40,000	3,800	22
40,000	60,000	8,200	24
60,000	80,000	13,000	26
80,000	100,000	18,200	28
100,000	150,000	23,800	30
150,000	250,000	38,800	32
250,000	500,000	70,800	34
500,000	750,000	155,800	37
750,000	1,000,000	248,300	39
1,000,000	1,250,000	345,800	41
1,250,000	1,500,000	448,300	43
1,500,000	2,000,000	555,800	45
2,000,000	2,500,000	780,800	49
2,500,000	3,000,000	1,025,800	53
3,000,000	3,500,000	1,290,800	57
3,500,000	4,000,000	1,575,800	61
4,000,000	4,500,000	1,880,800	65
4,500,000	5,000,000	2,205,800	69
5,000,000	....	2,550,800	70

Index

Index

237